Mike Meyers' CompTIA

A+™ Core 1

CERTIFICATION
PASSPORT

(Exam 220-1101)

D1216455

About the Series Editor

Michael Meyers is the industry's leading authority on CompTIA A+ and CompTIA Network+ certifications. He is the president and co-founder of Total Seminars, LLC, a major provider of computer and network repair curriculum and seminars for thousands of organizations throughout the world, and a member of CompTIA.

Mike has written numerous popular textbooks, including the best-selling *Mike Meyers' CompTIA A+ Guide to Managing and Troubleshooting PCs*, *Mike Meyers' CompTIA Network+ Guide to Managing and Troubleshooting Networks*, and *Mike Meyers' CompTIA Security+ Certification Guide*.

About the Author

Ron Gilster is a well-known best-selling author with over 40 published books on IT career certification, technology, business, and finance. Ron's career has spanned over multiple decades, ranging from punched-card equipment to senior executive and author. His books have covered CompTIA's A+, Network+, Server+, Security+, and Cloud+ as well as Cisco CCNA, CCDA, and several others. He has also been an educator, teaching IT, IS, networking, and cybersecurity at the high-school, baccalaureate, and graduate levels. Ron has always admired Mike and his books and videos and is honored to be working directly with Mike on this project.

About the Technical Editor

Chris Crayton is a technical consultant, trainer, author, and industry-leading technical editor. He has worked as a computer technology and networking instructor, information security director, network administrator, network engineer, and PC specialist. Chris has authored several print and online books on PC repair, CompTIA A+, CompTIA Security+, and Microsoft Windows. He has also served as technical editor and content contributor on numerous technical titles for several of the leading publishing companies. He holds numerous industry certifications, has been recognized with many professional and teaching awards, and has served as a state-level SkillsUSA final competition judge.

Mike Meyers' CompTIA

A+™ Core 1

CERTIFICATION PASSPORT

(Exam 220-1101)

Mike Meyers, Series Editor

Ron Gilster

New York   Chicago   San Francisco   Athens
London   Madrid   Mexico City   Milan
New Delhi   Singapore   Sydney   Toronto

Mike Meyers' CompTIA A+™ Core 1 Certification Passport (Exam 220-1101)

1 2 3 4 5 6 7 8 9   LCR   26 25 24 23 22

Library of Congress Control Number: 2022945488

ISBN   978-1-264-60565-1
MHID   1-264-60565-X

Sponsoring Editor	**Acquisitions Coordinator**	**Proofreader**	**Composition**
Tim Green	Caitlin Cromley-Linn	Rick Camp	KnowledgeWorks Global Ltd.
Editorial Supervisor	**Technical Editor**	**Indexer**	**Illustration**
Janet Walden	Chris Crayton	Claire Splan	KnowledgeWorks Global Ltd.
Project Manager	**Copy Editor**	**Production Supervisor**	**Art Director, Cover**
Tasneem Kauser, KnowledgeWorks Global Ltd.	Bart Reed	Thomas Somers	Jeff Weeks

Contents at a Glance

Contents

Acknowledgments

As with every book, a lot of work from a lot of people went into making it happen.

Our acquisitions editor, Tim Green, kept us on track with kind words and pointy sticks. Always a pleasure working with you, Tim!

Our acquisitions coordinator, Caitlin Cromley-Linn, did an outstanding job acquiring and coordinating, with gentle yet insistent reminders for us to get stuff to her on a timely basis. Likewise, our project manager, Tasneem Kauser at KnowledgeWorks Global Ltd. This was a fun project, and we look forward to the next one!

Bart Reed did great work as our copy editor. He transformed every awkward stumble of language into a grammatical gem.

Our technical editor, Chris Crayton, took what some would describe as gleeful delight in pointing out every technical error he found. But since he helped us fix every error too, we won't hold it against him. Thanks, once again, for your technical expertise.

The layout team at KnowledgeWorks Global Ltd. did a remarkable job, putting the prose and pictures into printable form, which you now get to enjoy!

Finally, thanks to our proofreader, Rick Camp, for catching every last error. There's no error too big or small—he'll find them all. Thank you.

Introduction

Your Passport to Certification

Hello! I'm Mike Meyers, series editor, co-founder of Total Seminars, and author of many best-selling certification books. On any given day, you'll find me replacing a hard drive, setting up a website, or writing code. The book you hold in your hands is part of a powerful book series called the *Mike Meyers' Certification Passports*. Every book in this series combines easy readability with a condensed format—in other words, it's the kind of book I always wanted when I went for my certifications. Putting a huge amount of information in an accessible format is an enormous challenge, but I think we have achieved our goal and I am confident you'll agree.

I designed this series to do one thing and only one thing—to get you the information you need to achieve your certification. You won't find any fluff in here. We packed every page with nothing but the real nitty-gritty of the CompTIA A+ Core 1 certification exam.

Your Destination: CompTIA A+ Certification

This book is your passport to CompTIA A+ Core 1 certification, the vendor-neutral industry standard certification for PC hardware technicians, the folks who build and fix PCs. To get fully CompTIA A+ certified, you need to pass two exams: 220-1101 (Core 1) and 220-1102 (Core 2). To help you prepare for the Core 2 exam, please see our companion book, *Mike Meyers' CompTIA A+ Core 2 Certification Passport (Exam 220-1102)*.

The CompTIA A+ Exams

The 220-1101 Core 1 exam concentrates on five areas: Mobile Devices, Networking, Hardware, Virtualization and Cloud Computing, and Hardware and Network Troubleshooting. This exam focuses on your understanding of the terminology and hardware technology used in each of the five subject areas.

The 220-1102 Core 2 exam works the same way, covering Operating Systems, Security, Software Troubleshooting, and Operational Procedures. The 1102 exam is focused mainly on Windows, including installing, updating, maintaining, troubleshooting, and more. The other operating systems covered—macOS, Linux, iOS, and Android—get more of a big picture view. Security and troubleshooting, in both Windows and applications, make up half the exam questions.

Speaking of questions, each exam consists of up to 90 questions. Each exam takes 90 minutes. You must score at least 675 on a scale of 100–900 to pass exam 220-1101 (Core 1) and at least 700 on a scale of 100–900 to pass exam 220-1102 (Core 2). Remember, you must pass *both* exams to achieve your CompTIA A+ certification.

Question Types and Examples

Both of the exams are extremely practical, with little or no interest in theory. When you take the exams, you will see three types of questions: multiple choice, drag-and-drop matching, and performance based (simulation).

The following is an example of the type of multiple-choice question you will see on the exams:

> A company is planning to upgrade its Fast Ethernet network to Gigabit Ethernet. The existing network uses a mixture of Cat 5, Cat 5e, and Cat 6 cables. Which of the following needs to be performed during the upgrade process?
>
> **A.** Replace all cables with Cat 6.
>
> **B.** Keep the same cables.
>
> **C.** Replace Cat 5 with Cat 5e or Cat 6.
>
> **D.** Replace all cables with Cat 5e.

The best answer is C, "Replace Cat 5 with Cat 5e or 6." The cable standards mentioned in Answers A and D support Gigabit Ethernet, but since some parts of the network already use these cables types, it is not necessary to replace them. You might also see multiple-response questions, essentially multiple choice with more than one correct answer.

Drag-and-drop questions involve dragging and dropping a picture onto the relevant text. For example, you might see the words "HDMI" and "DisplayPort," and then two video port illustrations next to them. You would need to drag the HDMI illustration onto the word "HDMI" and then drag the other illustration onto the word "DisplayPort."

Performance-based (simulation) questions ask you to re-create a real process used by techs when working on PCs. You might be asked to copy a file or change a setting in Control Panel, but instead of you picking a multiple-choice answer, your screen will look like a Windows desktop and you will follow the provided instructions, just like you were using the real thing.

Always read the questions very carefully, especially when dealing with performance-based and multiple-choice questions with two or more correct responses. Remember to look for the *best* answer, not just the right answer. Check the CompTIA website for the most up-to-date exam information, as CompTIA does make changes.

Signing Up for Your CompTIA A+ Certification Exams

So, how do you sign up to take the CompTIA A+ certification exams? As this book went to press, the procedure looks like this: Go to https://home.pearsonvue.com/CompTIA. Click the Sign In button or, if you don't already have a Pearson VUE account, click Create Account and create one. Then, click View Exams, select the 1101 or 1102 exam (you must pass both to get fully certified), select your preferred language, review the details, and click Schedule This Exam. Enter your username and password, choose an exam center, date, and time, and provide payment or an exam voucher when required. Repeat this process to schedule the other exam. Be sure to see the Pearson VUE website for the latest details.

You can also now take your tests over the Internet. To schedule an Internet-based exam through OnVUE, go to www.onvue.com. You'll need a solid Internet connection and a webcam, such as one built into most portable computers. Pearson VUE will accommodate any special needs, although this may limit your selection of testing locations.

A single exam voucher purchased directly from the CompTIA website is $239. However, there are many sources, including Total Seminars, that offer discounts. Some vendors offer bundles that include a free retest voucher. This book comes with a coupon code you can use to purchase a discounted exam voucher from the CompTIA Store. See the ad in the front of the book for more information on the code and the discount. Take it from me, you might like the opportunity to have a "mulligan" if you get test jitters!

CompTIA A+ certification can be your ticket to a career in IT or simply an excellent step in your certification pathway. This book is your passport to success on the CompTIA A+ Core 1 certification exam.

Your Guides: Mike Meyers and Ron Gilster

You get a pair of tour guides for this book—both me and Ron Gilster. I've written numerous computer certification books—including the best-selling *CompTIA A+ Certification All-in-One Exam Guide* and the *CompTIA Network+ Certification All-in-One Exam Guide*. More to the point, I've been working on PCs and teaching others how to make and fix them for a very long time, and I love it! When I'm not lecturing or writing about PCs, I'm working on PCs! My personal e-mail address is michaelm@totalsem.com. Please feel free to contact me directly if you have any questions, complaints, or compliments.

Ron has written or co-authored many books on career certification and books on hardware and software principles and troubleshooting, networking, and security. As an educator, he has developed and taught courses in computer technology, information systems, cybersecurity, and networking. He sees himself as a trainer, teacher, and guide and works to exhibit these qualities in his writing. Ron can be contacted at rgilster@pm.me.

About the Book

This *Passport* is divided into "Domains" that follow the exam domains. Each Domain is further divided into "Objective" modules covering each of the top-level certification objectives for the Core 1 exam. The goal is to facilitate accelerated review of the exam objectives in a quick-review format that will allow you to quickly gauge what you can expect to be tested on. Whether you want a last-minute review or you have enough experience that you don't need full coverage of every topic, this format is designed for you. This isn't meant to be a course in a book, but we hope you will find the *Passport* helpful as you prepare for your exam. If you find you need more in-depth coverage of the exam topics, we suggest using Mike's *CompTIA A+ Certification All-in-One Exam Guide, Eleventh Edition* to supplement your studies.

We've created a set of learning elements that call your attention to important items, reinforce key points, and provide helpful exam-taking hints. Take a look at what you'll find:

- Each Domain begins with a **Domain Objectives** list of the official CompTIA A+ Core 1 exam objectives, which correspond to the titles of the individual Objective modules in that Domain. The structure of each Objective module is based on the subobjectives listed under the corresponding exam objective.
- The following elements highlight key information throughout the modules:

 EXAM TIP   The Exam Tip element focuses on information that pertains directly to the exam. These helpful hints are written by authors who have taken the exam and received their certification—who better to tell you what to worry about? They know what you're about to go through!

Cross-Reference
This element points to related topics covered in other Objective modules or Domains.

 ADDITIONAL RESOURCES   This element points to books, websites, and other media for further assistance.

 CAUTION   These cautionary notes address common pitfalls or real-world issues.

 NOTE   This element calls out any ancillary but pertinent information.

- **Tables** allow for a quick reference to help quickly navigate quantitative data or lists of technical information.

Video Cable Type	Standard Name	Reduced-Size Version	Signal Types Supported	Notes
VGA	Video Graphics Array	N/A	Analog video	VGA displays can be connected to HDMI, DVI-I, and DisplayPort ports with suitable adapters.
HDMI	High Definition Multimedia Interface	Mini-HDMI	HD video and HD audio	Video signal is compatible with DVI.

- Each Objective module ends with a brief **Review**. The review begins by repeating the official exam objective number and text, followed by a succinct and useful summary, geared toward quick review and retention.

- **Review Questions and Answers** are intended to be similar to those found on the exam. Explanations of the correct answer are provided.

Online Content

For more information on the practice exams and other bonus materials included with the book, please see the "About the Online Content" appendix at the back of this book.

After you've read the book, complete the free online registration and take advantage of the free practice questions! Use the full practice exam to hone your skills, and keep the book handy to check answers.

When you're acing the practice questions, you're ready to take the exam.

Go get certified!

What's Next?

The IT industry changes and grows constantly, and so should you. Finishing one certification is just a step in an ongoing process of gaining more and more certifications to match your constantly changing and growing skills. Remember, in the IT business, if you're not moving forward, you are way behind!

Good luck on your certification! Stay in touch.

Mike Meyers, Series Editor
Mike Meyers' Certification Passport

Mobile Devices

Domain Objectives

- **1.1** Given a scenario, install and configure laptop hardware and components.
- **1.2** Compare and contrast the display components of mobile devices.
- **1.3** Given a scenario, set up and configure accessories and ports of mobile devices.
- **1.4** Given a scenario, configure basic mobile-device network connectivity and application support.

Objective 1.1 Given a scenario, install and configure laptop hardware and components

Although an increasing number of laptops have no user-replaceable parts, there are still many existing and new models from a variety of manufacturers that will need replacement keyboards, upgraded RAM or mass storage, or other types of upgrades. This objective gives you the "inside story" on what to expect.

Hardware/Device Replacement

Laptops can break, but when they do, the problem is usually a component that can be replaced.

The most common replacements (or upgrades) include keyboards and other input devices, hard drives, and RAM, but there are several additional components that you might be called upon to swap out. Many of these components can be seen in Figures 1.1-1 and 1.1-2.

FIGURE 1.1-1   The major components on the top side of a typical laptop system board

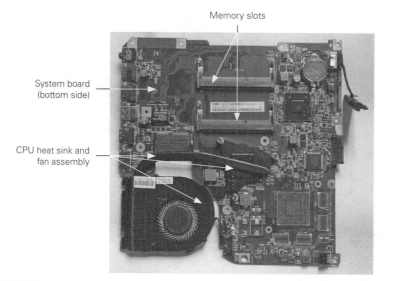

Memory slots

System board
(bottom side)

CPU heat sink and
fan assembly

FIGURE 1.1-2 The bottom side of a typical system board

Be sure to apply electrostatic discharge (ESD) precautions when upgrading or replacing laptop field replaceable units (FRUs). The companion book in this set, *Mike Meyers' CompTIA A+ Core 2 Certification Passport (Exam 220-1102)*, provides coverage on ESD protections and preventive measures.

 CAUTION Before attempting any laptop hardware or component replacement, refer to its service or owner's manual or access it online. Because laptops differ so much from brand to brand and model to model, the steps vary a great deal, and if you don't use proper procedures to disassemble a laptop, you might end up with more problems than when you started!

Keyboard

Replacing a laptop keyboard varies in difficulty from model to model. With some laptops, removing the old keyboard can be as easy as removing a retaining screw from the bottom of the laptop and pushing the keyboard up. However, some models require that almost all other components be removed before the keyboard can be removed.

 NOTE If the built-in laptop keyboard fails and can't be replaced right away, you can attach an external keyboard through a USB physical or wireless connection or through a Bluetooth connection.

FIGURE 1.1-3 The 2.5-inch and 3.5-inch drives are mostly the same.

Hard Drive

The term *hard drive* is used for a variety of mass storage devices using magnetic or solid-state technologies. You can replace a hard disk drive (HDD), solid-state drive (SSD), or solid-state hybrid drive (HHD or SSHD) easily in any recently manufactured traditional laptop; it's almost certainly a 2.5-inch SATA drive (most are 7 mm thick, but a few thicker drives won't fit into some laptops). Otherwise, no difference exists between 2.5-inch drives and their larger 3.5-inch brethren (see Figure 1.1-3).

Hard drive replacement is a little different on laptops than on desktops: find the hard drive hatch—either along one edge or on the bottom—and remove the screws (see Figure 1.1-4).

Remove the old hard drive, detach its mounting hardware, and install the mounting hardware on the new drive. The mounting hardware might include brackets, shock bumpers, or a protective cover over the drive's circuit board (see Figure 1.1-5).

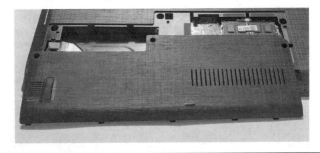

FIGURE 1.1-4 Removing the drive compartment hatch. Some laptops, like this one, use a single cover for access to hard drives and RAM.

Shock bumpers   Protective cover   Bumper attachment screws

FIGURE 1.1-5   The mounting hardware on this hard drive must be removed and attached to the new drive so it will fit properly in the computer.

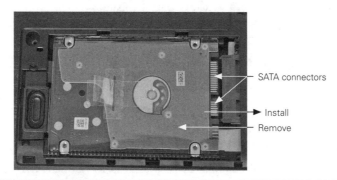

SATA connectors

Install

Remove

FIGURE 1.1-6   Inserting a replacement drive

Next, slide the new drive into its place (see Figure 1.1-6), making sure it is firmly connected to the drive interface and secured in place. Reattach the hatch, boot the computer, and install an operating system (OS) if necessary.

NOTE   Some laptops require the user to remove many components before upgrading the drive. Try to avoid upgrading these systems.

SSD vs. Hybrid vs. Magnetic Disk

One of the best laptop upgrades is to an SSD from a magnetic disk (HDD). It's less storage for the money, but SSDs are faster, lighter, quieter, cooler, use less power, and lack mechanical parts easily damaged by bumps, drops, and travel. SSDs are available in both the traditional 2.5-inch laptop form factor and smaller form factors, most notable the M.2 design.

SATA hard drive   M.2 SSD

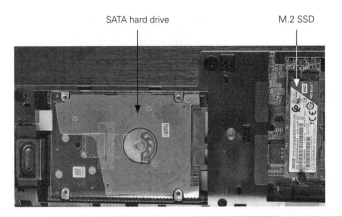

| **FIGURE 1.1-7** | A laptop with both SATA and SSD drives |

Some laptops, like the one shown in Figure 1.1-7, can use both. M.2 SSDs are available in two types: those that emulate SATA drives as well as versions known as NVMe drives. These connect to the PCIe bus, which is much faster than the SATA bus.

EXAM TIP   Make sure you are familiar with installing and configuring solid-state drives (SSDs) and magnetic hard disk drives (HDDs).

1.8 Inch vs. 2.5 Inch

Today, 2.5-inch HDDs and SSDs dominate laptop designs, as 1.8-inch HDDs have fallen out of favor due to flash memory usurping their role in portable music players and other small portables. These days, 1.8-inch HDDs are quite rare. If you encounter one, it almost certainly will be in an older portable on the small end of the scale.

Cross-Reference

For more on HDDs and SSD, see Domain 3.0, Objective 3.4.

Memory

Some laptops have upgradeable memory (RAM) slots, and other portables may not. RAM for portable devices, and especially laptop PCs, has its own small outline DIMM (SO-DIMM) form factor. Older SO-DIMMs (DDR and DDR2) were configured with 200-pin expansion cards. The DDR3 and DDR3L (low-voltage) cards used 204-pin SO-DIMMs, and the 260-pin DDR4 and 262-pin DDR5 SO-DIMMs. A DDR5 SO-DIMM has a 4800 MT/s (megatransfers per second) data rate and is currently available with 8 GB, 16 GB, and 32 GB memory capacities. Figure 1.1-8 shows examples of the DDR3, DDR4, and DDR5 SO-DIMMs.

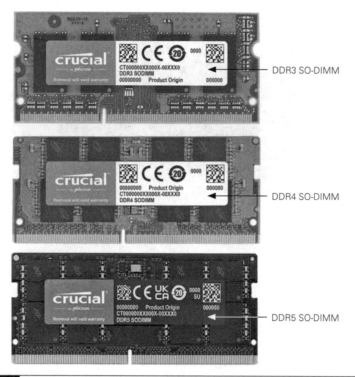

FIGURE 1.1-8   Examples of DDR3 (top), DDR4 (middle), and DDR5 SO-DIMMs (bottom) (images courtesy of Micron Technology, Inc.)

NOTE   The DDR5 SO-DIMM may not be backward compatible, even on DDR4 systems.

EXAM TIP   Memorize the SO-DIMM form factors—and the associated memory technologies—for the CompTIA A+ 220-1101 exam. (Note that the CompTIA objectives use "SODIMM," without the hyphen.)

When installing RAM, just like with a desktop, protect yourself and the portable by removing all power and taking ESD precautions. With portables, this includes removable batteries. If the portable has built-in batteries, consult the manufacturer's resources to check if and how you can safely work on it.

CAUTION   Some portables have both built-in and removable batteries.

FIGURE 1.1-9   Removing a RAM panel

Once you know you can work safely, consult the manufacturer's website or manual to confirm what kind of RAM the portable requires. Next, check the existing RAM configuration to confirm what you need to buy. To go from 4 GB to 8 GB, for example, you need to know if the portable has one 4-GB module or two 2-GB modules. You should also match the clock speed and timing of the existing module.

Second, locate the RAM slots. Depending on the system, the RAM slots might be under the same panel that you remove to access the hard drive (refer back to Figure 1.1-4) or under a separate panel (see Figure 1.1-9) on the bottom of the portable. Then you push out the retaining clips, and the RAM stick pops up (see Figure 1.1-10). Gently remove the old stick of RAM and insert the new one by reversing the steps.

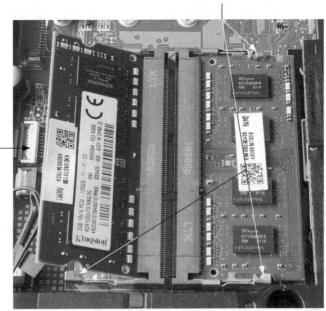

Retaining clips

RAM swings up after retaining clips are released

FIGURE 1.1-10   Releasing the RAM

Some portables (and desktops) have shared memory that enables the video card to borrow regular system RAM, providing performance comparable to its mega-memory alternative at a much lower cost. Unfortunately, the term *shared memory* is a bit misleading: the video card reserves this memory, and performance can suffer if the system runs out of it.

 EXAM TIP RAM and hard drives are usually the easiest components to replace.

Some CMOS utilities can change the amount of shared memory, while others can just toggle the setting. In both cases, more system RAM will improve overall performance when the OS and CPU get more usable RAM; the upgrade can also improve video performance if the system either shares a percentage of all RAM or lets you adjust the amount.

Cross-Reference

For more about laptop and desktop RAM types and specifications, see Domain 3.0, Objective 3.3.

Wireless Card

A wireless card is sometimes relatively easy to swap, as it may be accessible from the panel covering the hard drive and/or RAM. Before choosing an upgrade, make sure you check out the supported models, as an unsupported card won't be recognized by your system. If you upgrade a wireless expansion card, remember to reattach the antenna leads coming from the display in the correct locations. Depending on the age of the system, the wireless card might use a Mini-PCIe (refer back to Figure 1.1-1) or M.2 form factor.

 EXAM TIP Make sure you are familiar with the form factors used for wireless cards/Bluetooth modules.

Physical Privacy and Security Components

Laptop computers and other mobile devices don't stay in any one location, by design, which requires their physical security to be more specific to them than is the case for stationary devices. The physical security measures that protect desktop computers can also protect laptops, but only when the laptops are located within their coverage. A laptop that is moving about requires a special form of physical security that must also provide for data privacy as well.

Physical Security

The general objective of physical security is to restrict physical access to a device and, in turn, restrict logical access to its private content. Because a laptop is portable, its physical security must be portable as well. Certain aspects of physical security are difficult to apply to a laptop, such as preventing physical proximity, physical contact, and even physical possession. But wait, aren't those the physical aspects we need to secure? Yes, but more importantly, we need to secure any access to private or sensitive information or services located on the device. In other words, for a laptop, physical security amounts to denying access to the laptop's resources despite weak or nonexistent physical security.

The A+ Core 1 exam may include questions or content related to two of the methods used to secure laptops and their stored content: biometrics and near-field scanning.

Biometrics

Biometrics is used to both identify and authenticate someone attempting to gain access to a laptop and its resources. Biometrics involves the capture of one or more human traits for comparison against a prerecorded standard of the same measurements. Common biometric scans used with laptops and mobile devices include voice recognition, a fingerprint, the recognition of facial features, or an iris or retina scan of an eye.

Much like how a password is established as a control device, any of these biometric measurements and scans require a baseline capture to which future scans will be compared. Biometrics is, for the most part, reliable, and as the technology continues to develop, it becomes more and more reliable. However, biometric systems can produce two security flaws that, just like a password, require monitoring and the renewal of the baseline: false negatives and false positives.

A false negative occurs when the biometric scan of an authorized user results in the user being denied access. On the other hand, a false positive, which many be a more troublesome problem, occurs when an unauthorized supplicant is granted access in error.

 NOTE The Windows Biometric Framework (WBF), located on the Windows Control Panel, provides native support for the interface, management, and control of biometric devices interfaced to a computer.

Near-Field Scanners

Although the technology is more of a protective application than a pure security measure, near-field scanning can safeguard a computer from harm by detecting electromagnetic interference (EMI) within a configured range of a device. As mobile devices move about, EMI signals in an area may be strong enough to cause damage to system and power components.

A near-field scanner measures the amount of voltage in a time period or by frequency and quantifies it. The resulting metric is used to determine if a threat exists and, if so, to alert the user. Older near-field scanning systems used an onboard antenna, but more recent systems employ a scanner receiver to detect any electrical charges in its vicinity. Understand, though, that near-field scanning works over relatively small distances.

REVIEW

Objective 1.1: Given a scenario, install and configure laptop hardware and components Laptop hardware and component issues you might deal with include the following:

- Keyboard replacement
- Hard drive (2.5 inch) removal and installation
  - Use an SSD (2.5 inch or M.2), if you can, to improve performance and durability.
- Memory (SO-DIMM) types and their removal and installation
- Wireless card removal and installation
- Biometric devices for authentication and identification security

1.1 QUESTIONS

1. Your client wants you to upgrade the RAM, wireless cards, and storage in a collection of laptops from different vendors. Which of the following do you need to perform the work successfully? (Choose all that apply.)
   A. Service manual for each model
   B. Specialized tools
   C. Specifications
   D. All of the above

2. You are specifying the components you want in an ultimate gaming laptop. Which of the following standards provides the best opportunity for high-performance mass storage?
   A. SATA
   B. USB
   C. M.2
   D. Mini-PCIe

3. Which of the following laptop components typically requires the least disassembly to swap or upgrade?
   A. Hard drive
   B. RAM
   C. CPU
   D. Smart card reader

4. Your client wants to switch from SATA hard disk to SATA SSD storage in their fleet of laptops. Which of the following pieces of advice is most likely to be correct?

   A. Buy M.2 drives because all laptops have M.2 slots.

   B. SSDs are no faster than hard disk drives, so don't bother switching.

   C. Replacing hard disk drives with SSDs can provide better performance.

   D. SSDs are more fragile than hard disk drives.

5. Your client has stripped components from retired laptops to use for replacement parts in more recent laptops. Which of the following is most likely to be compatible with a newer laptop?

   A. Hard drive

   B. RAM

   C. Wireless card

   D. Optical drive

1.1 ANSWERS

1. **D** A service manual provides detailed teardown and reassembly instructions; specialized tools help you open cases without breaking parts; specifications inform you of standard features and supported upgrades.

2. **C** M.2 drives using NVMe are the fastest mass storage devices.

3. **B** Most laptops with upgradeable RAM have the modules under an easy-to-remove panel on the bottom of the case.

4. **C** SSDs in the SATA form factor provide faster performance than SATA hard disk drives.

5. **A** As long as a SATA 2.5-inch hard drive will physically fit into a laptop, it can be used as a replacement (a few hard drives are too thick for some laptops, but that is rare).

Objective 1.2 **Compare and contrast the display components of mobile devices**

The displays on or in mobile devices, including those on laptop computers, are very complex components. As a certified A+ technician, you can expect to encounter, troubleshoot, and diagnose the displays across the gamut of mobile devices, which will likely include smartphones, tablet, laptop, and notebook PCs, and other smaller handheld devices. This objective covers the subjects, topics, and content you can expect to see on the A+ Core 1 exam (220-1101).

Types of Displays

As mentioned, mobile devices are available in an expanding range of sizes and capabilities, which are determined by the technology each uses to create a displayed image. The overall size of a mobile device is largely a function of its display's size and its technology. A mobile device's display, which is commonly a liquid crystal display (LCD) or an organic light-emitting diode (OLED), typically ranges from 3 inches to as much as 20 inches on some laptop PCs.

LCD

An LCD display is backlit with light-emitting diodes (LEDs). Mobile devices incorporate three LCD display types: twisted nematic (TN), vertical alignment (VA), and in-plane switching (IPS). Table 1.2-1 compares these display types for performance and quality.

 ADDITIONAL RESOURCES For some additional information on the different LCD types, read the article "Monitor Panel Types | TN, IPS, VA Pros and Cons Explained – Pick the Right Display Technology!" by Dusan Stanar at the VSS Monitoring website (https://www.vssmonitoring.com/monitor-panel-types/).

 EXAM TIP Know the differences between the IPS, TN, and VA LCD technologies.

LED

An LED display on a mobile device uses light-emitting diodes (LEDs) to construct and show images, typically on a flat-screen display. An LED display provides a bright color image with higher efficiency that other types of monitors, including an LCD. In fact, an LED display consumes as much as 50 percent less power than an LCD, which is important to the life of the battery in a mobile device.

TABLE 1.2-1 LCD Displays on Mobile Devices

Criteria	TN	VA	IPS
Performance	Faster than VA and IPS	Slower than TN and IPS	Worse than TN, better than VA
Display	Worse than VA and IPS	Better than TN, worse than IPS; good color; best contrast and image depth	Better than TN and VA; best viewing angles; best color

An LED is a type of semiconductor that emits light when electricity is passed through it. An LED contains red, green, and blue sub-pixels that can blend to produce a particular color or shade. There are four primary types of LED displays:

- **Edge-lit LED**   This is actually an LCD monitor that has LEDs along the edges of the display that shine light toward the center of the display to light an image. The LEDs enable the displayed image to be viewed from several angles.

- **Full-array LED**   As its name implies, a full-array LED display has LEDs throughout the display area to produce sharp images and finer dimming. This type of display is popular on gaming and video streaming systems.

- **Direct-lit LED**   This type of LED display places LEDs in rows, which limits its capability to produce true colors, including black. Its images are in gray tones only.

- **Organic LED (OLED)**   OLEDs provide a superior display quality without separate backlighting. OLEDs illuminate pixels using negatively and positively charged ions. The three other forms of LEDs, and LCDs as well, use backlighting to sharpen their images, but OLED pixels provide all the light needed.

Display Panel Components

The display panel of a mobile device, especially laptops and notebook PCs, typically contains more than just the display. The display panel typically also houses the Wi-Fi antenna and the onboard webcam and microphone. There is a difference between a display panel, which is essentially the "lid" of the mobile PC, and the display assembly, which is only the display itself and its connecting wires and components.

Because the same panel can work in a wide variety of laptop models, finding a compatible display panel is easier than finding a compatible display assembly, and purchasing only a panel is less expensive than purchasing an assembly. In a few cases, it might be possible to switch screen types (from matte to glossy, for example). When swapping the panel only, take particular care to note the *placement* of component wires and how they are routed around the panel.

The following sections cover the system components commonly included in a display panel.

 EXAM TIP   Expect a question or two on the A+ 220-1101 exam involving a typical scenario that requires the replacement of the screen or components in the screen (for example, a cracked display panel, digitizer/touchscreen failure, Wi-Fi antenna malfunction, and so on).

Wi-Fi Antenna Connector/Placement

A broken mobile device display can be serviced in one of two ways: replace the entire display assembly or swap the display panel only.

 NOTE CompTIA's specific language for the antenna is *Wi-Fi antenna connector/placement* (although the industry-standard term is *Wi-Fi*). This refers to the wireless antenna wires that run along the top and sides of the screen assembly and connect to the Wi-Fi card.

When you're swapping a display assembly, it's important to note how the Wi-Fi antenna wires are connected to the wireless card. Even if you are only swapping a panel, you might need to move the wires out of the way. When you find it necessary to move them, it's important to properly position the Wi-Fi antenna wires around the panel and reconnect them to the wireless card. If they are pinched or broken, the laptop's Wi-Fi will stop working.

Figure 1.2-1 illustrates the position of Wi-Fi antenna wires and other components in a typical laptop display assembly.

Camera/Webcam

The camera/webcam (refer to Figure 1.2-1) is also built into the display assembly. The webcam can be replaced if it stops working. However, it's usually easier to replace a failed webcam with a USB version. If you decide to replace the webcam, be sure to note how it is attached to the display assembly and connected to the system board.

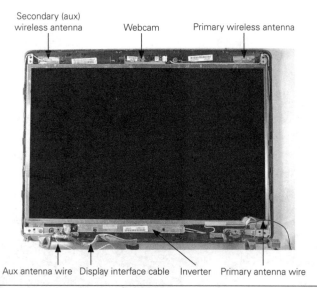

FIGURE 1.2-1 Wi-Fi antennas and other components in a typical laptop display panel

Microphone

Some laptops include a microphone in the screen assembly, while others place the microphone in the base of the laptop. If the laptop has a microphone in the screen assembly, be sure to disconnect it before swapping the screen assembly and be sure to reconnect it during the replacement process.

Inverter

Laptops that use older LCD screens with cold cathode fluorescent lamp (CCFL) backlighting require an inverter to convert DC power to AC power to control the backlight (refer to Figure 1.2-1). If the inverter fails, the screen will be extremely dim (use a flashlight to see if the screen still works). Replacing an inverter is a relatively easy and inexpensive repair to make because it is accessed from the bottom of the display assembly and is a plug-in component.

Touchscreen/Digitizer

Older laptops often used a separate touchscreen/digitizer layer, making repairs both expensive and more complicated. (A *digitizer* is the component that provides the "touch" part of a touchscreen. The digitizer's fine grid of sensors under the glass detects your finger's touch and signals to the OS its location on the grid.) Recent touchscreen laptops typically use display panels with integrated touchscreens, making the process of swapping the panel easier.

REVIEW

Objective 1.2: Compare and contrast the display components of mobile devices   A typical laptop display assembly includes the following:

- LCD panel (standard) or OLED panel (only very recent laptops)
  - LCD has a fluorescent or LED backlight.
  - OLED has no backlight.
- Wi-Fi antenna wires
- Camera/webcam
- Microphone (might be built into the base on some models)
- Inverter, but only on older LCD screens with fluorescent backlights
- Touchscreen/digitizer (might be a separate display panel layer on older models)
- LCD technologies, including IPS, TN, and VA

1.2 QUESTIONS

1. Your client has a cracked laptop screen, but the laptop still works. Which of the following might be the most cost-effective solution?

   A. Replace the display panel.

   B. Replace the display assembly.

   C. Replace the laptop.

   D. Replace the laptop with a desktop.

2. Your client decided to have a laptop display assembly swapped. Now, the Wi-Fi connection doesn't work. Which of the following is the most likely cause?

   A. The webcam was plugged into the wireless card.

   B. The Wi-Fi card was not reconnected to the wireless antennas.

   C. The new assembly is not compatible with the current wireless card.

   D. Wi-Fi wires were broken during the swap.

3. A user reports that an older laptop isn't displaying anything. However, when you plug in an external display, the laptop can be used. Which of the following would you check first?

   A. Digitizer

   B. Microphone

   C. Inverter

   D. Wi-Fi antennas

4. The wireless antennas in a laptop display assembly are usually located where?

   A. Lower-left and lower-right corners of the display

   B. Bottom center of the display

   C. Top center of the display

   D. Top-left and top-right corners of the display

5. Your client uses a laptop for live chats with her salesforce, but her webcam has failed. The weekly chat is in two hours. What should you do?

   A. Arrange for an express swap of her display assembly.

   B. Connect a USB webcam.

   C. Reimage a spare laptop.

   D. Advise her to cancel the chat.

1.2 ANSWERS

1. **A** Replace the display panel. The other components in the display assembly are working, so replacing only the panel is likely to be cheaper and probably faster than swapping the entire display assembly.

2. **B**   The Wi-Fi card is in the laptop base, so the wireless antenna wires must be disconnected to swap a display assembly. It's easy to forget to reattach them.

3. **C**   Check the inverter (on older laptops so equipped). When it fails, the built-in display becomes extremely dim.

4. **D**   The antennas usually are located in the upper-left and upper-right corners of the display assembly.

5. **B**   A USB webcam will work fine, may have better image quality than the built-in webcam, and can be installed and configured in plenty of time for the meeting.

Objective 1.3 Given a scenario, set up and configure accessories and ports of mobile devices

Mobile devices are small and portable, but thanks to a variety of wired and wireless connections, they can also be versatile. In this objective you are introduced to the main types of accessories available for mobile devices and the ways in which they can be connected.

Connection Methods

Mobile devices have many of the same types of connections and options as desktop devices do. These include wired ports, wireless devices, and accessories. Wired connections can be used for data synchronization and transfer to a larger computer, for charging, and for tethering to share a cellular connection. You need to be able to identify several wired connection types for the CompTIA A+ 220-1101 exam.

Universal Serial Bus

The universal serial bus, which is most commonly referred to as USB, connects a wide variety of devices to other devices, such as printers, external storage devices, keyboards, mice, and other controllers. USB has replaced the standard serial and parallel interfaces for the most part. Like these interfaces, USB provides for data transmission but also supplies 5 volts (5V) of power through a standard connection and cable. This allows low-voltage devices (those needing 5V of power or less) to connect and operate without requiring additional external power sources. A single USB jack has the capability of supporting as many as 127 USB devices using a series of unpowered USB hubs. USB devices that need more than 5V of power can connect through a powered USB hub that connects directly to a power source.

Since their introduction in the mid-1990s, the USB standards have expanded to a variety of versions and connector configurations, often distinguished by their overall size and pin array.

USB connectors are identified in a confusing overlap of types (aka generations and form factors) and versions that specify the cabling and transfer speeds, among other characteristics. Types and versions are commonly used interchangeably and in combination. However, simply put, USB types are denoted by letters (as in A, B, and C) and USB versions by numbers (such as 2, 3, and 4). The sections that follow explain the USB types and versions you should know for the A+ Core 1 exam.

NOTE   USB standards advanced from the original USB 0.7 to the developing USB 4.0. Market acceptance, or the lack of it, drove the early developments, but the first version to gain acceptance was USB 1.1. USB versions 1.0 and 1.1 were later renamed as USB 2.0 LowSpeed and USB 2.0 FullSpeed, respectively.

There are three basic USB types or form factors:

- **Type-A**   The original and likely most commonly used USB connector
- **Type-B**   Smaller, squarish-shaped connector compatible with nearly all other USB types
- **Type-C**   Asymmetric and slightly oval connector

Figure 1.3-1 shows each of these USB types.

USB-C

A USB-C cable, shown in the upcoming Figure 1.3-3, uses Type-C 24-pin connectors for transferring power of up to 100 watts and data as fast as 10 Gbps. These capabilities make the USB-C cable suitable for connecting video devices, such as monitors, transferring data between computers or phones, and charging any compatible devices. A standard USB-C cable has Type-C connectors at each end, but there are USB-C to USB-A converters that can be used for interfacing with USB Type-A ports. One of the better features of a USB-C/Type-C connector is that it is completely reversible and can be inserted into a plug with either side up.

Type-A   Type-B   Type-C

FIGURE 1.3-1   The three basic USB connector types

FIGURE 1.3-2 A micro-USB cable with a USB 3.0 connector

Micro-USB

The micro-USB connector is the smallest of the USB types and has been commonly used for connecting and charging mobile devices, such as MP3 players, smartphones, cameras, and more. There are several varieties of micro-USB cables, each intended to connect a micro-USB device to another USB port, commonly of a different type and typically a USB 3.0 or Type-C connector. Figure 1.3-2 and Figure 1.3-3 show examples of this cable.

There are a variety of micro-USB cables, each having a different USB type connector on the other end of the cable. Commonly used micro-USB cables are the micro-USB to Type-A, micro-USB to Type-B, and the USB 3.0.

Mini-USB

The mini-USB is essentially a sub-family of USB cables that includes versions with Type-A, Type-B, and hybrid Type-AB connectors. The most commonly used mini-USB connector is the 5-pin Type-B, which is popular in card readers, MP3 players, digital cameras, and many mobile PC storage devices. All mini-USB interfaces are sealed and essentially waterproof and dustproof. However, because they are smaller in size than other USB types, which is both a plus and a disadvantage, they are easily misplaced and can be difficult to remove from a device.

FIGURE 1.3-3 From left to right: USB-C, micro-USB, and Lightning cables

Lightning Connector

The Lightning connector was introduced in 2012 along with the iPhone 5 and several other Apple products for use in charging and synchronizing its devices. Apple continues to use the Lightning connector for its iPhones but has switched some devices to the USB-C interface. An example of a Lightning cable is shown in Figure 1.3-3.

Lightning is an 8-pin digital signal connector that can be attached to a device with dual-orientation, meaning no up or down sides. Each of the pins is connected directly to the reverse side pin in its position.

Cross-Reference

To learn more about these cables, their features, and how they are used, see Domain 3.0, Objective 3.1.

Serial Interfaces

The A+ Core 1 exam objectives indicate that you may encounter serial interfaces on the 220-1101 exam. So, let's take a quick look at this topic.

At one time, the peripheral devices on a PC were connected primarily as either a serial or a parallel interface. Simply defined, a serial interface sends or receives data one bit at a time in a series or in what is known as a temporal (time) format. In comparison, a parallel interface transmits data on a set of parallel carriers, usually wires, as a spatial group. Here's the short version: serial is one bit at a time on one wire and parallel is more than one bit at a time and more than one wire. Serial interfaces are used by USB and Serial Attached SCSI (SAS) devices.

Near-Field Communication

Near-field communication (NFC) uses chips embedded in mobile devices that create electromagnetic fields when these devices are close to each other or touching each other (typical ranges are anywhere from a few centimeters to only a few inches). The fields can be used to exchange contact information, small files, and even payment transactions through stored credit cards using systems like Apple Pay and Google Pay.

The OS determines the exact features of a smartphone. For example, Apple supports NFC only for Apple Pay, while Android smartphones also support file transfer.

Bluetooth

Bluetooth is a short-range wireless technology that can be used for personal area networking, connections to wireless speakers, mice, and keyboard devices, as well as connections to headsets, microphones, and wearables. Bluetooth implementations in mobile devices generally have a range of no more than 10 meters (about 33 feet).

Hotspot

Many smartphones and tablets with cellular support can share their cellular Internet connection with other devices by enabling a hotspot. The hotspot feature turns the device into a wireless router with an SSID (service set identifier) and password. When the hotspot device shares that information with Wi-Fi-enabled devices, those devices can connect to the Internet. The range of a hotspot connection varies according to the Wi-Fi standard used by the smartphone and the location (outdoors has a longer range than indoors).

 EXAM TIP   Be able differentiate the wireless connection types, including NFC, Bluetooth, and hotspot.

Accessories

Although mobile devices have many built-in features, they can use accessories to provide even more functionality. The following sections describe the accessories you need to understand for this objective.

Touch Pens

Also known as a stylus, a touch pen is a handheld pointing device that can be used on capacitive touchscreens. Touch pens can be used on smartphones, tablets, and other devices with touchscreen displays. A touch pen works much like your finger in that it absorbs the electricity of the touchscreen and identifies a specific location on the display.

Headsets

Headsets can connect to mobile devices via traditional 3.5-mm mini-jacks, USB, or wirelessly via Bluetooth. Headsets designed for use with smartphones or gaming include microphones.

Speakers

Mobile devices often have very small speakers with limited power. To increase volume and make it easier for groups to hear music, connect external speakers via 3.5-mm speaker jacks or wirelessly via Bluetooth.

Webcams

A webcam is a small digital camera that can be connected to a computer to capture video images in real time. Like any digital camera, a webcam captures images using a matrix of light detectors in a light-sensing chip, which is either a charge-coupled device (CCD) or a CMOS image sensor (the most common these days). The name "webcam" refers more to its software that formats the video for the Web.

FIGURE 1.3-4   Port replicator (bottom) versus docking station (top)

Docking Station

Business-oriented laptops can connect (*Transformers* style) with *docking stations* that provide a host of single- and multi-function ports. The typical docking station uses a proprietary connection but adds ports or devices not available on the original laptop, such as a network port, optical drive, and so on (see Figure 1.3-4, top device).

Port Replicator

A *port replicator* provides a permanent home for video, network, and audio cables that you would otherwise attach to and detach from a laptop as you move it around. Port replicators typically connect to the highest-bandwidth port (such as USB 3.0, 3.1, 3.2 and USB-C or Thunderbolt) and subdivide the bandwidth among port devices. Figure 1.3-4 shows a typical port replicator for a MacBook Pro or Air compared with a docking station for a Microsoft Surface Pro.

 EXAM TIP   The difference between port replicators and docking stations is sometimes unclear. For purposes of the CompTIA A+ 220-1101 exam, a docking station connects to a proprietary port, whereas a port replicator connects via a standard port. The Microsoft Surface Dock shown in Figure 1.3-4 is a true docking station because it plugs into the proprietary charging/docking port on the Surface Pro and adds a network port. The third-party port replicator for macOS-based laptops connects to a Thunderbolt port on a MacBook, MacBook Air, or MacBook Pro.

Trackpads and Drawing Pads

A *trackpad* is a user interface device that senses downward pressure and movement that is converted into cursor or pointer locations and movements. Also known as a *touchpad,* a trackpad is included in many laptop computers as an alternative to an external mouse. Trackpads and drawing pads, which are typically used with a stylus, work much like touchscreens and touch pens in that the touch device grounds the pad and its location is passed to the computer to move a visible cursor.

REVIEW

Objective 1.3: Given a scenario, set up and configure accessories and ports of mobile devices Mobile devices feature various types of connections and accessories, including the following:

- Universal serial bus (USB), including USB-C, micro-USB, and mini-USB
- Lightning
- Serial interfaces
- Near-field communication (NFC)
- Bluetooth
- Hotspots
- Touch pens
- Headsets
- Speakers
- Webcams
- Docking stations use a proprietary connection but add ports or devices not available on the original laptop, such as a network port and optical drive.
- Port replicators provide a permanent home for video, network, and audio cables that you would otherwise attach to and detach from a laptop as you move it around.
- Trackpads/drawing pads are typically used with a stylus and work much like touchscreens and touch pens in that the touch device grounds the pad and its location is passed to the computer to move a visible cursor.

1.3 QUESTIONS

1. Which of the following is not a wired connection type found on many mobile devices?
   A. Micro-USB
   B. Mini-USB
   C. USB-C
   D. NFC

2. Bluetooth can be used for which of the following accessories? (Choose all that apply.)

   A. Headset

   B. Battery pack

   C. Game pad

   D. Speaker

3. Your supervisor asks you about using a smartphone to make a payment at a convenience store. Which feature needs to be activated?

   A. USB

   B. Tethering

   C. NFC

   D. Hotspot

4. Your client has just purchased a new model iPad Pro. Which type of charge/sync cable does she need to use?

   A. Lightning

   B. USB-C

   C. Thunderbolt

   D. 30-pin

5. You're prevented from connecting your laptop computer to a video display because the laptop lacks an HDMI port. Which of the following devices could be used to solve this problem?

   A. Lightning cable

   B. USB-C hub

   C. Port replicator

   D. Serial cable

1.3 ANSWERS

1. **D**   An NFC connection is a type of wireless interface. The other answers are common types of wired connectors into which a matching cable can be inserted.

2. **A C D**   Bluetooth cannot be used for battery charging but works with Bluetooth-equipped speakers, headsets, game pads, and other input/output devices.

3. **C**   Near-field communication (NFC) can be used for cardless payment at convenience stores.

4. **B**   The newest iPad Pro models have switched from Lightning to USB-C.

5. **C**   A port replicator or docking station may supply the missing HDMI port.

Given a scenario, configure basic mobile-device network connectivity and application support

In this objective, you learn how to configure mobile devices, including cellular and wireless devices, for e-mail and other mobile applications.

Wireless/Cellular Data Network (Enable/Disable)

The majority of today's mobile devices are able to connect to two different communication technologies to access a network, including the Internet: cellular (cell phone) and wireless (Wi-Fi) networks. Only recently has either of these mediums been a viable means of connecting to a network from a mobile device.

Mobile Device Communication

Cellular networks became a usable way to connect to a network, and especially to the Internet, with the introduction of the fourth-generation (4G) long-term evolution (LTE) cellular technologies. The emerging 5G standard will improve the performance of cellular-based network access and provide the technology to support a merger of cellular networking with Wi-Fi standards.

A Wi-Fi network connection applies the IEEE 802.11 standard that is appropriate and compatible with the wireless communication technology of the particular mobile device. Wi-Fi communications are over the air radio frequency (RF) communications.

> **Cross-Reference**
>
> For more information on the IEEE 802.11 wireless networking standards, see Domain 2.0, Objective 2.3.

Regardless of the technology used to access a network from a mobile device, this capability likely needs to be configured and enabled (or disabled, if so desired). Generally, these actions are performed in the Settings or Preferences page of a system, using roughly the same steps.

By default, cellular-enabled devices, such as smartphones and some tablets, are enabled for communication to cellular data networks. However, on non-cellular (that is, Wi-Fi) devices such as laptops, notebooks, and some tablets, these connections must be configured and enabled manually.

Mobile devices such as laptops, notebooks, and some tablets running a full operating system, such as Windows, macOS, or Linux, have defined methods for configuring and enabling a connection to one or both of the communication mediums. Tablets, personal digital assistants (PDAs), and smartphones that are running a specialized version of Windows or macOS, or a version of Android or IOS, use a process that is particular to that system to enable or disable network communications over either technology.

 EXAM TIP For the A+ Core 1 exam, you should know the general process involved to enable, share, and disable access to a network over a cellular or Wi-Fi network on a mobile device.

Enabling/Disabling Cellular Communication

Smartphones and cellular-based tablets, by default, have a Subscriber Identification Module (SIM) card or an embedded SIM (eSIM) that permits the device to connect and communicate with a specific cellular network service such as LTE or broadband. Some laptops and tables may have an eSIM, but for the most part, these devices must connect to a cellular service though a USB cellular modem (see Figure 1.4-1) or a cellular router device. Cellular modems commonly have their own specific configurations that are typically set by default.

The process used on a Windows laptop to configure and enable a connection to the Internet using a cellular network involves the following steps:

1. Insert the SIM card into its holder, slot, or USB modem. Without a SIM or eSIM, cellular communications cannot be configured.

2. Access the Start menu and click the gear wheel icon on the left edge of the window to open Settings.

3. On the Setting menu page, click the Network & Internet selection.

FIGURE 1.4-1 A USB cellular modem with a SIM card adapter

4. On the Network and Internet page, select Cellular from the left-hand panel and do the following:

    a. In the Data Roaming Options drop-down menu on the right-side of the page, select either Don't Roam (which is the default selection) or Roam.

 NOTE   The preceding action sets a value for the InternetAlwaysOn DWORD of the HKEY_LOCAL_MACHINE\SOFTWARE\Microsoft\WwanSvc\RoamingPolicyForPhone\ key.

    b. Close Settings.

 ADDITIONAL RESOURCES   For information on a few other options for using a cellular connection on a Windows 10 or 11 system, visit https://support.microsoft.com/en-us/windows/cellular-settings-in-windows-905568ff-7f31-3013-efc7-3f396ac92cd7.

Enabling/Disabling Wi-Fi Communication

On a Windows 10 system, the steps used to access the settings to enable or disable Wi-Fi are found by choosing Settings | Network & Internet | Wi-Fi. On the Wi-Fi page, this service can be set on (enabled) or off (disabled) using a slide switch, as shown in Figure 1.4-2. (This figure also shows the other connection options available. If a cellular service is available, it would also be listed.) On handheld mobile devices, you should refer to the user's manual for how to enable or disable Wi-Fi services.

Making a Wi-Fi connection on a smartphone or tablet is essentially the same as the process used on a laptop. The settings involved are relatively intuitive: on an iPhone they are under Wi-Fi, and on an Android device they are under Wireless and Networks. Much like with other mobile devices, the Wi-Fi networks within range are listed and you can select one to connect with temporarily or configure one as the default Wi-Fi network.

Wireless Generations

To date, there have been five major "generations" of wireless and cellular communications. Figure 1.4-3 illustrates the path of the generations. Each generation provided important improvements in the technologies and capabilities of wireless telecommunications. Here is a brief summary of each of the generations:

*   The first generation (1G) cellular network provided narrow band analog service with a very limited number of simultaneous callers.
*   The second generation (2G) introduced digital transmissions on wider frequency bands with greater mobility. 2G introduced digital encryption of conversations.

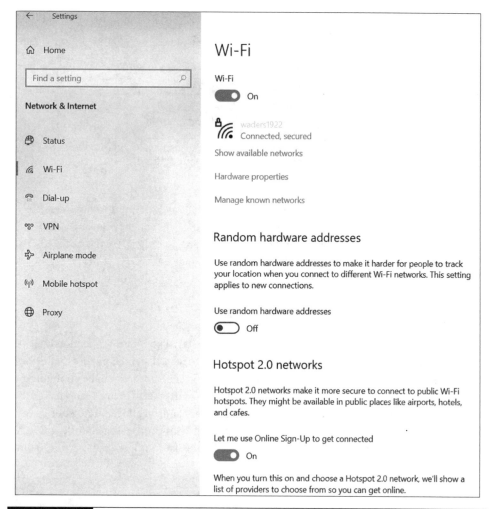

FIGURE 1.4-2   The Network & Internet settings page on a Windows 10 system

- The third generation (3G) added several security features, transmission types, global roaming, and data transmission speeds, which are in the range of 144 Kbps to a theoretical 2 Mbps. 3G provided features that included video conferencing, instant messaging, and cellular VoIP. 3G provided for two-way authentication between a phone and a network.

- The fourth generation (4G) uses an IP-based system and higher transmission rates. 4G provides data speeds of 50 Mbps to 80 Mbps (LTE+) to a maximum distance of 31 miles (endpoint device to tower). 4G provides security features such as secured data in transit, authenticated access, and support for 3DES and AES encryption.

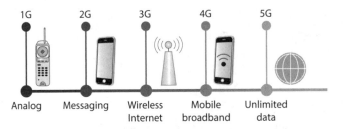

Each of the five generations in telecommunications introduced major developments in mobile and cellular communications.

- The fifth-generation (5G) telecommunications standards define a radio access technology (RAT) separated into two frequency ranges: Frequency range 1 (FR1) supports the sub-6 GHz bands of the earlier standards and the 410 MHz to 7.125 GHz spectrum. Frequency range 2 (FR2) supports the range 24.25 GHz to 52.6 GHz. 5G, which is built on the 4G LTE standard, provides data speeds of multiple Gbps or more.

Hotspot

A mobile *hotspot* device creates a Wi-Fi network to share its cellular data connection (3G, 4G, 4G LTE, or 5G) with other Wi-Fi devices. Wireless providers sell standalone hotspot devices for their network, but many smartphones and tablets with cellular access can be configured to act as a hotspot. As illustrated in Figure 1.4-4, enabling a smartphone (in this case, an Android smartphone) involves enabling a cellular data connection and toggling the hotspot setting. The hotspot configuration enables the device to interact with the Wi-Fi network and serve as a router between it and the cellular network. You should also configure a password to limit access to the hotspot.

FIGURE 1.4-4 The sequence of screens (left to right) and selections for configuring an Android phone as a Wi-Fi hotspot

NOTE   Some devices use the term *tethering* as a synonym for *hotspot*.

GSM vs. CDMA

The two primary service protocols used for cellular phone systems are Global System for Mobile Communications (GSM) and code division multiple access (CDMA). GSM is the generally deployed standard and is replacing CDMA slowly, but there are still CDMA networks deployed. Both of these network standards provide about the same features and capabilities, but their major difference is their portability. A GSM SIM card can be removed and installed into a new device with the same provider or that of another provider. CDMA devices are tied to a provider and must remain so.

Preferred Roaming List Updates

As mobile devices travel, they frequently have to pass through areas that don't have strong signals, or into areas that the carrier does not service, and maintain connection by roaming on another carrier's network. Your phone's firmware gets occasional updates to its *preferred roaming list (PRL)*, a priority-ordered list of other carrier networks and frequencies, sent via your phone's cellular connection (called baseband updates, or over-the-air updates) or through normal OS updates. Updates to the PRL are also sent to cell towers. As the PRL is updated, devices can roam further from their own providers' coverage area.

CDMA devices may also receive *product release instruction (PRI)* updates that modify a host of complex device settings. Don't worry about specifics, here—but a device may need PRI updates if the network is evolving during the lifetime of the device, the device is moving to a new network, or the device has a new owner.

 EXAM TIP   PRL updates are handled automatically during firmware/OS updates. They are only for CDMA networks. No one but the nerdiest of nerds will ever see these updates.

Bluetooth

As discussed in the previous objective, Bluetooth is a popular way to connect many different types of accessories. Table 1.4-1 covers the process of using Bluetooth on a mobile device.

 EXAM TIP   Given a scenario, know the setup process for Bluetooth pairing.

TABLE 1.4-1 Bluetooth Setup Process

Step	What It Does
Enable Bluetooth.	Turns on Bluetooth connectivity.
Enable pairing.	Enables the device to find and be found by other Bluetooth devices.
Find a device for pairing.	Locates and lists nearby Bluetooth devices available to pair with (headset, keyboard, and so on).
Enter the appropriate PIN code or press a button on the device.	Makes the pairing connection between the Bluetooth host and device.
Test connectivity.	Confirms that the devices can communicate. Use the Bluetooth device to play music, record audio, type, and so on.

Two or more paired Bluetooth devices create a *personal area network (PAN)*. Figure 1.4-5 illustrates a very simple PAN, in which each device is paired with other devices in range to create a network. Another Bluetooth network topology is a *scatternet*, which combines two PANs by connecting a device from either side to link the PANs. Figure 1.4-6 illustrates a simple scatternet.

Cellular Location Services

Cellular location services use real-time location tracking to identify a mobile device's physical and geographical locations. This technology tracks your location constantly, not just at one

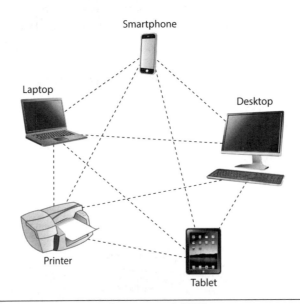

FIGURE 1.4-5 A Bluetooth personal area network (PAN)

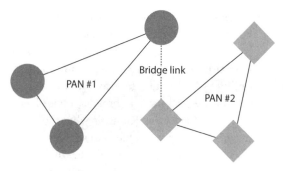

FIGURE 1.4-6   A Bluetooth scatternet connects two or more PANs.

particular moment. A mobile device commonly includes one or more technologies able to determine its current location. In most cases, these technologies are GPS, radio frequency ID (RFID), Wi-Fi, and cellular RF technology. In order to function, a mobile device uses one or more of these technologies to interact with other devices, which may include geopositioned satellites, network routers, and cell and communication towers. This interaction, which involves a mobile device communicating with one of the multiple types of communication hubs, is used to nail down a device's precise location. This feature, known as Location Services in iOS and Location in Android, is used by mapping and several other types of apps, but only you provide the apps with permission to use this feature.

Most cellular systems use a triangulation method to determine the general location of a trackable device. As shown in Figure 1.4-7, the distance to each of three (and possibly more) cellular service towers can cause the transmitted signal strength to weaken. The degree to which the signal does weaken is used to determine the distance to the tower. The distance calculations for each tower are combined to locate the device.

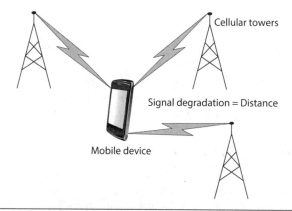

FIGURE 1.4-7   A process called triangulation is used to determine the location of a device.

There are many pros and cons to enabling location services on a cellular or mobile device. Enabling location services can provide a route-finder application with a starting point and the capability of tracking progress. In an emergency, first responders are able to pinpoint the phone's exact location. You can also let selected friends see your location on their smartphones. There are many other possibilities with location services turned on.

On the other hand, it may not always be safe to broadcast your location. You can't be sure exactly who may be receiving that information. Knowing where you are could lead to stalking or robbery. And knowing where you aren't could lead to someone breaking into your home. It's debated whether the police or a government agency knowing and tracking your location, without a warrant to do so, could be a violation of your civil rights.

Disabling location services on a mobile device won't completely mask its location. Several applications, and even phone calls, connect to the nearest cell tower, which has a location. Perhaps the only way you can hide your personal location is to not have the device with you. Much of the sharing of a mobile device's location is done by misconfigured application permissions and settings. Being aware of which apps use location services and carefully assigning their permissions can reduce the chance of location services being used for bad.

 ADDITIONAL RESOURCES   To learn more about location-based services, read the article "What are location-based services?" at the Ancoris website (https://www.ancoris.com/blog/what-are-location-based-services).

GPS

One of the primary technologies used by location-based services is the *Global Positioning System (GPS)*, which is built into most mobile devices, along with Bluetooth, Wi-Fi hotspots, and cellular towers, to determine the device's location.

GPS is based on 24 satellites that transmit their location and time to Earth-based GPS receivers. The most common purpose-built GPS device is the navigational aid that mounts on a vehicle's dashboard or windshield, and you can buy the equivalent for boats, airplanes, bicycles, and more. There are even handheld versions tailored to scuba diving, hiking, hunting, and so on, with features better suited to their niche, such as preloaded special-purpose maps, waterproofing, impact resistance, route memory, bookmarking, stored locations, low-power use, simple replaceable batteries, and other useful sensors or tools. Figure 1.4-8 illustrates a simplified version of GPS integrated into a communications system.

Securing Mobile Devices

Mobile device management (MDM) is a type of security software that enables organizations to secure, monitor, manage, and enforce policies on employees' mobile devices. MDM is often linked with or based on the use of mobile application management (MAM) software.

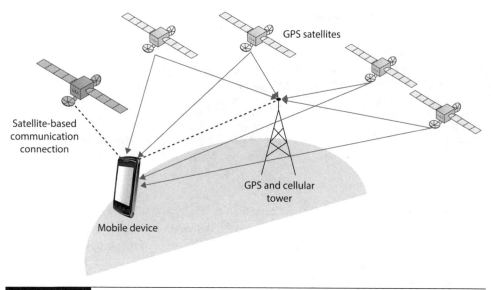

FIGURE 1.4-8   An example of a GPS network

Mobile Device Management

MDM involves the use of monitoring, securing, and managing any mobile devices that have access, gain access, or connect to a company's network and data resources. Employees and possibly customers or suppliers may be allowed to directly connect mobile devices on an internal network. Their activity must be tracked to protect the data asset by applying a carefully thought-out data management program. The purpose of the MDM is to provide the internal IT administrators with the information needed to manage and administer the security of a network. MDM solutions allow IT teams and admins to control and distribute security policies to the mobile devices.

Mobile Application Management

MAM encompasses the entire software development life cycle (SDLC) process for mobile software developed internally or externally, as well as updates, fixes, and retirement of mobile software. MAM can also include the management of application licenses, user account access permissions, and the operating configuration of mobile software. Here are some examples of how MAM is applied:

- **Corporate e-mail configuration**   A corporate or even a small business e-mail system must be configured and fine-tuned to provide e-mail services to mobile devices. Commonly this may also be accomplished through the configuration on the mobile device itself. The information commonly used includes account type, e-mail address, password, logical domain, and the user's account name.

- **Two-factor authentication** Unfortunately, shoulder surfing and phishing are often successful in learning a user's login credentials. The use of a two-factor authentication (2FA) process at login helps to ensure that a mail client is who they claim to be. In a 2FA scheme, the user's account name and password count only as one factor. A second security factor is commonly a phone number, a PIN code, or a generated code sent to the supplicant's device.

 EXAM TIP Be sure you understand the concept and use of two-factor (multifactor) authentication and the use of biometrics as a part of the MAM process.

- **Corporate applications** The management of application software on a mobile device is very much like the management of software on an internal network. For example, if a corporation has a customer relationship management (CRM) system, whether the user is local and using a device on the internal network or is remote and several thousand miles away, the client/server nature of the application must be the focus for its confidentiality, integrity, and availability.

 EXAM TIP Know the differences between MDM and MAM. MDM concentrates on centrally managing device updates and securing mobile devices, whereas MAM focuses on specific corporate applications.

Mobile Device Synchronization

People generally want their contacts and calendars to match across their devices, so for the CompTIA A+ 220-1101 exam, you need to know how to configure mobile devices to synchronize data across two or more devices to maintain a single set of contacts, one e-mail inbox, one calendar, and perhaps even one set of up-to-date files, folders, or directories. Whether you wish to synchronize a desktop with a mobile device or two, most personal productivity applications and suites now include support to *synchronize,* or *sync,* data.

 EXAM TIP Be sure you understand the difference between the synchronization of data and files and performing a backup of the same.

Having the same data available on different mobile (and stationary) devices is the primary benefit of data synchronization. The requirements for this process are a data source, a target for the data, and an application to transfer and synchronize the data on both devices. A source device could be a mobile phone or a desktop computer, and the target device may be any mobile device or desktop PC, or any other combination of devices, provided a synchronization application is available.

Data synchronization is important to anyone who relies on data stored on a mobile device to be just as accurate and timely as the same data stored on a base system. Data synchronization is a two-way street, meaning that the data source could very well be a mobile device, and the target device could be a user's desktop computer, a cloud application, or even another mobile device.

Data synchronization processes are defined by their targets. The following briefly describes the three target categories.

- **Synchronizing to a desktop** Mobile devices can synchronize data by connecting to a laptop or desktop computer via USB, Wi-Fi, or Bluetooth. Another way that a mobile computing device can sync to a desktop is using OneDrive or Dropbox as an intermediary. However, this method may only work for data that isn't updated frequently.

- **Synchronizing to the cloud** Cloud-based storage sites can be used to pass data between devices, especially when the devices might not be able to communicate directly. Cloud services like NetApp's Cloud Sync, Apple's iCloud, and Microsoft Azure AD Connect provide the capability to schedule backups, synchronization, and other data harmonization features.

- **Synchronizing to an automobile** The latest models of automobiles use synchronization to push firmware and software updates to systems in a vehicle, usually without the owner being involved or even knowing that it happens. The car may also provide data back to the manufacturer regarding the performance of certain onboard systems. Drivers may want to synchronize their smartphone to the sound system for hands-free use or to play music stored on the smartphone.

The types of data and information that can be synchronized between two devices includes just about everything: e-mail messages, calendars and contacts, applications, photos, audio files, video files, browser bookmarks, documents, e-books, and even passwords.

You should expect to encounter a question or perhaps just a reference to the synchronization processes of Microsoft 365, Google Workspace, and Apple iCloud application suites. The synchronization processes for these and other similar products are relatively the same, but the setup processes do vary. Since the primary resource that is synchronized to a mobile device relates to e-mail, the following are some examples of how each is set up.

Synchronize Apple iCloud to an Android Device

iCloud is an application in the Apple system environment. Before you can sync to it, you must establish an account. If you already have an @mac.com or @me.com e-mail account, you are set. If not, you must create one. After doing so, you can then set up synchronization.

On an Android device, perform the following steps:

1. Access the Apps menu and select Settings.
2. Choose Accounts and then Add An Account.

3. Select the appropriate Account Type and, if necessary, the Account Sub-Type.

4. Enter the e-mail address to be synchronized and its corresponding password and then tap Next to continue. You may be prompted for a username, password, or server. If so, provide this information.

5. Provide the SMTP server ID and the related port number and then tap Next.

6. You may be asked for some additional settings for this account, such as frequency, size, and the like. If so, enter this information and tap Next.

7. Assign a name to the account (it will be the name used for outgoing messages from the account). Select Next to create the account.

Synchronize Google Workspace to an Android or iOS Device

As in the previous example, in order to synchronize to a Google Workspace account, you must first have one. If you already have an @gmail.com account, you are good to go. Otherwise, you need to create one.

Next, sign in to the Gmail app:

- For an Android device, access the Gmail app and sign-in.
- For an iOS device:
    1. Choose Settings | Accounts & Passwords | Add Account | Gmail.
    2. Enter a name, address, and password and then click Next.
    3. Re-enter the address and click Next.
    4. Choose the items to be synced and click Done.

Synchronize Outlook (Exchange) to an Android or iOS Device

Before beginning to set up the synchronization, create a Microsoft account, if necessary, and install the Outlook for Android app on the Android device, if needed. Use the following steps to set up synchronization between Outlook and the device.

On the Android device:

1. Open the Email app and sign in.

2. Select Manually Setting and fill in the Domain/Username entry.

3. Enter the Exchange server password and choose the Use Secure Connection (SSL) option.

4. Set the frequency to be used for checking for updates in Accounts Options.

5. Give the account a name and tap Done.

On the iOS device:

1. Add the account using Settings | Accounts & Passwords | Add Account and indicate the account type being added.

2. Enter a name, e-mail address, e-mail password, and description, if desired, and tap Save.

Synchronize Outlook (Exchange) to an iOS Device

Before you begin to set up the synchronization, create a Microsoft account, if necessary. Use the following steps to set up synchronization between Outlook and the iOS device:

1. The first step is to identify the Outlook/Exchange account to iOS using Settings | Passwords & Accounts | Add Account | Exchange. Then enter the e-mail address to be synchronized.

2. Enter how you wish to connect to the Exchange server, choosing either Configure Manually or Sign In.
   - Configure Manually requires that you set up an Exchange account using your e-mail account and its associated password, plus perhaps some other server-related information.
   - Sign In requires only your e-mail address and password, which are transmitted to the Exchange server for validation and to retrieve account information. If multifactor authentication is in use, you will be asked for the additional authentication information.

3. Add the account using Settings | Accounts & Passwords | Add Account and indicate the account type being added.

4. Enter a name, e-mail address, e-mail password, and description, if desired, and then tap Save.

One huge caution, though: if you are synchronizing to or from a cell phone or smartphone, keep the data transfer capacity limit (data cap) in mind. Some files, and probably most files, are larger than you think and may result in additional charges for data transfers.

REVIEW

Objective 1.4: Given a scenario, configure basic mobile-device network connectivity and application support

- The five generations of cellular data networks and communication are 1G, 2G, 3G, 4G, and 5G.
  - 1G offered narrow band analog service with a limited number of simultaneous callers.
  - 2G provided wider frequency bands and greater mobility. 2G introduced digital encryption.

- 3G added security features, transmission types, global roaming, faster data transmission speeds, and two-way authentication.
- 4G uses IP-based system with data speeds of 50 Mbps to 80 Mbps over a maximum range of 31 miles. Also, it secures data in transit with 3DES and AES encryption, and access is authenticated.
- 5G defines a RAT that is separated into two frequency ranges: FR1 with sub-6 GHz bands, and FR2 built on the 4G LTE, which provides Gbps data speeds.
- A mobile hotspot device creates a Wi-Fi network that shares its data connection with other Wi-Fi devices. A hotspot is also called tethering.
- The primary service protocols for cellular phone systems are Global System for Mobile Communications (GSM) and code division multiple access (CDMA).
  - GSM is the generally deployed standard and is replacing CDMA. A GSM SIM card can be removed and installed into a new device.
  - CDMA devices are tied to a provider and must remain so.
- A preferred roaming list (PRL) contains networks and frequencies used by other carriers. CDMA devices may receive product release instruction (PRI) updates.
- Bluetooth setup includes the following steps: enable Bluetooth, enable pairing, locate a device for pairing, enter the PIN code, and test connectivity.
- Location services use GPS, RFID, Wi-Fi, or cellular RF technology to identify a device's location.
- Mobile device management (MDM) is security software that enables organizations to secure, monitor, manage, and enforce policies on employees' mobile devices.
- Mobile application management (MAM) is a methodology for mobile software development but can also cover operations of mobile software, including corporate e-mail configuration, two-factor authentication, and corporate applications on mobile devices.
- Data synchronization helps to ensure that the same data is available on different devices.

1.4 QUESTIONS

1. Which of the cellular technology generations added security features, transmission types, global roaming, and data transmission speeds of 144 Kbps to 2 Mbps?

   A. 1G

   B. 2G

   C. 3G

   D. 4G

   E. 5G

2. What technology allows a SIM card to be removed and installed into a new device?

 A. CDMA

 B. GSM

 C. TDMA

 D. 5G

3. What feature is used by mapping and location-based apps on mobile devices?

 A. Location Services

 B. Maps

 C. Find My

 D. Tips

4. You are getting ready to try out a new Bluetooth headset for your smartphone. After you enable Bluetooth and turn on the headset, which of the following do you need to do to use the headset?

 A. Tether the headset.

 B. Connect to the hotspot on the phone.

 C. Pair the headset with the phone.

 D. Run a program.

5. What types of data can be synchronized between a PC and another device?

 A. Only text-based data

 B. Only e-mail

 C. All data

 D. No data

1.4 ANSWERS

1. **C**   3G added security features, transmission types, global roaming, faster data transmission speeds, and two-way authentication.

2. **B**   GSM SIM cards are portable and can be removed from one device and inserted into another device, regardless of the service provider.

3. **A**   Apple's Location Services feature provides location information to mapping and location-based apps. (The same is true for Google's Location feature.)

4. **C**   You must pair a new Bluetooth device with your mobile device before you can use the new device.

5. **C**   Virtually all types of data can be synchronized between two devices or between a source and a target.

Networking

Compare and contrast Transmission Control Protocol (TCP) and User Datagram Protocol (UDP) ports, protocols, and their purposes

In the standard network reference models, such as the TCP/IP and OSI models, the respective Transport layers define two protocols: the Transmission Control Protocol (TCP) and User Datagram Protocol (UDP), which are the primary data transfer protocols of any TCP/IP network. Although both are used to transport information, they are as different as an eye dropper and a fire hose—a difference we explore in this objective.

Ports and Protocols

Protocols handle data transfer details, such as how to pack and unpack data into protocol-specific *packet* formats. The Internet runs on the *Transmission Control Protocol/Internet Protocol (TCP/IP)* suite, which is a stack (collection) of protocols and services that individually are designed to manage, package, transmit, and operate networks large and small.

NOTE   The terms *packet* and *frame* are often used interchangeably. However, they are actually two different message formats used on separate layers of a network reference model. A *frame* is a Data Link layer message format, most commonly used in Ethernet networks. A *packet* is a Network or Internet layer message format typically associated with TCP/IP networks, such as the Internet.

TCP and UDP both use port numbers to identify the type of connection being used. Table 2.1-1 provides a quick reference to application protocols and the TCP port numbers they use. Table 2.1-2 provides a quick reference to utility protocols (protocols that are hidden "behind the scenes" protocols) and the TCP and UDP port numbers they use.

EXAM TIP   Be able to identify the various TCP/UDP ports and the associated protocol of each port.

ADDITIONAL RESOURCES   Apps with network support use many additional TCP and UDP ports. To see a comprehensive real-time report on TCP and UDP activity on a computer running Windows, download the free LiveTcpUdpWatch utility from NirSoft at https://www.nirsoft.net/utils/live_tcp_udp_watch.html.

TABLE 2.1-1   Application Protocols

TCP Port Number	Application Protocol	Function
20/21	FTP (File Transfer Protocol)	File transfer control data (20) and file data (21)
22	SSH (Secure Shell)	Encrypted terminal emulation
23	Telnet	Terminal emulation (not secure)
25	SMTP (Simple Mail Transfer Protocol)	Outgoing e-mail
80	HTTP (Hypertext Transfer Protocol)	Web pages (not secure)
110	POP3 (Post Office Protocol 3)	Incoming e-mail
143	IMAP (Internet Message Access Protocol)	Incoming e-mail
443	HTTPS (HTTP Secure, HTTP over SSL)	Secure web pages
3389	RDP (Remote Desktop Protocol)	Remote Desktop

TABLE 2.1-2   Utility Protocols

Port Number	Protocol Type	Utility Protocol	Function
53	UDP	DNS (Domain Name System)	Allows the use of DNS naming
67, 68	UDP	DHCP (Dynamic Host Configuration Protocol)	IP addressing provided by a DHCP server (67) to network client (68)
137–139	TCP/UDP	NetBIOS/NetBT (NetBIOS over TCP/IP)	Enables legacy (pre-TCP/IP) apps to run on TCP/IP networks
161, 162	UDP	SNMP (Simple Network Management Protocol)	Remote management of network devices; SNMP manager (161) and SNMP agent (162)
389	TCP	LDAP (Lightweight Directory Access Protocol)	Querying directories
445	TCP	SMB/CIFS (Server Message Block/Common Internet File System)	Windows naming/folder sharing and cross-platform file sharing

Connection-Oriented vs. Connectionless

When transmitting data over a network, whether it's over the same network or between two different networks, the protocol in use and the communication interfaces of the sending and receiving stations determine which of the two available connection types is to be used. The two connection types are connection-oriented and connectionless.

A *connection-oriented* protocol, as its name implies, focuses on creating, managing, and operating the connections and data transmission over the circuit established between them.

A *connectionless* protocol, as its name implies, doesn't create formal connections and focuses instead on the data transmission.

Connection-Oriented

The connection-oriented communication method is an outgrowth of the telephone system. Before signals can be transmitted over an end-to-end link, each end of the link must agree to the configuration of the line and the protocol in use. The link is confirmed using what is called a handshake, which involves an exchange of specialized packets that represent a request to synchronize (SYN), a request to send (RTS), indications that the line is clear to send (CTS), and the acknowledgments (ACKs) for each packet sent and received by either end. Once the connection is verified, data packets are transmitted and received in a fixed serial order. Because of its rigid protocol requirements, TCP, which is a connection-oriented protocol (COP), is considered to be a reliable communication protocol.

Connectionless

Earlier TCP and UDP were likened to an eye dropper and a fire hose, respectively. With its fixed requirements for establishing and managing a communication link, the connection-oriented TCP is something like an eye dropper. A connectionless protocol—namely, UDP—is then more like a fire hose. A connectionless protocol doesn't manage the connection, the transmission link, or the data flow. Data is merely transmitted on the line without the use of RTSs, CTSs, or ACKs. Data flows at the speed available, much like water through a fire hose. UDP, which is a connectionless protocol (CLP), is considered to be an unreliable protocol.

Figure 2.1-1 shows a simplified comparison of connection-oriented and connectionless protocols.

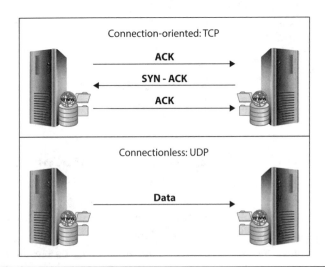

FIGURE 2.1-1   A comparison of the connection methods used by TCP and UDP

TCP vs. UDP

TCP accomplishes the reliable transfer of data with communication rules that require both machines to acknowledge each other to send and receive data. Thus, TCP is referred to as a connection-oriented protocol.

UDP is much faster because it lacks these checks—which is fine if your data can tolerate some errors, or if the chance of errors is low. For example, speed might be more important than a few dropped packets for a Voice over IP (VoIP) call or video chat. Because UDP simply sends data without checking to see if it is received, it is referred to as a connectionless protocol.

When data moving between systems must arrive in good order, we use the connection-oriented *Transmission Control Protocol (TCP)*. If it's not a big deal for data to miss a bit or two, the connectionless *User Datagram Protocol (UDP)* is the way to go. Most TCP/IP applications use TCP (that's why we don't call it UDP/IP) because it transfers data reliably.

Other Connection-Oriented Protocols

Although TCP is often given as the primary example of a connection-oriented protocol, there are others. In situations where an assurance of integrity or confidentiality is needed, there is very likely a COP that fits the bill. Other commonly used COPs are HTTPS, FTP, SMTP, and SSH. TCP, HTTPS, and SSH are the COPs you can expect to see on the A+ Core 1 exam. Let's look at the latter two a bit deeper.

Hypertext Transport Protocol Using TLS

At one time, the *S* in HTTPS represented the Secure Sockets Layer (SSL), but SSL is in the process of being replaced by the Transport Layer Security (TLS) protocol, but more on that later. First, it's important to understand how HTTPS incorporates connection-oriented communication.

Like TCP, an HTTP session involves an exchange of messages between the requester and the server, which can require several back-and-forth messages. These messages help the client and the server come to an agreement on the characteristics of the transmission, such as bandwidth, speed, and more. However, one of these characteristics isn't security, and HTTP data packets are plain text, which is why TLS is added to the mix. HTTPS encrypts the standard HTTP packet within a TLS wrapper (packet). So, in this relationship, HTTP provides the connection-oriented assurance of the communication and TLS supplies the security.

Secure Shell

The Secure Shell (SSH) protocol is a secured replacement for the unsecured Telnet protocol, which is a COP for unencrypted communication between network nodes. In addition to a lack of security, Telnet doesn't provide authenticate policies or encryption.

The SSH protocol is included in all later versions of macOS and Linux, but a utility, such as PuTTY, is required for Windows systems. SSH operates on a client/server model using TCP port 22 and uses a TCP authentication handshake to verify a session and, once verified, sets up the secure shell and connection.

Other Connectionless Protocols

There are functions and services performed by several TCP/IP protocols that require less assurance and more efficiency than would be possible with a connection-oriented protocol. Some of the more commonly used connectionless protocols are UDP, Internet Protocol (IP), Internet Control Message Protocol (ICMP), Dynamic Host Configuration Protocol (DHCP), and Trivial FTP (TFTP). The A+ Core 1 exam may include questions or references about DHCP and TFTP.

Dynamic Host Configuration Protocol

The Dynamic Host Configuration Protocol (DHCP) is a connectionless protocol that functions on UDP. DHCP is a client/server model protocol that responds to a client's request for IP configuration data with data drawn from a pool of predefined values. DHCP also manages the "lease" period for the data supplied to the client and its renewal or expiration. DHCP operates as a connectionless service because the data is needed immediately by the requesting station.

Trivial File Transfer Protocol

The legacy File Transfer Protocol (FTP) is a connection-oriented service based on the need for accuracy in the transfer. However, smaller files, command sets, or files not requiring verification can use a connectionless service. Trivial FTP (TFTP) is a lightweight version of FTP that operates without authentication and a structured flow control as a connectionless protocol.

REVIEW

Objective 2.1: Compare and contrast Transmission Control Protocol (TCP) and User Datagram Protocol (UDP) ports, protocols, and their purposes

- Application protocols use TCP ports to perform functions such as file transfer, terminal emulation, web page transfers, and remote desktop connections.
- TCP ports are connection-oriented, meaning that both ends of a connection must acknowledge the connection. TCP connections are more reliable but slower than UDP connections.
- Utility protocols use primarily UDP ports, as well as some TCP ports, to perform functions such as file and directory services, folder sharing, and services discovery.
- UDP ports are connectionless, meaning that a service using UDP does not verify that the connection is working. UDP connections are faster but less reliable than TCP connections.
- HTTPS and SSH are connection-oriented protocols.
- DHCP and TFTP are examples of connectionless protocols.

2.1 QUESTIONS

1. An incorrect firewall setting results in port 110 being blocked. Which of the following services will not work until the port is unblocked?

   A. Secure web pages

   B. Receiving POP3 e-mail

   C. Remote desktop

   D. Upgrading to Windows 11

2. A computer that uses automatic IP addressing relies on which of the following ports?

   A. 21

   B. 25

   C. 143

   D. 67, 68

3. Which of the following protocols are considered connection-oriented? (Choose two.)

   A. HTTPS

   B. SSH

   C. DHCP

   D. TFTP

4. Sometimes, for greater security, e-mail providers change the default ports used for sending and receiving e-mail. If an e-mail provider changes from port 143 to a different port, which of these services would need to be configured to use the new port?

   A. POP3

   B. SMTP

   C. IMAP

   D. HTTP

   E. SSH

5. A user reports that she can connect to insecure websites (http://) but not to secure websites (https://). Which port is being blocked by a firewall?

   A. 80

   B. 445

   C. 25

   D. 443

2.1 ANSWERS

1. **B**   The default port used by POP3 to receive e-mail is 110.

2. **D**   The ports used by the DHCP service for automatic IP addressing are 67 and 68.

3. **A B**   HTTPS and SSH are connectionless protocols.

4. **C**   IMAP normally uses port 143.

5. **D**   443 is the port used for HTTPS (secure HTTP).

 **Objective 2.2** # Compare and contrast common networking hardware

Networks are all about interconnecting computing devices (also called hosts) so they can communicate. More specifically, your *local host* can communicate with *remote hosts* to access the *resources* (such as printers, files, web pages, and so on) those systems share, and to share its own resources. In each exchange, the system providing a resource is the *server,* and the system using the resource is the *client*; when we call an entire system a server, what we really mean is that the system's primary job is serving some resource(s) to clients.

For a variety of different devices to share resources over a network, the network components need a shared connectivity standard, an addressing method clients and servers can use to find and communicate with each other, and shared software protocols that each system in an exchange understands. Let's look at many of the concepts and components that come together to form a network.

Routers

A router is a device that connects LANs to a WAN (see Figure 2.2-1). Hosts send signals for destinations outside of the LAN to the router, which routes traffic between networks.

FIGURE 2.2-1   Two broadcast domains connected by a router—a WAN

FIGURE 2.2-2 Two broadcast domains—two separate LANs

Switches

Switches connect hosts on a *local area network (LAN)* and pass signals between them. Switches memorize the MAC address of each device to smartly repeat signals to the appropriate host. A group of computers connected by one or more switches is a *broadcast domain* (see Figure 2.2-2).

> **EXAM TIP** A LAN is a group of networked computers within a few hundred meters of each other, whereas a *wide area network (WAN)* is a group of computers on multiple LANs connected with long-distance technologies.

Managed

A *managed switch* is a switch in which each port can be configured with different settings. For example, you can set a single managed switch to function as two or more virtual LANs (VLANs), control quality of service (QoS) settings on a per-port basis, and more.

Unmanaged

An *unmanaged switch* is the type of switch sold for small office/home office (SOHO) use, such as the one shown in Figure 2.2-2. It has no management features, and all devices connected to it are in the same LAN.

> **EXAM TIP** Be ready to identify the various networking hardware devices. Know the differences between routers, managed switches, and unmanaged switches.

FIGURE 2.2-3   Device that acts as access point, switch, and router (inset shows ports on back side)

Access Points

An *access point (AP)* centrally connects wireless network nodes into a wireless LAN (WLAN) in the same way a switch connects wired devices into a LAN. Many APs also act as high-speed switches and Internet routers (see Figure 2.2-3). APs are sometimes referred to as *wireless APs (WAPs)*.

Patch Panel

A *patch panel* (shown in Figure 2.2-4) has a row of permanent connectors for horizontal cables on the back and a row of female port connectors on the front, enabling you to use short

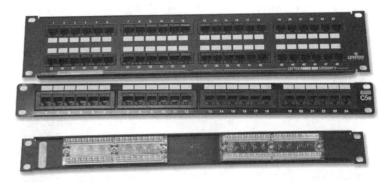

FIGURE 2.2-4   Typical patch panels

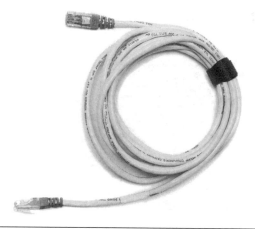

FIGURE 2.2-5 Typical patch cable

stranded-core UTP *patch cables* (shown in Figure 2.2-5) to connect the patch panel to the switch. Premade patch cables make it simple to get multiple colors for organization and often come with booted (reinforced) connectors.

 NOTE A patch cable is a specific length (usually short but can be up to 100 feet) of cable terminated at each end with a plug or socket. Also called a patch cord.

Firewall

Firewalls generally protect an internal network from unauthorized access to and from the Internet at large with methods such as hiding IP addresses and blocking TCP/IP ports, but firewalls at internal boundaries can also help limit the damage a compromised node can do to important resources. *Hardware firewalls* are often built into routers (or standalone devices), whereas *software firewalls* run on individual systems.

Hardware firewalls protect your LAN from outside threats by filtering packets before they reach your internal network and its resources and devices. You can configure a SOHO router's firewall from its browser-based settings utility provided by virtually all hardware firewalls. Hardware firewalls use *stateful packet inspection (SPI)* to inspect individual packets and block incoming traffic that isn't a response to your network's outgoing traffic. You can even disable ports entirely, blocking all traffic in or out.

Most software firewalls don't provide the advanced features found on larger hardware firewalls, but they are primarily designed to protect a single host computer rather than entire networks or enterprise systems. Figure 2.2-6 shows a sampling of the firewall settings on the Comodo Internet Security Pro system.

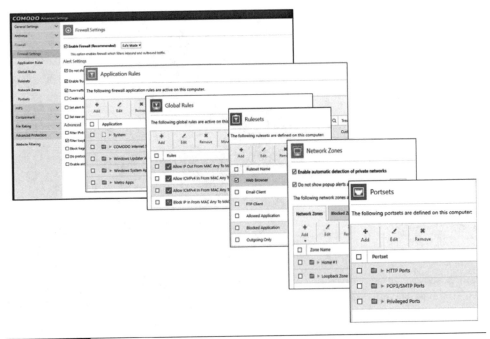

FIGURE 2.2-6 The configuration settings on a software firewall

Power over Ethernet

Most network hardware, including APs, draw power from an electrical outlet. Advanced APs and networked devices such as security cameras can instead operate on electricity supplied by a *Power over Ethernet (PoE) injector* or *PoE switch*. Both types of devices enable a standard Ethernet cable to carry power and data simultaneously.

PoE Standards

PoE provides electrical power from power sourcing equipment (PSE), such as a PoE switch, to a powered device (PD) over Ethernet cables that carry both the electrical power and transmitted data. PoE standards, discussed next, are developed and published by the IEEE (Institute of Electrical and Electronics Engineers) primarily to control how much power is supplied to different types of PDs.

The PoE standards define four types or levels of power, detailed in IEEE 802.3af, IEEE 802.3at, and IEEE 802.3bt, which defines two types. Each of these PoE standards specifies the minimum power a PSE can source and the maximum power a PD can expect to receive. The three standards, which are defined within the IEEE 802.3 Ethernet group, are as follows:

- **IEEE 802.3af (Standard PoE)** Also known as Type 1, this standard defines a power source of 44–57 volts and the maximum power output of a port to be no more than 15.4 watts. Used for voice over the Internet (VoIP) and Wi-Fi APs.

| **TABLE 2.2-1** | IEEE PoE Standards |

IEEE Standard	Type	PD Min. Power	PSE Max. Power	Cable
802.3af	1	12.95 W	15.4 W	Cat5e
802.3at	2	25 W	30 W	Cat5e
802.3bt	3	51–60 W	60 W	Cat5e
802.3bt	4	71–90 W	100 W	Cat5e

- **IEEE 802.3at (PoE+)**   Also known as Type 2, this standard is essentially an update to the 802.3af standard. However, the 802.3at standard doesn't replace or obsolete the earlier standard and is backward compatible with it. PoE+ supplies a range of 50–57 volts. Each port of a PSE can supply up to 30 watts of power, but not less than 25 watts. PoE+ supports LCD displays, biometric sensors, and tablets.
- **IEEE 802.3bt (PoE++)**   Also known as Type 3 and Type 4, these two standards increase the maximum PoE power by sending additional power over two or more previously unused pairs of Ethernet cables:
  - **Type 3 (PoE++)**   Carries up to 60 watts on each PoE port with a minimum power of 51 watts on a single RJ-45 cable.
  - **Type 4 (higher-power PoE)**   Supplies maximum power of 100 watts on each port of a PSE and ensures a minimum of 71 watts.

Table 2.2-1 summarizes the specifications of the PoE standards.

Injectors

A *PoE injector* (also known as a midspan) is plugged into a standard Ethernet cable coming from a switch and a source of AC power. The injector adds the power to the Ethernet cable running from the injector to the PoE device.

Switch

A *PoE switch* detects whether connected devices are standard Ethernet devices or PoE devices. It supplies power to PoE devices but does not supply power to standard Ethernet devices.

Hub

An Ethernet *hub* resembles a switch but takes a signal from one *port* and blindly broadcasts it out the others. This slows down traffic, and to make matters worse, hubs subdivide the total bandwidth of the network by the number of connected devices. Take, for example, a 100Base-T (Fast Ethernet) network. Use a switch, and you get the full 100-Mbps speed to each port. Replace that switch with a hub, and if you have four devices connected, the effective speed per port is only 25 Mbps. Don't use Ethernet hubs (USB hubs, on the other hand, are very useful).

Optical Network Terminal

Fiber-to-the-curb/-cabinet (FTTC), fiber-to-the-premises (FTTP), and fiber-to-the-home (FTTH) are becoming more and more available throughout the United States and in many countries around the world. If you subscribe to a fiber optic service for Internet, you'll find that just like most all other communication service types, there is a device that serves as the demarcation point (demarc). In a fiber installation, the demarc is a device for which the responsibility for the service connection is divided. The service provider is responsible for all aspects of the service (quality, availability, speed, and so on) from its originating source, like a central office (CO). The subscriber is responsible for the service either at or beyond the demarc (as it enters the premises). The responsibility of the demarc and the service responsibility change are typically tied to who owns the demarc.

In a fiber optic service, the demarc can be an *optical network terminal (ONT)*, or the service provider may install a termination unit as the demarc, as illustrated in Figure 2.2-7. This device operates like a modem that is converting digital to analog and back again. An ONT, however, converts light signaling into electrical impulses, and vice versa. An ONT device can be about the same size as a cable modem but may also be the size of a bathroom medicine cabinet. Typically, an ONT is installed out of sight in a utility or service area.

Cable/DSL Modem

At one time, DSL was one of the more common types of broadband services for SOHO networks. However, it's now just one of several services available for SOHO Internet connections, along with cable, satellite, and wireless. The A+ Core 1 (220-1101) exam focuses on only two of these services: cable and DSL. This section looks at the differences between these services and their respective modem interfaces.

Cable Modem

Cable uses regular RG-6 or RG-59 cable TV lines to provide upload speeds from 1 to 20 Mbps and download speeds from 6 Mbps to 1+ Gbps. *Cable Internet* connections are theoretically

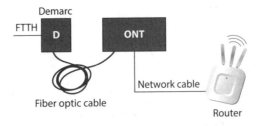

FIGURE 2.2-7   An ONT provides the conversion between fiber optic service and a premises network.

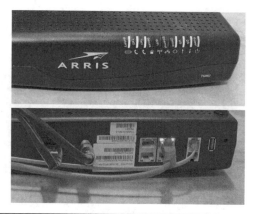

FIGURE 2.2-8   Cable modem with VoIP telephone support

available anywhere you can get cable TV. The cable connects to a cable modem that itself connects (via Ethernet) to a small home router or your NIC. Some cable modems also include support for VoIP telephony, such as the one shown in Figure 2.2-8.

DSL Modem

A *digital subscriber line (DSL)* modem connects to a standard RJ-11 telephone line, enabling the conversion of high-speed digital signals to and from the telephone line. DSL modems frequently are combined with wireless routers and are referred to as *DSL gateways*. DSL speeds vary widely from location to location because the greater the distance from the DSL modem to the telephone company's central switch, the slower the performance.

Cross-Reference

To learn more about DSL service, see the "DSL" section in Objective 2.7.

Network Interface Card

A *network interface card (NIC)* was originally an add-on card that connected a computer to an Ethernet or other wired network. Although most computers and network devices use integrated wired or wireless network connections instead of a card, the term NIC is used for both network cards and integrated network adapters. Older computers can use PCI-based NICs, while current computers can use PCIe NICs, such as the wireless NIC shown in Figure 2.2-9.

If a computer needs an upgrade to a faster or more capable NIC, it's usually easier to use a USB NIC, like the one shown in Figure 2.2-10. Tablets and other devices with USB ports but no Ethernet ports can use a USB to Ethernet adapter (see Figure 2.2-11).

FIGURE 2.2-9 Wireless PCIe add-on NIC

FIGURE 2.2-10 External USB wireless NIC

FIGURE 2.2-11   External USB to Ethernet adapter

Each network adapter (or NIC) has a 48-bit built-in binary *media access control (MAC) address* that uniquely identifies it. Before a NIC sends data out, it breaks that data into transmission-friendly *frames* (see Figure 2.2-12), each tagged with the MAC address of the sender and recipient, along with information the receiver can use to detect any possible errors. A *network switch* uses the MAC address to forward frames to the port on which the correct host can be reached.

 NOTE   A cyclic redundancy check (CRC) is a common mechanism for detecting data transmission errors.

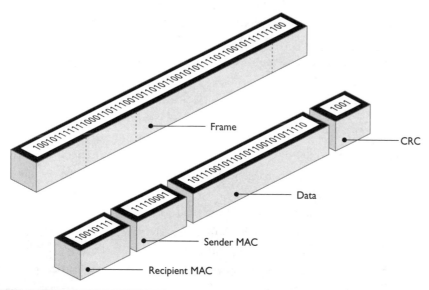

FIGURE 2.2-12   Generic frame

Software-Defined Networking

Unlike hardware-based networking—where the configurations of a network's switches, routers, and firewalls specify its operations, pathing, and decisions—*software-defined networking (SDN)* provides an approach to network management that enables the network configuration to be set using dynamic, programmatic settings to define the network environment. SDN provides a more flexible way to configure a network's operation, performance, and monitoring functions. SDN is more like cloud computing than traditional hardware-based network management.

An SDN network is defined on three layers: an application layer, a control layer, and an infrastructure layer. This architecture isn't something you need to know for the exam, but what each layer represents may help you to answer a question in which SDN is material. The application layer of an SDN contains hardware or software edge devices, such as a load balancer or a firewall (or both) and other mechanisms that operate at the edge of the network. The control layer contains the device (for example, a router or switch) that runs the software and acts as the brains for the network. The infrastructure layer is made up of the switching systems and devices that direct the flow of network traffic. The most important element of all of this is that the functions and interactions of the SDN layers are software-defined.

REVIEW

Objective 2.2: Compare and contrast common networking hardware

- Networks interconnect devices for communication and sharing resources. Network components share a connectivity standard, an addressing method, and protocols.
- A router connects LANs to WANs, and a switch connects devices on a LAN. Switches use the MAC address of a device, and routers use IP addresses to forward data to a destination.
- A LAN is a group of networked computers in close proximity, and a WAN is a group of computers on multiple LANs connected with long-distance technologies.
- Each port on a managed switch can be configured with different settings. An unmanaged switch has no management features.
- An AP centrally connects wireless network nodes into a WLAN.
- A firewall protects an internal network from unauthorized access to and from external networks. A network firewall can be either hardware or software.
- PoE devices provide electrical power over cables that carry both electrical power and transmitted data.
- An Ethernet hub takes a signal from one port and broadcasts it to all its other ports.
- An ONT is a fiber optic service's demarc that converts light into electrical impulses, and vice versa.

- A DSL modem converts high-speed digital signals to and from the telephone line. A cable modem performs the same function on a cable service line.

- An SDN network is defined on three layers: an application layer, a control layer, and an infrastructure layer, which contain hardware or software edge devices, the control software, and the switching systems, respectively, that define and control a network.

2.2 QUESTIONS

1. Company A wants to create two separate networks in a building but only wants to use a single-point connection. Which of the following does the company need?
   A. Unmanaged switch
   B. Router
   C. Hub
   D. Managed switch

2. You wish to install a digital PoE security camera over an outside storage area that requires 60 watts of power. To operate, what is the minimum PoE standard for this camera?
   A. PoE+
   B. Standard PoE
   C. Type 3 PoE++
   D. PoE is not available for digital cameras.

3. Company B has just moved into a new building and has found an existing Internet connection that use RG-6 wiring. Which of the following is being used?
   A. Cable
   B. DSL
   C. PoE
   D. Fiber

4. Your client is a company that has two locations in the same city, both of which get their Internet service from the same provider in the same city. Both locations use the same type of service, but one location has service that is about three to five times faster than the other. What type of service is most likely being used?
   A. Cable
   B. Satellite
   C. DSL
   D. PoE

5. What feature of all network adapters can be used to determine which device a frame is sent from or going to?

   A. IP address

   B. MAC address

   C. Switch port

   D. Router

2.2 ANSWERS

1. **D** A managed switch can be used to create multiple networks.

2. **C** A 60-watt PoE device requires Type 3 PoE++ standard support.

3. **A** RG-6 is a type of wiring used for cable Internet and cable TV.

4. **C** DSL service varies widely in speed, which is dependent on the distance from a client site to the central switch (central office) used by the phone company; longer distances have slower connections.

5. **B** Every network adapter, including those built into other devices, has a unique 48-bit MAC address.

 **Objective 2.3** # Compare and contrast protocols for wireless networking

Setting up a small office/home office (SOHO) network is a great way to learn about networking and its benefits, such as easy file sharing and more flexible printing. The principles and methods you learn in this objective will help you understand the operations of wireless networking protocols.

Frequencies

The U.S. Federal Communications Commission (FCC) and the International Telecommunication Union (ITU) work together to provide interference-free transmission across the spectrum of RF bands. The ITU's authority also extends to assigning satellite orbits and developing and coordinating worldwide technical standards. Figure 2.3-1 shows a graphic of the frequency allocations in U.S. radio spectrum.

 ADDITIONAL RESOURCES For a better view of the poster shown in Figure 2.3-1, visit the National Telecommunications and Information Administration (NTIA) at www.ntia.doc.gov/files/ntia/publications/january_2016_spectrum_wall_chart.pdf.

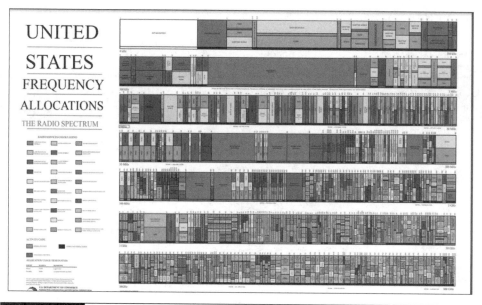

The two primary radio frequency bands used in SOHO wireless networks are those that contain the 2.4-GHz and 5-GHz frequencies. These frequency bands are unlicensed, meaning there is no registration or licensing fees or requirements for their use.

Industrial, Scientific, and Medical Bands

The Industrial, Scientific, and Medical (ISM) bands were originally designated for use by machinery that emits RF signals as a by-product of its use, such as welders, heaters, and microwave ovens. In 1985, these bands were opened for use with mobile communications and LAN networking.

The ISM bands are open and free to use without restriction. However, the downside to using ISM bands is that ISM bands are used for other purposes beside Wi-Fi. Many household, first responder, microwave, and several other wireless connections are also permitted to use these frequencies.

As shown in Table 2.3-1, the ISM bands used in Wi-Fi are in the 2.40-GHz to 2.48-GHz band and the 5.73-GHz to 5.83-GHz band. ISM bands are the basis of two IEEE 802.11 standards: 802.11b and 802.11g. Within these standards, wireless devices communicate over non-overlapping channels (channels 1, 6, and 11), as shown in Figure 2.3-2. All other channels overlap one or more other channels, making them unreliable to use.

TABLE 2.3-1	Bandwidth for the ISM RF Bands	
Band Designation	**ISM Band/Devices**	**Max Bandwidth**
Industrial	902–928 MHz	26 MHz
Scientific	2.4–2.48 GHz	100 MHz
Medical	5.725–5.825 GHz	150 MHz

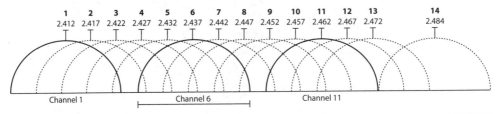

FIGURE 2.3-2 The channels in a wireless frequency band

Unlicensed National Information Infrastructure Bands

The Unlicensed National Information Infrastructure (UNII) bands include three separate frequency bands: UNII-1 (lower bands), UNII-2 (middle bands), and UNII-3 (upper bands), as shown in Table 2.3-2. Each of these frequency groupings is 100 MHz wide. Like the ISM bands, UNII bands are unlicensed.

Channels

Each of the 802.11-based wireless network standards uses a single frequency range in either of the two radio band allocations (ISM or UNII) for sending and receiving data. Although 14 ISM channels are defined internationally, not all the channels can be used in certain countries. In the U.S., the FCC identifies only 11 channels, for example. Each of the 11 U.S. channels is 5 MHz in width. Unfortunately, in the 11-channel designation, only channels 1, 6, and 11 are available for use on a wireless local area network (WLAN), as these channels aren't overlapped by other channels, as illustrated in Figure 2.3-2.

TABLE 2.3-2	Standard UNII Bands
Band Designation	**ISM Band/Devices**
UNII-1 Low	5.15–5.25 GHz
UNII-2 Middle	5.25–5.35 GHz
UNII-3 Upper	5.725–5.825 GHz

| TABLE 2.3-3 | UNII Non-overlapping Channels |

UNII Band	Non-overlapping Channels Available
UNII-1	36, 40, 44, 48
UNII-2	52, 56, 60, 64
UNII-3	149, 153, 157, 161, 165

The UNII frequencies have 24 non-overlapping channels that can be used on a WLAN, but not all are available on each of the UNII band levels. Table 2.3-3 lists the non-overlapping channels available for each of the bands.

Wireless Networking Standards

Wi-Fi, or wireless networking, is made up of a series of standards published by the IEEE. These standards define different levels of range, bandwidth, and compatibility with other standards for the medium in a WLAN. For each of the Wi-Fi standards, all of which are in the 802.11 series, two primary measurements are used to differentiate them: speed and frequency.

Speed designates the amount of data a standard can transmit from one wireless device to another in millions of bits per second, or Mbps. *Frequency* specifies the RF frequency of the wireless medium. Table 2.3-4 lists these characteristics for the current wireless standards.

 EXAM TIP You should know the characteristics of the various Wi-Fi/802.11 standards for the A+ Core 1 exam.

| TABLE 2.3-4 | Current Wireless Network Standards |

Name	Standard	Speed	Range Indoor/Outdoor	Frequency
Wi-Fi 1	802.11b	11 Mbps	115 feet/460 feet	2.4 GHz
Wi-Fi 2	802.11a	54 Mbps	115 feet/390 feet	5 GHz
Wi-Fi 3	802.11g	54 Mbps	125 feet/460 feet	2.4 GHz
Wireless-N/ Wi-Fi 4	802.11n	100 Mbps	230 feet/820 feet	2.4 GHz/ 5 GHz
Gigabit Wi-Fi/ Wi-Fi 5	802.11ac	1.3 Gbps	115 feet	5 GHz
AX Wi-Fi/ Wi-Fi 6	802.11ax	9.6 Gbps	200 feet/3000 feet	2.4 GHz/ 5 GHz
Wi-Fi 6E	802.11ax	10.8 Gbps	50 feet	6 GHz

NOTE   Wi-Fi 5, or 802.11ac, operates only in the 5-GHz band. However, Wi-Fi 4, Wi-Fi 6, and after are dual-band and operate in either the 2.4-GHz or 5-GHz band.

Bluetooth

As explained in Objective 1.4, Bluetooth devices communicate directly with each other. Whereas a wireless LAN needs an intermediary device, such as a router or an access point, Bluetooth devices are able to connect directly by "pairing." Bluetooth data transmission uses a limited-distance frequency between 2.1 and 2.48 GHz that a wireless network may also use.

A Bluetooth device operates on either Bluetooth Low Energy (LE), which is the more popular of the two types, or legacy Bluetooth, which is also called Basic Rate/Enhanced Data Rate (BR/EDR). Bluetooth LE has a lower data transfer rate (1 to 2 Mbps) than the Bluetooth BR/EDR, which operates at 3 Mbps.

Bluetooth devices, such as computing and handheld devices, can be all or part of a personal area network (PAN), which is accomplished by pairing Bluetooth devices together (important to remember for the exam). The following section provides a basic outline of the pairing process for a Bluetooth device.

Enabling and Pairing Bluetooth

Before you can connect via Bluetooth one device with another, you must first enable the Bluetooth capability on the device(s). Enabled Bluetooth devices can then be *paired* to establish interaction between them. For example, you can pair two smartphones together or a PC to a keyboard, mouse, printer, or another Bluetooth device. Assuming the device you wish to pair with has Bluetooth active and ready, the following sections describe the steps you need to take on a Windows, macOS, or Linux device to enable and pair it.

Windows 10/11

To enable Bluetooth on a Windows 10 or Windows 11 device, do the following:

1. Open the Settings app from the Start menu.
2. Choose Devices to open the Bluetooth & Other Devices page.
3. Move the slide switch to On to enable Bluetooth (see Figure 2.3-3).

Once Bluetooth is enabled on a Windows device, it can be paired with (connected to) another Bluetooth device. On a Windows device, open the Settings | Devices | Bluetooth & Other Devices page, as described. Click the plus sign associated with the Add a Bluetooth or Other Device option, and the Add a Device applet page will appear (see Figure 2.3-4). Choose Bluetooth to open the page that lists the Bluetooth devices within range to which your device can be paired. Choose the device to complete the pairing.

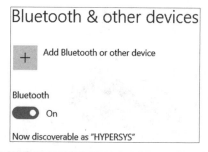

FIGURE 2.3-3 The Bluetooth & Other Devices settings page

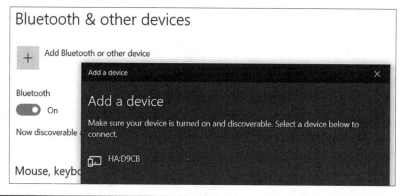

FIGURE 2.3-4 The Add a Device applet is used to pair Bluetooth devices to a Windows device.

Many Bluetooth devices, such as wireless headsets, mice, keyboards, and the like, will ask for a PIN code (number) to complete the pairing. For most devices, the pairing process is timed, which means you only have about 30 seconds (or less) to complete the pairing. Typically, this code is found in the device's user manual or on a sticker on the device itself. If you cannot find the code cannot, access the manufacturer's website or contact them directly.

macOS

To enable Bluetooth on an Apple macOS device, use the following steps:

1. On the Control Center or on the menu bar, click the Bluetooth icon (see Figure 2.3-5).
2. Click the Bluetooth switch to On (to enable) or Off (to disable).

 NOTE On a macOS system, turning off Bluetooth may also disable hotspot and other services.

FIGURE 2.3-5   The Bluetooth symbol

To pair a Bluetooth device to macOS, make sure the device is on and Bluetooth is enabled. Open System Preferences on the Apple menu and click Bluetooth to list the devices in range and choose the device. Enter the passcode if required.

Linux

On a Linux system, depending on its distro, the required daemons are bluez, gnome-bluetooth, Xfoe, LXDE, and i3, all of which are typically available in the blueman package. To start the Bluetooth daemon, enter the command **sudo apt-get Bluetooth start** in the Terminal.

To pair a Bluetooth device to a Linux system, use the following series of commands at the command line:

1. Check the Bluetooth status: **sudo systemctl status Bluetooth**
2. Enable Bluetooth discovery: **bluetoothctl discoverable on**
3. List Bluetooth devices in range: **bluetoothctl scan on**
4. Pair with a device: **bluetoothctl pair <MAC address>**
5. Connect to the paired device: **bluetoothctl connect <MAC address>**
6. Set the paired device to trust status: **bluetoothctl trust <MAC address>**
7. List paired devices: **bluetoothctl paired-devices**

Long-Range Fixed Wireless

Often the cost of pulling cable over long distances to provide access to rural homes and businesses isn't feasible. In this case, alternative solutions, such as digital subscriber line (DSL), satellite, and fixed wireless access (FWA), can provide access to Internet-based resources.

DSL may not be a viable solution in all situations. It has distance limitations and may not be available. Satellite and FWA may also not be viable as they are point-to-point and typically line-of-sight (LoS) services. Satellite services require the installation of a dish and typically have expensive bandwidth increments. FWA does require an antenna, but it is smaller than a satellite dish. Like satellite, FWA doesn't require long pulls of fiber optic and copper cables for last mile connection.

If you have a satellite service, such as Dish Network, DirectTV, or Hughes Internet, you are already using a form of FWA. FWA isn't a new technology, and it's possible you use some form of it, in one way or another, including 4G/LTE and Wi-MAX, both of which have proven to be expensive to install and operate. The deployment of 5G Fixed Wireless Access (5G-FWA) or any of the fixed wireless legacy systems, such as Local Multipoint Distribution Services (LMDS) and ISM 2.4-MHz point-to-point services, will depend on local ordinances and policy.

IEEE 802.11ah

The IEEE 802.11ah standard defines a WLAN that operates on an unlicensed 1-GHz band. Its lower frequency gives it a longer transmission range than other Wi-Fi WLAN standards. IEEE 802.11ah is used for extended-range hotspots and cellular traffic offloading.

Local Multichannel Distribution Service

Local multichannel distribution service (LMDS) has proven to be a cost-effective two-way wireless LoS microwave service for all Internet media types. In the U.S., LMDS operates on the 28-GHz frequency band (the EU uses 40 GHz), which is limited to a range of two or three miles, depending on what may be encountered in its path.

Licensed Frequencies

In the U.S., the Federal Communications Commission (FCC) controls who can broadcast on the available RF spectrums. Licensed bands of the RF spectrum are assigned (for a fee) to broadcasting and cellular networks, among others. A licensed RF band grants the holder the sole right to broadcast their signals over one specific frequency in a specified geographic area (for example, your favorite radio station might broadcast on the licensed frequency of 98.7 FM).

EXAM TIP For the A+ Core 1 exam, you should know and understand what long-range fixed wireless is and how it's used as well as the difference between licensed and unlicensed frequencies. You should also have a general understanding of the power and signal strength elements of wireless signaling.

WLAN Devices: Power and Signal Strength

In a WLAN, transmitting and receiving devices convert wired signals to wireless signals and back again. The signals transmitted between the wireless devices are in the form of radio frequency signals, which can attenuate over set distances, depending on the signal strength. The primary signal strength and the power of the transmission are defined by the following:

- **Radio transmit power** Measured in decibel mW to indicate the power level of a transmitted signal.
- **Equivalent isotopically radiated power (EIRP)** The equivalent of the transmit power less the signal strength loss between the transmitter and the antenna plus the signal strength gain of the antenna.
- **Received signal strength indicator (RSSI)** As its name says, this is the measurement of the signal strength received at any receiver within the range of a WLAN. It indicates the signal strength residual after distance and obstacle attenuations.

Near-Field Communication

Near-field communication (NFC) allows wireless devices to communicate with other wireless devices within a range of 4 centimeters (cm), or about 1.6 inches. NFC transmits and receives RF waves, which can make it seem much like Bluetooth, RFID, or even Zigbee, but NFC differs because its signal generation is produced from electromagnetic induction. This allows passive devices with no power source to transmit to an active device, such as a smartphone or tablet, that enters its range.

NFC has three modes of operations: read/write, card emulation, and peer-to-peer, which has been redacted. NFC is most commonly used with tap-to-go payment systems, such as Apple Pay, Google Pay, and other form of cashless payment services.

Radio-Frequency Identification

Radio-frequency identification (RFID) is a technology in which digital data, burned into labels or tags, is emitted as RF waves that can be received by nearby readers. RFID is an automatic identification and data capture (AIDC) technology that automatically identifies objects, collects data about them, and inputs the data into another system without external intervention.

At its core, an RFID system has three components: an RFID tag or label, a reader, and an antenna. An RFID tag or label contains an integrated circuit and an antenna that transmits data to an RFID reader on a receiver device. The reader converts the signal into usable data that is transferred to a host computer system and then stored. RFID devices can be used for asset, inventory, and people tracking as well as to limit access into controlled areas. RFID technology is also used in ID badges.

REVIEW

Objective 2.3: Compare and contrast protocols for wireless networking

- The two primary RF spectrums used in SOHO wireless networks are the unlicensed ISM and UNII spectrums (2.4 GHz and 5 GHz, respectively).
- ISM WLAN devices communicate over non-overlapping channels (channels 1, 6, and 11).
- The IEEE 802.11 wireless networking standards have evolved from the 802.11a to the current 802.11ax.
- Wi-Fi 802.11 standards use two measurements to differentiate them: speed and frequency. Speed designates the data transmitted in Mbps. Frequency specifies the RF frequency.
- Bluetooth devices communicate directly, but a WLAN requires an intermediary device, such as a router or an access point. Bluetooth transmits on a limited-distance frequency between 2.1 and 2.48 GHz in the ISM frequencies.
- NFC wireless devices communicate in a range of 4 cm. NFC has three modes of operations: read/write, card emulation, and peer-to-peer.
- RFID labels or tags emit RF waves that can be received by nearby readers. RFID systems have three components: an RFID tag or label, a reader, and an antenna.

2.3 QUESTIONS

1. The wireless LAN RF frequencies are specified in the 2.4-GHz and 5-GHz ranges, which are known commonly as what? (Choose two.)
   - **A.** ISM
   - **B.** WLAN
   - **C.** NTIA
   - **D.** UNII

2. Bluetooth transmits on a limited-distance frequency between which two ISM frequencies?
   - **A.** 2.57 GHz to 2.8 GHz
   - **B.** 2.1 GHz to 2.48 GHz
   - **C.** 5.725 GHz to 5.825 GHz
   - **D.** 28 GHz to 36 GHz

3. Which of the following is not one of the factors used to define the primary signal strength and transmission power of an RF wireless signal?
   - **A.** Radio transmit power
   - **B.** EIRP
   - **C.** RSSI
   - **D.** DHCP

4. What is the maximum range of NFC wireless devices?

  A. 4 cm

  B. 4.6 inches

  C. 4 mm

  D. 4 mW

5. Which of the following is not a component of an RFID system?

  A. RFID tag

  B. RFID label

  C. RFID printer

  D. RFID reader

6. Which Wi-Fi standard has a maximum speed of 9.6 Gbps and uses the 2.4-GHz and 5.8-GHz frequencies?

  A. 802.11ac

  B. 802.11n

  C. 802.11ax

  D. 802.11z

2.3 ANSWERS

1. **A D**   ISM frequencies begin with 2.4 GHz, and UNII frequencies begin with 5 GHz.

2. **B**   Bluetooth transmits on a limited-distance frequency between 2.1 GHz to 2.48 GHz.

3. **D**   DHCP is not a factor of the primary signal strength and transmission power of an RF wireless signal.

4. **A**   The maximum range of NFC wireless devices is 4 cm.

5. **C**   RFID systems are wireless and do not print physical elements.

6. **C**   802.11ax, also known as Wi-Fi 6, has a maximum speed of 9.6 Gbps and uses the 2.4- and 5.8-GHz frequencies.

Objective 2.4 # Summarize services provided by networked hosts

Network hosts can be used as servers to provide file, print, and other types of services; as network appliances to provide security and network protection features; and as embedded and legacy devices to provide ATM, traffic light, machine control, and other specialized services.

Server Roles

A server is any computer or device that provides services to connected devices. Depending on the size and types of networks in use, some servers are built into devices such as routers, and some computers on the network can perform server roles. The following sections describe these roles.

 EXAM TIP   Know the various server roles by name and function. For example, know that a syslog server is used to store (log) events and can send alerts to administrators.

DHCP Server

A Dynamic Host Configuration Protocol (DHCP) server provides IP addresses, default gateways, and other network settings such as DNS server addresses to connected devices. Typically, a DHCP server's function is incorporated into a device such as a router on a small office/home office (SOHO) network. However, larger networks might use dedicated DHCP servers.

DNS Server

A Domain Name Service (DNS) server maintains a database of IP addresses and their matching host names. When a host name, such as www.totalsem.com, is entered into a web browser, the DNS server used by that system matches that host name to the appropriate IP address.

DNS servers are provided by ISPs as well as by public DNS services such as Google DNS and OpenDNS. Although your device typically is configured with DNS servers by the DHCP server, it is possible to manually configure the DNS servers you prefer.

File Server

A *file server* or a *file share* stores files that are used by other computers and devices on a network. For residential or small business networks, a file server–like function can be enabled through file sharing on Windows, Linux, or macOS computers. Larger organization networks typically use dedicated file servers and computers. File server hardware generally features very large high-speed storage devices, high-performance network adapters, and sufficient memory to support the server software it hosts.

Print Server

A *print server* manages a network print queue for printers that are attached to the server or are connected directly to the network. Depending on the network, a single physical server might be used for both file and print server tasks, or separate servers might be used.

Mail Server

A *mail server* sends and receives e-mail. Incoming servers (where you check for new e-mail) typically use *Post Office Protocol version 3 (POP3)* or *Internet Message Access Protocol version 4 (IMAP4)*, while outgoing servers (where you send e-mail) use *Simple Mail Transfer Protocol (SMTP)*. These addresses come from your e-mail provider (usually your ISP, company, school, or other organization).

Syslog

Syslog is a protocol that network devices use to send event messages to a server that logs them for viewing. The syslog server can send alerts that can be reviewed by network administrators. Syslog is not natively supported on Windows, but third-party software can be used to convert messages from Windows apps into syslog-compatible messages.

 ADDITIONAL RESOURCES   To learn more about syslog, see the article "The Original Windows Syslog Server" at https://www.winsyslog.com/.

Web Server

A *web server* runs software designed for serving websites. For example, Microsoft Internet Information Services (IIS) functionality is available as an optional feature of Windows Server and business-oriented editions of Windows 10 and Windows 11. Most Linux distributions include Apache or Nginx web servers. Apache can also be used on macOS.

Authentication, Authorization, and Accounting Server

An *authentication, authorization, and accounting (AAA) server* program processes user requests to authenticate (identify) that the requestor is valid, may be authorized for specific access levels, and is to be tracked by audit and accounting functions. Authentication typically requires the verification of a user name and password, but additional factors can be used or required. Authorization assigns the predefined rights and permissions of an authenticated user to control access and action with resources. Accounting is the tracking mechanism in use to record the actions and results of the user.

An AAA server verifies the user's identity and controls and tracks access to system resources while the user is logged in to a network. Examples of AAA servers include RADIUS servers used by WPA2 and WPA3 encryption on corporate networks and servers that inspect RSA tokens provided by users with RSA key fobs.

Internet Appliance

Internet appliances are special-purpose devices that are incorporated into networks, typically to provide various types or levels of network security. The following sections provide a brief overview of the types of Internet appliances you need to know for the CompTIA A+ 220-1101 exam.

Spam Gateways

Anti-spam appliances (aka *spam gateways*) are devices that use onboard software to filter out incoming spam e-mail messages and instant messaging (or "spim") to prevent them from entering a system. Spam gateway devices are primarily in use in enterprise organizations, but many ISPs, academic institutions, and small businesses also employ some version of this function.

Unified Threat Management

Unified threat management (UTM) involves the use of hardware or software to provide a combination of several security functions. Typically, a UTM device provides security protections that may include firewall, remote access, VPN support, web traffic filtering, anti-malware, and network intrusion prevention. UTM replaces the need to install separate devices or systems for each of its supported security functions. A UTM solution can be a specialized appliance that is placed between an internal network and an end or gateway device, or it may be installed on a virtual machine running cloud-based services.

EXAM TIP   Know the purposes of and understand the differences between Internet appliances such as UTM devices, intrusion detection systems (IDSs), and intrusion prevention systems (IPSs). For example, an IDS can identify threats and send alerts. However, the more powerful IPS can actually act on the threat and possibly stop it!

Load Balancers

The purpose of a *load balancer* is to spread out the processing required to respond to incoming request traffic as evenly as possible, or desired, across a group of network or specific-purpose servers. Load balancers typically sit on the network between client devices and the servers to be balanced. Incoming requests are assigned to the next available server with the capability of processing the request.

Proxy Server

A *proxy server* is an intermediary between its users and the resources they request. Applications send requests to the proxy server instead of trying to access the Internet directly, and the proxy server fetches the resources on behalf of the users. This enables the proxy server to monitor usage, to restrict access to or modify insecure or objectionable content, as well as to cache, compress, or strip out resources to improve performance—and more. Enterprise proxy servers are usually implemented as software running on a multipurpose server.

 EXAM TIP Many security appliances include context-based rules called data loss prevention (DLP) to avoid data leaks. DLP scans outgoing packets and stops the flow if they break a rule.

Legacy/Embedded Systems

Networked devices don't necessarily look like computers. Many are, but you can find narrow-purpose computers or servers embedded in all sorts of machines and other equipment—CompTIA calls these *legacy/embedded systems*. It can be easy to overlook networked devices embedded in this equipment, but they may represent massive investments your network must remain compatible with. Some examples of legacy/embedded systems include machine controllers, digital watches, digital music players, traffic light controllers, aviation equipment, bank ATMs, and more. If these systems are running operating systems that are no longer supported with security or other patches (such as Windows XP or Windows 7), they represent a significant security threat.

Supervisory Control and Data Acquisition

Supervisory control and data acquisition (SCADA) systems perform real-time data collection for analysis of the efficiency, cost reduction, and operation improvements in an industrial setting. Because there can be an almost overwhelming amount of data available, SCADA is used to help organizations select and access specific data and control the functions of the equipment and machinery involved. SCADA applications can be used to view, collect, analyze, and graph a range of process characteristics, such as temperature, power consumption, operating levels, and many other measurable conditions.

Internet of Things Devices

Internet of Things (IoT) devices, also called "smart devices," include those devices and objects capable of being connected to a WAN or the Internet. IoT devices, or "things," is an ever expanding group, but characteristically they are devices that have the capability to send and receive data over a network. This includes automobiles, home appliances, smartphones and watches, residential and security lighting, home security detection and alarm systems, and more. For example, a car may have a system that helps it locate an empty parking space, or a refrigerator can alert its owner when the inventory of a required food or liquid item falls below a certain level.

REVIEW

Objective 2.4: Summarize services provided by networked hosts

- Web servers run software that serves websites.
- File servers store files and folders for use on the network.
- Print servers manage network print queues.
- DHCP servers provide IP addresses to connected devices.
- DNS servers handle DNS/IP address lookups.
- Proxy servers reroute requests for Internet content to their own copy of that content, or they can block requests.
- Mail servers send and receive e-mail.
- Authentication servers verify a user's identity.
- The syslog protocol is used to send event messages to a server where they can be logged and viewed.
- Internet appliance categories include spam gateways, load balancers, IDSs, IPSs, UTM devices, and end-point management servers, all of which can be used to protect the network.
- Legacy/embedded systems such as ATMs and machine controllers represent a significant security threat if their operating systems are no longer being patched. SCADA systems perform real-time data collection for analysis of the efficiency, cost reduction, and operation improvements in an industrial setting.
- IoT devices include automobiles, home appliances, smartphones and watches, residential and security lighting, home security detection and alarm systems, and more!

2.4 QUESTIONS

1. Microsoft IIS and Apache are examples of which type of server?
   - **A.** DHCP server
   - **B.** File server
   - **C.** Web server
   - **D.** Print server

2. Company H is setting up a RADIUS server as part of its wireless network. This server will perform which of the following tasks?
   - **A.** Mail server
   - **B.** Authentication server
   - **C.** Proxy server
   - **D.** Print server

3. Company J wants to install an Internet appliance that will provide protection as well as load balancing and VPN services. Which of the following categories has the device they need?

   A. IPS

   B. DLP

   C. IDS

   D. UTM

4. Your client's network is able to receive e-mail but unable to send it. Which of the following is not working?

   A. SMTP

   B. UTM

   C. Authentication server

   D. DNS server

5. Your department is considering an Internet appliance. Which of the following is the most likely reason to get one?

   A. Print serving

   B. Security

   C. Wireless AP

   D. Web server

2.4 ANSWERS

1. **C**   These are examples of web servers.

2. **B**   A RADIUS server is used for authentication on a WPA2 or WPA3 Wi-Fi enterprise network.

3. **D**   UTM (unified threat management) includes broad protection against threats as well as bundles network security services.

4. **A**   SMTP (Simple Mail Transfer Protocol) is used to send e-mail messages. If this protocol is disabled or blocked, e-mail cannot be sent.

5. **B**   Internet appliances are used to provide additional security features to an Internet connection.

Objective 2.5 # Given a scenario, install and configure basic wired/wireless small office/home office (SOHO) networks

Small office/home office (SOHO) networks tend to be simpler in design and layout, and they typically have fewer components than the networks in larger organizations and enterprises. This doesn't mean that the same network functions aren't required, because they are. A SOHO network often uses a single device to implement multiple network processes, but this capability isn't always available. This objective provides an overview of the processes used to configure and install a basic network, wired or wireless, in a SOHO setting.

Internet Protocol Addressing

The most important activity in the configuration of a network, regardless of its size, is the assignment of its Internet Protocol (IP) addressing scheme. On Ethernet networks, which most SOHO networks are, the addressing choices are *Layer 2 Media Access Control (MAC) addresses* (also called physical addresses) and *IP version 4 (IPv4)* or *IP version 6 (IPv6) addresses* (also called logical addresses).

MAC addresses are the default addressing on any Ethernet network. Each component capable of communicating on the network's medium is permanently assigned a MAC address by its manufacturer. If the communication between one network node and another remains totally on the local network, only the MAC address is needed. However, should network communication need to exit the local network and be forwarded on a WAN or the Internet, IP addressing becomes a necessary part of the configuration of the network and each of its nodes.

A *network address,* also called a *logical address,* must uniquely identify any device capable of communicating on the network medium, regardless of the medium being wireline (or wired) or wireless. A network address becomes the means by which a device is located on the network. In the addressing schemes of a TCP/IP network, an *IP address* identifies both a device and the network on which it resides. There are two versions of IP: IPv4 and IPv6. The following sections cover their essentials features and differences.

 EXAM TIP   Know the differences between IPv4 and IPv6. For example, an IPv4 address uses 32 bits while an IPv6 address uses 128 bits.

IPv4 Addresses

An IPv4 address is expressed in *dotted-octet notation,* which formats the address in four sets of eight binary numbers (octets), separated by periods (or dots). Network devices see IP addresses in binary form (for example, 11001010.00100010.00010000.00001011), but this isn't human-friendly. Therefore, the dotted-decimal form is used to express the IPv4 address (for example, 202.34.16.11), which is easier for people to read.

The IPv4 standard reserves certain address ranges for special purposes and uses. Table 2.5-1 lists these special-purpose address ranges.

Loopback Addresses

An IPv4 loopback address is the logical address assigned to the network adapter in a computer or network-capable device. On most computers, the loopback address refers to the network interface controller (NIC) or its network adapter. Because the address range of the lookback address block is a set standard, the loopback address is almost always the same on all network-enabled computers. This means that on any single PC, the loopback address is likely to be 127.0.0.1. The same is true for any other PC, even if it's on the same network. Network-capable devices, especially computers, can have multiple network adapters (referred to as being "multihomed"). In this case, each of the network adapters is assigned a different loopback address from the 127.0.0.0–127.255.255.255 loopback address range.

Private Addresses

When it began to be apparent that the available IPv4 addresses were running out, one of the changes made to the IPv4 standard was to set aside three blocks of addresses, one from each address class, that could be used repeatedly for local area networks (LANs) and other private networks. To ensure that these addresses could be reused on different networks and to avoid any possible routing problems, these addresses, designated as *private addresses,* were blocked from being forwarded outside of an organization's edge routers. Similar to the reusability of loopback addresses, multiple LANs in the same or in different organizations may use the same block of private addressing.

All IPv4 addresses that are not in the set-aside ranges of private addresses are *public addresses.* This means that unlike private addresses, a public address cannot be duplicated anywhere on the Internet or on the WANs and LANs that make up the Internet.

TABLE 2.5-1   Reserved IPv4 Nonroutable Addresses

Purpose	IPv4 Address Range
Loopback/localhost	127.0.0.0–127.255.255.255
Private addresses	10.0.0.0–10.255.255.255
	172.16.0.0–172.31.255.255
	192.168.0.0–192.168.255.255
Link-local (APIPA)	169.254.0.0–169.254.255.255

Link-Local Addresses

Sometimes a node on a local network is unable to obtain its configuration data from a Dynamic Host Configuration Protocol (DHCP) server. Rather than being blocked from communicating on the local network, which typically uses MAC addresses, the node's operating system can assign a placeholder *link-local address,* which is an address that's valid only for interactions within the network segment (broadcast domain) on which its node is located. This address is blocked from communicating outside of its LAN until it can obtain a valid IPv4 address.

On a Windows system, the link-local address that is assigned is an *Automatic Private IP Addressing (APIPA)* address, which is chosen randomly from the reserved IPv4 address range of 169.254.0.1 to 169.254.255.254 and assigned with a Class B 16-bit subnet mask (255.255.0.0). To ensure that the address assigned is unique to the local network, the system broadcasts the random address and uses it if there is no response.

EXAM TIP   If your system can communicate with other systems on your local network but can't reach the Internet, chances are the DHCP server is down and you have been assigned an APIPA address. You can find out if you are using an APIPA address by running ipconfig.

IPv6 Addresses

IPv6 is a Network layer protocol that was first defined by the Internet Engineering Task Force (IETF) in a draft proposal in December 1998 because of a concern that we would soon be running out of IPv4 addresses to assign. In September 2015, the American Registry for Internet Numbers (ARIN) announced that officially there were no more IPv4 addresses to issue. In July 2017, IETF issued the IPv6 standard to expand the available address pool and to supersede IPv4. The format of an IPv6 address is shown in this example:

2001:0000:0000:3210:0800:200C:00CF:1234

The structure of IPv6 involves the following characteristics:

* It has 128 bits in its addressing scheme, which provides for 340 undecillion (2^{128}) addresses.
* It has eight hexadecimal number groups separated by colons.

An IPv6 address can be shorted using the following rules:

* Leading zeros may be omitted from a group; therefore, 00CF becomes CF, and 0000 becomes 0.
* Any number of consecutive all-zero groups (0000) can be omitted and indicated with two-colon separators from the beginning and end of the string.

For example, the shortened version of the IPv6 address

2001:0000:0000:3210:0800:200C:00CF:1234

is

2001::3210:800:200C:CF:1234

 EXAM TIP   IPv6 addresses aren't case sensitive and can use either uppercase or lowercase letters. You may encounter lowercase or uppercase notation on the exam.

Operating system (OS) developers have two options for the last 64 bits (host ID) of an IPv6 address. Windows OS generates a random value when a NIC is configured, and that number never changes. Linux and macOS build the host ID (called the *Extended Unique Identifier-64-bit,* or *EUI-64*) from the MAC address of the NIC.

IPv6 includes a loopback address for a network adapter that can be used for testing. The full address is 0000:0000:0000:0000:0000:0000:0000:0001/128, which can be abbreviated as ::1/128 (using the two-colon abbreviation for consecutive all-zero groups).

IPv4 vs. IPv6

IPv4 and IPv6 differ in many ways. Table 2.5-2 helps you compare the differences.

TABLE 2.5-2   IPv4 vs. IPv6

Feature	IPv4	IPv6
Number of address bits	32 bits	128 bits
Address format	Four groups of binary octets, separated by periods	Eight four-digit groups of hex numbers, separated by colons
Zero compression	N/A	Uses :: (double colon) to replace one or more contiguous fields of zeros
Address example	192.168.0.1	2001:0000:0000:3210:0800:200C:00CF:1234 or 2001::3210:800:200C:CF:1234
Loopback address	127.0.0.1	0000:0000:0000:0000:0000:0000:0000:0001/128 or ::1/128
Maximum number of public IP addresses	Over 4 billion (2^{32})	Over 340 undecillion (2^{128})

Dynamic Address Assignment

Dynamic address configuration on a Windows, Linux, or macOS computer is performed by the TCP/IP protocol DHCP. Dynamic addressing allows a network's devices to be possibly configured with a different IP address each time it connects to a network. A node configured through dynamic address assignment is able to use network services like DNS and communication protocols based on UDP or TCP.

Dynamic Host Configuration Protocol

On a local network, or multiple LANs connected via a relay, the DHCP infrastructure consists of one or more DHCP servers and usually one or more network nodes or DHCP clients. The DHCP server supplies IP configuration information from a pool configured by the network administrators in response to requests made by DHCP clients.

The primary elements of a DHCP implementation are as follows:

- **DHCP server** As a server in a client/server arrangement, a DHCP server responds to IP configuration or lease requests to provide an IP address, monitor it during its lease period, and renew the lease if it expires.
- **DHCP client** As a client in a client/server arrangement, a DHCP client is the endpoint that requests and receives configuration data from a DHCP server. Most network clients receive DHCP configuration data by default.
- **IP address pool** The IP address provided to a network node is drawn from a pool of unassigned addresses defined in a pool of available addresses.
- **IP address lease** DHCP configuration items, including the IP address, have expiration dates. This data indicates the time period (present to future) in which a DHCP client can hold its DHCP configuration. If the lease expires, the affected client must renew it.

 NOTE Each time a DHCP client reboots, the DHCP configuration is assigned without regard to any configuration data previously assigned.

IPv4 DHCP

DHCP is the default dynamic addressing service for Windows and macOS and can be configured on most Linux distros. In response to a request from a node, DHCP automatically provides an IP address (IPv4, IPv6, or both), the associated subnet mask, the default gateway address, and the primary DNS address. The addressing provided is selected from a configured pool of available addresses.

To view the address assignment configuration of a Windows system, use the following steps:

1. Open the Control Panel and select Network and Sharing Center.
2. Click Change Adapter Settings.
3. Select the adapter that provides the primary connection to the network.
4. Click Properties.
5. Click Internet Protocol Version 4 (as shown in Figure 2.5-1).
6. Click Properties. Figure 2.5-2 shows a typical example of the settings for dynamic IP addressing on a Windows system.

Here are the steps used in the DHCP client/server configuration acquisition process, as illustrated in Figure 2.5-3:

1. **Discover**   After the client has completed its startup or if the ipconfig/ifconfig command is used, the client broadcasts a message asking the DHCP server to identify itself with its network addressing.
2. **Offer**   The DHCP server responds to the client with an IP address assigned from its pool of available addresses. If no addresses are available, the server sends a non-acknowledgment (NAK) message, and the client assigns itself a link-local address and terminates the dialog.

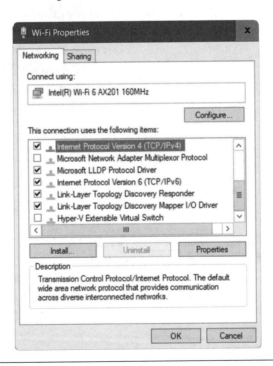

FIGURE 2.5-1   The adapter properties dialog box

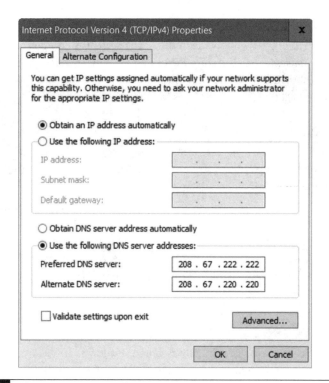

FIGURE 2.5-2 | Network adapter configured to get an IP address from a DHCP server automatically

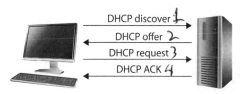

FIGURE 2.5-3 | The DHCP client/server configuration acquisition process

3. **Selection**   On some larger networks, there may be two or more DHCP servers offering IP address configurations, each sending its own DHCP offer. The client can respond to each of the offers with a DHCP request for additional information or merely respond with a request to the server that provided the first offer it received.

4. **Acknowledgment**   When the server receives the DHCP request message from the client, it creates an Address Resolution Protocol (ARP) mapping and responds to the client directly (unicast) with a DHCP ACK message.

IPv6 Link-Local Address

When a computer running IPv6 boots or restarts, the system is configured with a link-local address using the *Stateless Address Autoconfiguration (SLAAC)* service. SLAAC provides IPv6 systems with most of their link-local configurations. The first 64 bits of a link-local address are always FE80:0000:0000:0000 (which shortens to FE80::).

IPv6 DHCPv6

Whereas IPv4 DHCP (DHCPv4) uses broadcasting requests and responses, IPv6 DHCP (DHCPv6) uses multicasting (IPv6 doesn't include a broadcasting capability). One limitation of DHCPv6 is that it doesn't provide a default gateway to a node.

DHCP Reservations

A *DHCP reservation* is a DHCP-supplied IP address that never changes. It is meant for devices whose IP address needs to remain constant (for example, a print server). DHCP reservations are created on the DHCP server. This feature is available in DHCP servers as well as in some SOHO routers.

Static Addresses

A *static IP address* is a permanent, manually assigned IP address. Typically, static IP addresses are used in networks for systems that must always have the same IP address because they are used as servers or because they use different protocol settings than other devices on the network. When a static IP address is used, the IP address, subnet mask, default gateway, and DNS servers must also be assigned. See Figure 2.5-4 for a typical example.

 EXAM TIP Know the various IP addressing concepts, including static, dynamic, APIPA, and link local. Practice using the **ipconfig** and **ipconfig /all** commands at a command prompt to see if you can identify any of these IP address assignments.

Gateway

A *gateway* is a link connecting two networks. When a computer uses DHCP for its IP address, it receives the default gateway's IP address as part of its configuration. However, if you configure a device with a static IP address, you must also provide the default gateway's IP address. The default gateway on most private networks is an address such as 192.168.0.1 or 192.168.1.1.

To see the current IP address, subnet mask, default gateway, and DNS servers in Windows, open a command prompt and use the command **ipconfig /all**. Scroll to the current local area connection after running the command (a typical example is shown in Figure 2.5-5). The comparable command to use in Linux and macOS is **ifconfig**.

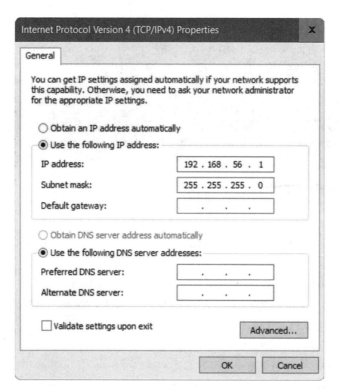

FIGURE 2.5-4 Network adapter configured with a static IP address

```
Wireless LAN adapter Wi-Fi:

    Connection-specific DNS Suffix  . : hsd1.wa.comcast.net
    Description . . . . . . . . . . . : Intel(R) Wi-Fi 6 AX201 160MHz
    Physical Address. . . . . . . . . : 44-AF-28-B3-D4-09
    DHCP Enabled. . . . . . . . . . . : Yes
    Autoconfiguration Enabled . . . . : Yes
    IPv6 Address. . . . . . . . . . . : 2603:3023:81d:e300::336b(Preferred)
    Lease Obtained. . . . . . . . . . : Tuesday, February 22, 2022 12:43:14 PM
    Lease Expires . . . . . . . . . . : Saturday, March 12, 2022 7:23:50 AM
    IPv6 Address. . . . . . . . . . . : 2603:3023:81d:e300:24b5:f7ca:631b:8cec(Preferred)
    Link-local IPv6 Address . . . . . : fe80::24b5:f7ca:631b:8cec%5(Preferred)
    IPv4 Address. . . . . . . . . . . : 10.1.10.253(Preferred)
    Subnet Mask . . . . . . . . . . . : 255.255.255.0
    Lease Obtained. . . . . . . . . . : Sunday, February 20, 2022 2:25:36 PM
    Lease Expires . . . . . . . . . . : Monday, March 14, 2022 7:37:01 AM
    Default Gateway . . . . . . . . . : fe80::bcc1:daff:fee2:1300%5
                                        10.1.10.1
    DHCP Server . . . . . . . . . . . : 10.1.10.1
    DHCPv6 IAID . . . . . . . . . . . : 71610152
    DHCPv6 Client DUID. . . . . . . . : 00-01-00-01-29-A4-43-35-44-AF-28-B3-D4-09
    DNS Servers . . . . . . . . . . . : 2001:558:feed::1
                                        2001:558:feed::2
                                        208.67.222.222
                                        208.67.220.220
    NetBIOS over Tcpip. . . . . . . . : Enabled
```

FIGURE 2.5-5 Using ipconfig /all to display the current IP configuration on the author's PC

EXAM TIP   Make sure you know how to use **ipconfig /all** and how to identify the settings displayed by **ipconfig /all**. Practice using **ipconfig** and **ipconfig /all** (or **ifconfig** and **ifconfig -a**) on different computers.

NOTE   The "(Preferred)" after an IP address in an adapter's ipconfig display indicates the address assigned to the interface. This address has no restrictions on its use.

REVIEW

Objective 2.5: Given a scenario, install and configure basic wired/wireless small office/home office (SOHO) networks

- A dynamic IP address is received from a DHCP server by a device on the network.
- An APIPA address is generated if the DHCP server cannot be reached.
- A link-local address is IPv6's equivalent to an APIPA address.
- A static IP address is an address that is manually assigned.
- If a static IP address is assigned, a DNS server must also be assigned.
- A DHCP reservation is a DHCP-supplied IP address that doesn't change.
- IPv4 uses dotted-octet notation and a subnet mask.
- IPv6 uses up to eight groups of numbers and supports methods to shorten its address.
- A gateway is a link connecting two networks.

2.5 QUESTIONS

1. A user cannot connect to the Internet. When you ask her for her current IP address, she tells you it is 169.254.0.18. Which of the following is not working?
   A. APIPA
   B. Static IP
   C. Link-local
   D. DHCP

2. An IPv4 address of 10.10.10.10 is best described as which of the following?
   A. Class C address
   B. Loopback address
   C. Private address
   D. DHCP address

3. Which of the following are characteristics of an IPv6 address? (Choose two.)

    A. Link-local

    B. 128 bits

    C. Zeroes omitted

    D. Colon separated

4. A DHCP-provided IP address that never changes is classified as which of the following?

    A. IP permanency

    B. IP reservation

    C. Link-local

    D. APIPA address

5. A network node using IPv6 can get its IP configuration from which of the following services and protocols? (Choose two.)

    A. VPN

    B. SLAAC

    C. DHCPv6

    D. ipconfig

2.5 ANSWERS

1. **D**   The IPv4 address 169.254.x.x is generated when the DHCP server cannot be reached.

2. **C**   Three address ranges are reserved for use as private network addressing.

3. **B D**   IPv6 addresses are 128 bits in length and formatted into eight groups of four-digit hex numbers separated by colons.

4. **B**   An IP reservation is an address set up by a DHCP server that doesn't change.

5. **B C**   DHCP is not a default configuration method in IPv6, but SLAAC is. Optionally, DHCPv6 can be configured.

Objective 2.6   **Compare and contrast common network configuration concepts**

To enable a network to work properly, an IP address must be assigned to each device on the network, a mechanism must be available for translating between website names and IP addresses, and methods must exist for connecting different networks to each other. This objective explains these features.

DNS

The *Domain Name System (DNS)*, also referred to as the *Domain Naming Service*, exists because humans use the Internet. In the site-to-site operations of the Internet, the binary-encoded addresses of the sites, whether IPv4 or IPv6, guide the transfer of data across the network. A binary IPv4 address like 10010000.10101000.11001010.10110110 could be hard to remember. For this very reason, DNS was developed as a means to convert the binary addressing and its decimal equivalent (such as 144.168.202.182) into a uniform resource locator (URL) or a fully qualified domain name (FQDN).

DNS Operation

Figure 2.6-1 illustrates the interaction of a local device with DNS to request a URL from a DNS server. Although greatly simplified, this illustration shows the process involved to resolve a URL to an IP address.

1. The user enters a URL into a browser.
2. DNS responds with the IP address associated with that URL.
3. The browser sends out an HTTPS request with the IP address.
4. The appropriate web server provides the requested content.

DNS Record Types

DNS matches IP addresses to host names (and the reverse). Each device on an IP network must have access to at least one DNS server. By default, DNS values are assigned by a DNS server, but they can be manually entered. Although DNS appears to be a simple lookup application,

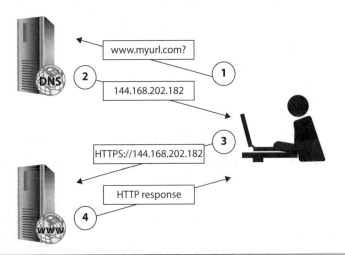

FIGURE 2.6-1   A request and response between a local device and a DNS server

it's really not. More than 30 separate record types define the relationships between a URL or FQDN and an IP address. The following list includes the DNS record types you are likely to encounter on the A+ Core 1 (220-1101) exam:

- **A record**   An A record associates a domain name with its corresponding IPv4 address, and it defines the following characteristics for the domain name:
  - **The domain name**   If an "at" sign (@) follows the domain name, the name is a root domain name.
  - **The IP address associated with the domain name**   A records can only hold IPv4 addresses.
  - **The TTL (Time to Live) in seconds**   The default is 14400 (240 minutes or 4 hours). This is the time at which DNS must request new information for this record type.

  Here is an example of an A record:

  www.myurl.com @ A 144.168.202.182 14400

- **AAAA record**   An AAAA record performs the same function and contains essentially the same data as an A record. However, an AAAA record associates an IPv6 address to a domain name. Remember that A is for an IPv4 address and AAAA is for an IPv6 address.

- **MX record**   Mail exchanger (MX) records provide SMTP instructions for e-mail to use to reach a particular mail server, which must have an active A record that provides its IP address. In addition to the fields in an A record, the MX record includes a priority. In the example that follows, the MX record has a priority of 10. There is no scale, but the lower the priority in an MX record, the higher its privilege.

  Here is an example of an MX record:

  www.myurl.com @ MX 10 mail.myurl.com 14400

- **TXT record**   A text (TXT) record can be combined with any other DNS record type to store comments or descriptions that cannot be included in other record types. In a TXT record, the IP address field is replaced with a comments or "value" field that can contain up to 255 alphanumeric characters. As explained in the next section, TXT records can also be used to help prevent spam.

  Here is an example of a TXT record:

  www.myurl.com @ TXT "IP expires 10-31-24" 14400

EXAM TIP   The important elements and concepts to remember about DNS for the A+ Core 1 exam are addressing, A records, AAAA records, TXT records, and MX records.

E-mail Protection in DNS

The DNS server's MX records indicate where e-mail messages are to be forwarded. Specifically, MX records identify the mail servers that can receive messages addressed to a domain name. MX records identify specifically who (which senders) is authorized to send messages to a mail client or mail box. There are other DNS record types that can help to set up controls on the deliverability of e-mail. For the A+ Core 1 exam, you should know the DMARC, SPF, and DKIM record types and their purposes, as explained in the following sections.

DMARC Record

DMARC stands for *Domain-based Authentication, Reporting, and Conformance.* DMARC records are composed in DNS TXT record types to help prevent spoofing on the domain in an e-mail address. Essentially what a DMARC does is define what should happen to a message if the sender cannot be authenticated. One of two actions can be taken:

- The receiving mail server is advised to quarantine the message, reject the message, or accept the message for delivery to the addressee.
- The receiving mail server reports to the message's recipient e-mail address (or addresses) with information on messages received from the sending domain.

SPF Record

A *Sender Policy Framework (SPF)* record is another type of a DNS TXT record. An SPF record identifies the specific mail servers that are authorized to send out e-mail from a particular domain. One of the primary protections offered by an SPF record is that it can prevent spam being generated from the domain with a spoofed From address. In other words, SPF records act as an e-mail authentication agent that protects against e-mail spoofing.

DKIM Record

The *DomainKeys Identified Mail (DKIM)* DNS record attempts to authenticate whether a message's content can be trusted and has not been modified or tampered with while in transit. DKIM records are also TXT records. An SPF record is often compared to the return address of a message, and DKIM raises the level of a message to something like that of a USPS certified letter, providing enhanced trust to both sender and receiver.

DHCP

Although the *Dynamic Host Configuration Protocol (DHCP)* was discussed in the previous objective, we'll look a bit deeper into some of its characteristics and functions in this section.

DHCP Operations

DHCP operates with a four-step interactive process to provide an IP configuration to a network node. The steps involved, and the transaction types used, are as follows:

1. When a network node powers up onto a network, typically a LAN, it has no ability to communicate on the network. To gain this ability, it broadcasts a DHCPDISCOVER message to the network with a source address of 0.0.0.0 and a destination address of 255.255.255.255. The local network DHCP server continuously scans for these messages on UDP port 67.

2. The DHCP server responds to the DHCPDISCOVER message with a DHCPOFFER message that includes all of the configuration settings the node needs to become active on the network. The node, which is now a DHCP client, uses the content of the DHCPOFFER message to complete its network configuration.

3. The client replies to the DHCPOFFER message with a DHCPREQUEST message to accept the configuration it was provided.

4. The server acknowledges the client's DHCPREQUEST message with a DHCPACK message granting permission to the client to use the configuration provided.

DHCP Leases

As explained in the previous objective, DHCP configuration data is not assigned permanently to a network node. In effect, the configuration is assigned for a specific period of time after which it expires and must, if possible, be renewed.

Why is this mechanism needed? Well, at one time, an organization could have more networked workstations needing Internet access than it had IP addresses. So, to give each one the network time needed, IP addresses were pooled and assigned by DHCP on fixed-time leases. The lease time set the number of seconds a client could use the IP configuration before it expired and then possibly assigned to a different node. On networks that allow clients to renew their leases, a lease is renewed when the lease period is about half over. However, if a node with a current DHCP configuration is powered off, the next time it restarts, the complete cycle starts over from scratch.

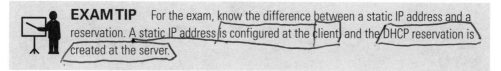

EXAM TIP   For the exam, know the difference between a static IP address and a reservation. A static IP address is configured at the client and the DHCP reservation is created at the server.

DHCP Scope

A *DHCP scope* defines a range of IP addresses and other configuration settings available for assignment to requesting network nodes. DHCP scopes can be defined as one of three different types:

- **Normal**   A normal DHCP scope is created through the DHCP Management Console and the Scope Wizard.

- **Multicast**   A multicast scope is created and managed by the Multicast Address Dynamic Client Allocation Protocol (MADCAP).
- **Superscope**   A DHCP server with a superscope is able to provide DHCP configuration settings to clients on multiple subnets.

All DHCP scopes share a common format that includes the following data:

- Network ID for the range of IP addresses in the scope
- Subnet mask for the network ID
- The range of IP addresses assigned to the scope
- The IP address of the network gateway or router
- The range of any IP addresses excluded from the scope
- The lease duration in seconds
- An administrative alphanumeric name for the scope

EXAM TIP   You can expect to encounter questions about or references to DHCP leases, reservations, and scope types on the A+ Core 1 exam.

VPN

A *virtual private network (VPN)* sets up endpoints at each end of an encrypted tunnel between computers or networks to join them into a private network as if they were on a directly connected LAN (though they obviously won't perform like it). In order to pull off this trick, the endpoint on each LAN gets its own LAN IP address and is responsible for handling traffic addressed to and from the remote network (see Figure 2.6-2).

NOTE   When your mobile or portable device connects to an untrusted Wi-Fi hotspot, you can connect to another network with a VPN and do all of your browsing (or other work) through the secure tunnel.

In Windows 10/11, type **VPN** at the Start screen and select VPN Settings. Enter your VPN server information, which your network administrator should provide, in the resulting dialog box (see Figure 2.6-3). This creates a virtual NIC that gets an IP address from the DHCP server back at the office.

To set up a VPN connection in macOS, open System Preferences | Network, click Add, and choose VPN. Select the VPN type, server address, account name, and authentication settings and then click OK. Click Connect to connect.

To set up a VPN connection in Linux, check the distro's documentation.

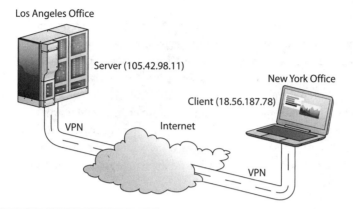

FIGURE 2.6-2   Typical VPN tunnel

FIGURE 2.6-3   The Add a VPN Connection dialog box in Windows 11

VLAN

A *virtual local area network (VLAN)* is a Layer 2 logical construct of switch ports that connect a set of nodes to create a broadcast domain. Typically, a VLAN is created by configuring ports on a managed network switch into a single VLAN. Other VLANs may be configured on the same switch by placing other interfaces into a VLAN configuration. A VLAN is essentially a subgroup of switch ports on an Ethernet LAN. A VLAN is its own broadcast and collision domain and subnetwork, thus increasing the number of domains while reducing the size of each. For example, a 48-port managed switch could be subdivided into six eight-port VLANs. Figure 2.6-4 illustrates a common VLAN in which all of the network hosts exist on the same collision and broadcast domain. Figure 2.6-5 shows an example of how VLANs are configured across a network.

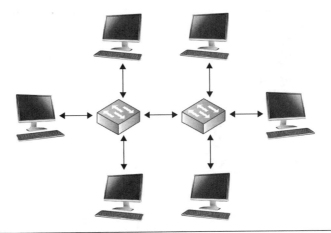

FIGURE 2.6-4   A VLAN with all of the hosts in the same broadcast domain

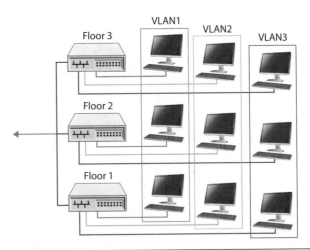

FIGURE 2.6-5   VLANs do not need to be configured in a single location or on a single switch.

ADDITIONAL RESOURCES   To learn more about VLANs, go to www
.lifewire.com and search for the article "What Is a Virtual LAN (VLAN) and What Can
It Do?"

REVIEW

Objective 2.6: Compare and contrast common network configuration concepts

- DNS record types contain specific content:
  - The following are the important address records:
    - A records associate a domain name with an IPv4 address.
    - AAAA records associate a domain name with an IPv6 address.
    - MX records provide SMTP instructions.
    - TXT records hold comments and descriptions.
  - DKIM records are a version of TXT records that provide message authentication.
  - SPF records identify the mail servers authorized to send e-mail from a domain.
  - DMARC records prevent domain spoofing.
- A VPN is a virtual private network. It enables secure connections over an insecure network such as the Internet.
- A VLAN is a collection of ports that act as a separate physical network, and it requires a managed switch.

2.6 QUESTIONS

1. Which of the following is used to define DNS-based security for e-mail?
   A. DKIM
   B. DMARC
   C. SPF
   D. MX

2. Company K has a sales force that typically uses insecure wireless networks in hotels and coffee shops. Which of the following should you advice the salespeople start using to enhance security?
   A. VLAN
   B. VPN
   C. NAT
   D. IPv6

3. A DHCP-provided IP address that never changes is known as which of the following?

   A. IP permanency

   B. IP reservation

   C. Link-local

   D. APIPA address

4. Your client wants to buy a single switch to create three separate wired networks. What type of networks does the client want to create?

   A. VPN

   B. Link-local

   C. VLAN

   D. IPv6

5. Which of the following DNS record types is a TXT record intended to prevent spoofing of an e-mail address domain?

   A. MX

   B. AAAA

   C. DMARC

   D. SPF

2.6 ANSWERS

1. **D**   DMARC, SPF, and DKIM records are defined using a TXT record.

2. **B**   A VPN is a virtual private network, which creates a secure "tunnel" for carrying network traffic through insecure connections.

3. **B**   An IP reservation is an address set up by a DHCP server that doesn't change.

4. **C**   A VLAN is a group of ports on a managed switch that performs as if it's on a separate network from other ports on the switch.

5. **C**   DMARC records help to block spoofing of a domain name.

Objective 2.7 **Compare and contrast Internet connection types, network types, and their features**

There are many different methods for connecting to the Internet as well as many different network types. They work together to connect devices into networks ranging in size from small LANs to worldwide networks.

Internet Connection Types

When you want to connect a LAN to the Internet, you need some way of connecting the LAN to an available data transmission medium. This can only be done through hardware that interconnects your computer, LAN, or WLAN to the data transmission medium and the software that speaks to the hardware. However, this hardware and its associated software as well as where the hardware is located can vary.

 EXAM TIP Make sure you can explain the differences between these Internet connection types: satellite, fiber, cable, DSL, dial-up, cellular, and wireless Internet service provider (WISP).

Connection Hardware

The type of hardware device used to connect to an Internet service largely depends on the ISP and the type of service it provides. Each of the different Internet connection types uses a different proprietary device suited to the signal type and format. Table 2.7-1 lists the hardware device type used for each of the Internet service types you may encounter on the A+ Core 1 exam.

 NOTE Each PC OS has settings to share a direct Internet connection with a LAN or other systems. For example, Windows 10 uses a virtual network adapter and Internet Connection Sharing (ICS), and Windows 11 provides a wireless hotspot.

Satellite

Satellite connections beam data to a professionally installed satellite dish at your house or office (with line of sight to the satellite). Coax connects the satellite to a receiver or satellite modem that translates the data to Ethernet, which can connect directly to your router or the NIC in your computer.

TABLE 2.7-1 Internet Service Connection Devices

Internet Service	Connection Device(s)
Dial-up	Modem
Digital subscriber line (DSL)	Modem
Cable	Modem and router or modem/router combo
Satellite	Modem/router combo (plus satellite disk)
Cellular (3G/4G/5G)	Cellular Internet gateway

Real-world download speeds in clear weather run from a few to about 25 Mbps; upload speeds vary but are typically a tenth to a third of the download speed. They aren't stunning, but satellite can provide these speeds in areas with no other connectivity.

NOTE   Keep in mind satellite latency—usually several hundred milliseconds (ms). It isn't highly obvious for many purposes but can affect real-time activities like gaming or video/voice calls.

Fiber

Telephone system providers are in the process of making fiber optic services available. The two primary service types for network (WAN and Internet) are fiber-to-the-node/fiber-to-the-neighborhood (FTTN) and fiber-to-the-premises (FTTP) services. FTTN connections run from a provider's central office (CO) to a distribution box in a neighborhood. Your home or office connects to the distribution box over coaxial or Ethernet cable. An FTTP connection links the provider's CO directly to a home or office with fiber cabling the whole way.

NOTE   Other types of fiber services available include fiber-to-the-curb/fiber-to-the-cabinet (FTTC), fiber-to-the-home (FTTH), and fiber-to-the-building (FTTB). Fiber is also commonly spelled as "fibre."

Fiber services are becoming more available in cities, with several telco and resell providers offering a variety of service packages. These services offer a range of speeds (100 to 5000 Mbps) and subscription costs ($39 to $55 per month).

Cable

It may seem counterintuitive that a cable TV service could also provide high-speed Internet service. The coaxial cable used to carry the two signal streams is capable of transmitting multiple MHz of signals. The TV service uses only a 6-MHz channel to transmit the available channels and more. The remaining space can then be used for other services, including Internet and possibly telephone. Typically, the service enters a premises through either a modem or router (or a combination of the two) and is capable of supporting either a wired or a wireless SOHO network.

The cable Internet services offer a relatively wide range of speeds, mostly asymmetric, meaning a service offers different upload speeds (5 Mbps to 50 Mbps) and download speeds (50 Mbps to 5 Gbps). *Cable Internet* connections are theoretically available anywhere you can get cable TV.

DSL

A *digital subscriber line (DSL)* connects to a provider's CO on what is called either the plain old telephone system (POTS) or the public switched telephone network (PSTN). A switching device at the CO, a DSL access multiplexor (DSLAM), supports an always-on Internet connection. There are several "flavors" of DSL, and depending on a number of factors, any or all may not be available to any given location.

Distance is DSL's primary limiting factor. DSL's speed diminishes as the distance between the subscriber's premises and the provider's CO increases. In general, DSL has a very limited range in which its maximum speeds are available, commonly less than 18,000 feet (3.4 miles), measured along the cable path of the provider.

 NOTE   The most common forms of DSL are asynchronous (ADSL) and synchronous (SDSL).

Cellular

Access to an Internet connection has become a necessity for households and SOHOs. Most cellular service providers now offer home and office cellular Internet plans. Cellular Internet connections are increasingly available in 3G, 4G, and 5G in more locations. In addition to being available in smartphones, cellular connections are available for tablets and laptops as an additional wireless feature alongside the usual Wi-Fi and Bluetooth connections.

To connect an office or a residence to a cellular Internet service requires a router or a hotspot that connects to a cellular service provider's network, in the same way that a cellular phone does. A router provides for a wireless LAN, and a hotspot essentially extends the cellular service into the premises. One major limitation on cellular Internet services is that they may be subject to data plans. The amount of data transferred may be included in the cell service plan's cost, usually with a cap, such as a 10-Gigabit download limit, on a single cellular subscription. Exceeding the data cap could be very expensive.

The data speed of the internal network largely depends on location. The closer you are to a cell tower, the higher the speed of the service between the router/hotspot and the tower will be. Another factor that can affect data speeds is congestion; as more devices connect to the tower, its speed can diminish. Weather may also become a factor, although rarely. Typically, the data speeds of a cellular Internet service for homes and offices tend to be lower than those of cable or FTTH server. It is anticipated that 5G services will greatly improve speed, bandwidth, and perhaps even cost.

Wireless Internet Service Provider

A *wireless Internet service provider (WISP)* is an ISP that uses wireless technology to provide Internet services to the home. WISP networks are called line of sight. *Line-of-sight wireless*

Internet service (also known as *fixed wireless*) is a popular choice in some smaller cities and nearby rural areas where cable or DSL Internet services are not available. This type of service uses high-powered directional antennas to connect to fixed locations up to about eight miles away. Speeds can vary from as little as 256 Kbps to 20 Mbps or more, depending on the distance and your ISP.

 ADDITIONAL RESOURCES   To learn more about this type of service, search the Web for "broadband fixed wireless."

Network Types

With more network types than ever before, the CompTIA A+ 220-1101 exam expects you to know the differences between LANs, WANs, and many more. See the following subsections for a brief introduction to the types you need to know.

 EXAM TIP   Make sure you can explain the differences between these network types: LAN, WAN, PAN, MAN, WLAN, and SAN.

LAN

A *local area network (LAN)* is a group of networked computers within a few hundred meters of each other. LAN connections typically use wired Ethernet or Wi-Fi.

WAN

A *wide area network (WAN)* is a group of computers on multiple LANs connected with long-distance technologies. The Internet is a WAN.

PAN

A *personal area network (PAN)* is a short-range network typically using Bluetooth. It is used to interchange data between personal devices such as smartphones, tablets, and laptops.

MAN

A *metropolitan area network (MAN)* is a network larger than a LAN but smaller than a WAN. The term MAN is often used to refer to city-wide or campus-wide networks that use fiber optic or fixed-base wireless networks.

WLAN

A *wireless local area network (WLAN)* is essentially a LAN with the wired medium replaced by an RF wireless medium, typically with similar range, attenuation, and strength. However, a WLAN can be less secure because its signal is transmitted through the air and can be intercepted.

SAN

A *storage area network (SAN)* interconnects two or more storage devices into a single address-able network node. A SAN, which can be connected directly to the network, a server, or a network node, commonly by a fiber channel (FC) protocol, is a self-contained network primarily for servicing data transfers. A SAN is recognized by an accessing device as a single data storage device, which serves to reduce latency and improves data transfer speeds. Because a SAN is made up of multiple storage devices, it can provide redundancy and scalability in that additional devices can be added to the SAN without impacting the existing system.

 NOTE   A SAN is commonly confused with a NAS (network attached storage), which is a control device with multiple storage devices attached. The storage devices of a NAS are typically in a RAID arrangement.

REVIEW

Objective 2.7: Compare and contrast Internet connection types, network types, and their features

- Internet service types use a variety of connection devices:
  - Dial-up and DSL services use a modem.
  - Cable service uses a modem and router or a modem/router combination.
  - Satellite service uses a modem/router combination.
  - Cellular (3G/4G/5G) uses a cellular Internet gateway.
- Satellite connections beam data to a satellite dish with a line-of-sight signal.
- The two primary options for Internet service over fiber are fiber-to-the-node (FTTN) and fiber-to-the-premises (FTTP).
- Cable TV services also provide highspeed Internet services on a coaxial cable able to carry the two signal streams.
- A digital subscriber line (DSL) provides Internet services over the PSTN.
- Cellular Internet connections are available in 3G, 4G, and 5G on smartphones as well as cellular Internet gateways.
- Line-of-sight wireless Internet service or fixed wireless service is a popular choice in rural areas where other types of Internet services aren't available.

- A local area network (LAN) is a group of networked computers within a few hundred meters of each other. LAN connections typically use wired Ethernet or Wi-Fi.

- A wide area network (WAN) is a group of computers on multiple LANs connected with long-distance technologies. The Internet is a WAN.

- A personal area network (PAN) is a short-range network typically using Bluetooth. It is used to interchange data between personal devices such as smartphones, tablets, and laptops.

- A metropolitan area network (MAN) is a network larger than a LAN but smaller than a WAN. The term MAN is often used to refer to city-wide or campus-wide networks that use fiber optic or fixed-base wireless networks.

- A wireless local area network (WLAN) is a LAN with an RF wireless medium that may be less secure because its signal is transmitted through the air and can be intercepted.

- A storage area network (SAN) interconnects two or more storage devices into a single addressable network node connected using a fiber channel protocol.

2.7 QUESTIONS

1. You are working with a client who needs Internet access but lives too far away from the city to use DSL or cable. They live on top of a hill. They need quick response and expect to use 15 GB or more of data per month. Which of the following Internet services would you recommend investigating?

   A. Satellite

   B. Cellular

   C. FTTP

   D. Line-of-sight fixed wireless

2. Your client has an old laptop with an RJ-11 port and an RJ-45 port built in. The laptop does not have wireless capabilities. Without buying or renting another component, the client is ready to use which of the following Internet connection types on this laptop?

   A. DSL

   B. Dial-up

   C. Cable

   D. Fiber

3. You are at a client's location preparing to install an update to Windows. Their Internet connection goes down. Which of the following is the best choice to use to install the update immediately?

   A. DSL

   B. Dial-up

   C. Mobile hotspot/tethering

   D. ISDN

4. Your client wants to build a network that will connect locations in various parts of a medium-sized city with each other. Which type of network does the client want to create?

   A. MAN

   B. WAN

   C. LAN

   D. PAN

5. Your company is considering upgrading its DSL service to a faster service. Which of the following types of services is likely to be the fastest?

   A. Cable

   B. FTTN

   C. Satellite

   D. FTTP

2.7 ANSWERS

1. **D**   Line-of-sight fixed wireless, if available, is the best choice because it has no data caps and, unlike satellite, has a quick response rate (that is, a fast ping rate).

2. **B**   The RJ-11 port indicates the laptop has a dial-up modem. Dial-up requires no additional equipment, only an account with a dial-up ISP.

3. **C**   The mobile hotspot/tethering option supported by many smartphones would enable you to perform the update onsite.

4. **A**   A metropolitan area network (MAN) connects locations in a single city that might be separated by some blocks of distance.

5. **D**   Fiber-to-the-premises (FTTP) will be the fastest because the fiber is connected directly to the office.

Objective 2.8 Given a scenario, use networking tools

Whether you build, repair, or troubleshoot wired or wireless networks, you need to understand how to use the networking tools covered in this section.

> **EXAM TIP**   Make sure you understand the uses for the following tools: crimper, cable stripper, Wi-Fi analyzer, toner probe, punchdown tool, cable tester, loopback plug, and network TAP.

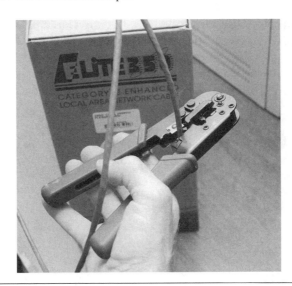

FIGURE 2.8-1 Crimper

Crimper and Cable Stripper

For a patch cable, use stranded unshielded twisted pair (UTP) cable matching the Cat level of your horizontal cabling. If you use cable with a lower Cat level than your existing cable, the network might run more slowly. The basic tool is a RJ-45 *crimper* (see Figure 2.8-1) with built-in *cable stripper* (also known as a wire stripper) and *wire snips*. Stranded and solid-core cable require different crimps; make sure you have the right kind. First, cut the cable square with the RJ-45 crimper or scissors; then use the built-in cable stripper to strip a half inch of plastic jacket off the end of the cable (see Figure 2.8-2). Once the cable is stripped, you're ready to wire the connector.

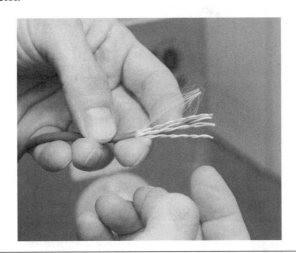

FIGURE 2.8-2 Properly stripped cable

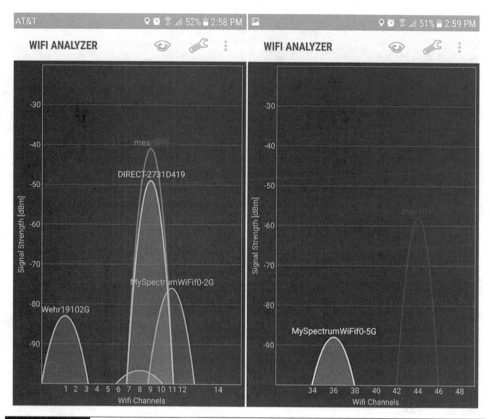

FIGURE 2.8-3   Typical 2.4-GHz (left) and 5-GHz (right) router activity as captured by Wi-Fi Analyzer from Farproc

Wi-Fi Analyzer

Which Wi-Fi channels are currently in use? How strong are the signals? To find out, you can use your Android or iOS smartphone with a free or paid *Wi-Fi analyzer* app, available from many vendors on the Google Play and Apple App stores. Figure 2.8-3 illustrates how a typical Wi-Fi analysis app (Wi-Fi Analyzer app for Android from Farproc) shows activity on the 2.4- and 5-GHz bands. After you review the information, you might want to change the channel(s) used by your router.

Toner Probe

Even in well-planned networks that don't turn into a rat's nest of cable, labels fall off and people miscount which port to label. In the real world, you may have to locate, or *trace,* cables and ports to test them.

Fox and Hound, a tone generator and probe (toner probe) made by Triplett Corporation

Network techs use a *toner probe,* also known as a *tone generator* and *probe* (see Figure 2.8-4). The tone generator connects to the cable with alligator clips, tiny hooks, or a network jack, and it sends an electrical signal along the wire. The toner probe emits a sound when it is placed near the cable carrying this signal.

Punchdown Tool

With a typical horizontal cabling run, you'll connect the work-area end to the back of a wall outlet with a female connector, and the telecommunications-room end will connect to the back of a patch panel's female connector. You typically use a *punchdown tool* (see Figure 2.8-5) to connect the cable to a *110 block* (also called a *110-punchdown block*), which is wired to the female connector. The punchdown tool forces each wire into a small metal-lined groove (shown in Figure 2.8-6), where the metal lining slices the cladding to contact the wire.

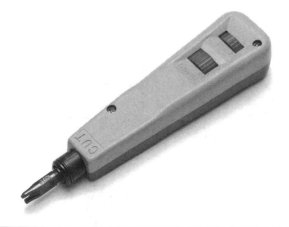

FIGURE 2.8-5   Punchdown tool

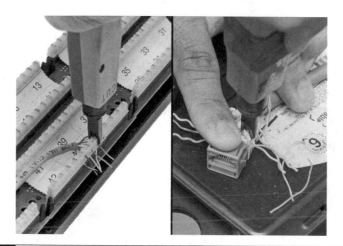

FIGURE 2.8-6   Punching down a patch panel (left) and modular jack (right)

 NOTE   The UTP connectors in outlets and patch panels also have Cat levels—for example, don't hamstring a good Cat 6 installation with outlets or patch panels that have a lower Cat level (such as Cat 5e or Cat 5).

A work-area wall outlet (see Figure 2.8-7) consists of one or two female jacks, a mounting bracket, and a faceplate.

FIGURE 2.8-7   Typical work area outlet

Cable Tester

A *cable tester* (shown in Figure 2.8-8) is used to verify the individual wires in twisted pair (TP) cable are properly located and connected. When testing cables, be sure to test patch cables as well as cable runs in the walls. To do so, unplug the patch cable from the PC, attach a cable tester, and go to the communications room. Unplug the patch cable from the switch and plug the tester into that patch cable.

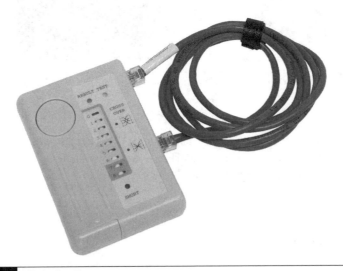

FIGURE 2.8-8   Typical cable tester

FIGURE 2.8-9   Loopback plug

Loopback Plug

A bad network interface card (NIC) can cause a length of network cable to appear to have failed. Unfortunately, the NIC's female connector is easy to damage. To determine if the card is bad, diagnostics provided by the OS or NIC manufacturer may include a *loopback test* that sends data out of the NIC to see if it comes back. A *loopback plug*.(see Figure 2.8-9) is attached to the NIC's RJ-45 cable port, and it loops transmit lines back to the receive lines. If the data that's sent and received is the same, the NIC port works. If not, the NIC needs repair or replacement.

Network TAP

A *network TAP* (test access point) is a piece of hardware that can be added to a network segment to track network traffic over the network medium. The TAP copies all network traffic, without impeding its flow. It provide access for other monitoring or measuring devices to all network activity flowing on the network medium.

As illustrated in Figure 2.8-10, a network TAP device is inserted into a network segment, typically between two interconnecting devices such as a switch and a server (as illustrated) or perhaps, on a wireless network, between an access point and a router. In either of these cases, the link is considered to be an "out of band" connection. The TAP provides connections for monitoring devices, such as an intrusion detection or prevention system or an VoIP recorder.

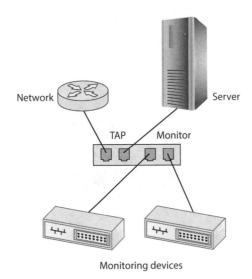

FIGURE 2.8-10 An example of how a network TAP can be used to capture network traffic information

REVIEW

Objective 2.8: Given a scenario, use networking tools

- A crimper is used to attach a connector to a UTP cable.
- A wire/cable stripper is used to remove the outer sheath from the cable to expose the UTP wires.
- A tone generator and probe (also known as a toner or toner probe) is used to find the specific cable for labeling or testing.
- A cable tester tests specific wires in a cable.
- A loopback plug checks the condition of a NIC port.
- A punchdown tool is used to connect the wires in a cable to a 110-punchdown block.
- A Wi-Fi analyzer is an app you can run on an iOS or Android smartphone to display signal strength and network usage for Wi-Fi networks.
- A network TAP monitors local network events.

2.8 QUESTIONS

1. Your client is reporting problems with some of their network cables. Unfortunately, none of the cables are labeled and the client's wiring closet is a mess. Which of the following should you use to help label the client's cables?

    A. Multimeter

    B. Toner probe

    C. Crimper

    D. Loopback plug

2. After labeling the cables for your client, you discover that one of the cables is connected to a workstation that can't connect to the Internet. To help determine if the problem is actually the NIC, which of the following would you use?

    A. Loopback plug

    B. Multimeter

    C. Cable tester

    D. Tone generator and probe

3. Your client's 2.4-GHz network once ran very quickly. However, several new houses have been built nearby and network performance is now very poor. Which of the following would help determine if different settings are needed?

    A. Mobile hotspot

    B. Cable tester

    C. Punchdown tool

    D. Wi-Fi analyzer

4. You are preparing to build some network patch cables for a Gigabit Ethernet network. Which of the following do you *not* need to use for this task?

    A. Punchdown block

    B. RJ-45 crimper

    C. Wire stripper

    D. Connector matching cable type

5. After an office remodeling project, some segments of your client's wired network are slow. The existing computers, switches, and routers were retained, but additional patch panels were installed. What might have gone wrong during the process? (Choose two.)

    A. Incorrect Cat level in patch panels

    B. Loopback plugs left connected to some workstations

    C. Incorrect Cat level in patch cables

    D. Hub used on some network segments

2.8 ANSWERS

1. **B** A toner probe helps determine which wire is which.

2. **A** A loopback plug is attached to the NIC's RJ-45 cable port, and it loops transmit lines back to the receive lines. If the data that is sent and received is the same, the NIC port works. If not, the NIC needs repair or replacement.

3. **D** A Wi-Fi analyzer displays the activity on the 2.4-GHz band by channel and router name.

4. **A** A punchdown block is not used to make patch cables. It is used for cables wired into a wall.

5. **A C** Using patch cables or punchdown blocks with Cat levels lower than the network hardware requires could slow down the network. For example, using Cat 5 (100 Mbps) on a system designed for Cat 6 (1000 Mbps) hardware capabilities.

Hardware

DOMAIN
3.0

Objective 3.1 **Explain basic cable types and their connectors, features, and purposes**

Cabling and wiring are the primary media for connecting circuits, printed circuit boards (PCBs), expansion slots, components, peripheral devices, and even other computers. Cables (and wires) are extremely important to a computing device's internal communications and, to a lesser degree, to its external communications with other devices. In this objective, we look at the various types of connection media, connector devices, and their use.

Network Cables and Connectors

Network cables interconnect computers and other devices on wired networks, primarily LANs, as well as provide a connection to an Internet gateway. There are three primary categories of network cables, each based on its core material:

- **Twisted pair (TP)**   This copper multiple-wire cable is the most used cable for Ethernet LANs and telephone connections.
- **Coaxial**   This cable type has a solid copper core and a metallic shielding for the transmission of cable TV and Internet services.
- **Fiber optic**   This cable type transmits a light stream over a glass or plastic strand. Fiber cabling can be used for LAN connections, but it's more commonly used for long-haul transmission in WANs.

 NOTE   Another very popular LAN medium is RF signaling, more commonly known as wireless networking, WLAN, or simply Wi-Fi. Domain 2.0 of the Core 1 exam (220-1101) covers wireless media.

 EXAM TIP   Be sure you are familiar with the network cable types identified in this objective and their speeds, characteristics, and any transmission limitations.

Copper Cables

Wired Ethernet networks were first interconnected (and continue to be) using copper-core wiring and cable. As defined earlier, the two primary types of copper cabling are twisted pair and coaxial cables. Of these two cable types, TP is by far the more commonly used with coaxial cabling used in special situations and for special purposes.

FIGURE 3.1-1   A Cat 6 twisted-pair cable

TP cable, as shown in Figure 3.1-1, is composed of eight solid or stranded copper wires arranged in four color-coded pairs. Table 3.1-1 compares the characteristics of the major categories of Ethernet cable in current use: Cat 5, Cat 5e, Cat 6, and Cat 6a.

NOTE   The Electronics Industry Association/Telecommunications Industry Association (EIA/TIA) classifies twisted-pair cable into categories, or *Cats*, each of which defines the construction, characteristics, and proper use of different twisted-pair cable types, such as the number of wires and nominal transmission speeds. Cats 1 through 4 are now considered to be defunct, and Cats 7 and 8 (40 Gbps) are now available.

EXAM TIP   Although most Ethernet installations use twisted-pair cabling, Ethernet networks can also use fiber optic or coaxial cable. Coaxial cable is still in use for hazardous environments, such as wet areas.

TABLE 3.1-1   Common Ethernet Cable Types

Category	Maximum Speed Supported	Network Types Supported
Cat 5	100 Mbps	Fast Ethernet (100-Mbps Ethernet)
Cat 5e	1 Gbps	Gigabit Ethernet (1000-Mbps Ethernet)
Cat 6	1 Gbps	Gigabit Ethernet (1000-Mbps Ethernet)
Cat 6a (Augmented)	10 Gbps	Gigabit Ethernet, 10-Gbps Ethernet (up to 100 meters), and Power over Ethernet (PoE)

TABLE 3.1-2 Common 802.3 Ethernet Cable Codes

IEEE Standard	Ethernet Cable Designation	Cable Medium
802.3	10Base5	Coaxial (Thicknet)
802.3a	10Base2	Coaxial (Thinnet)
802.3i	10BaseT	Twisted pair
802.3j	10BaseFL	Fiber optic
802.3u	100BaseTX	TP
802.3ab	1000BaseT	TP
802.3an	10GBaseT	TP

TP cabling used for Ethernet networks is also designated by the IEEE 802.3 standards with a more descriptive coding system, referred to only as the Ethernet standard. Table 3.1-2 lists the more commonly used of the Ethernet cable codes. As shown, the cable designations include three components: a data transfer speed, a transmission mode, and a medium designation. For example, a 10BaseT designation translates to 10 Mbps speed, baseband transmission, and twisted-pair medium.

 EXAM TIP For the A+ Core 1 exam, you should know the IEEE standards in Table 3.1-2. The Ethernet standards in this table are for informational and cross-referencing purposes only.

Unshielded Twisted Pair

Unshielded twisted pair (UTP) cabling consists of four to eight 22–26 AWG (gauge) insulated wires, each of which is twisted with a color-matched wire mate into a wire pair. The resulting four pairs are then enclosed in a common protective sheathing. The EIA/TIA 568 standards, which the A+ exam refers to as T568A and T568B, specify the pattern and sequence of the color-coded wires. UTP cabling is the most common cable type used for Ethernet local area networks. Figure 3.1-1 shows the construction of a Cat 6 UTP cable.

The twisting in each wire pair is done to diminish electromagnetic radiation between the wires in the pair and the crosstalk with adjacent wire pairs. In addition, the twisted wire pairs also help to reject electromagnetic interference (EMI) from outside the cable. Not that you really need to know this, but Alexander Graham Bell developed this concept.

Shielded Twisted Pair

Essentially, a *shielded twisted pair (STP)* cable has the same basic construction as a UTP cable. However, each wire pair is wrapped in a foil shielding to further increase its rejection of external EMI. STP is not frequently used in general network installations. It's more commonly used in EMI-heavy settings, such as a machine shop floor or any area with electric motors.

FIGURE 3.1-2   Cat 6 cable showing the identification on the sheathing

Most Ethernet cables are marked with a Cat number, as shown in Figure 3.1-2.

The EIA/TIA 568 standard, discussed later, sets the maximum distance for a single Cat 5, 5e, or 6 cable run (between two network devices). For Cat 5, Cat 5e, and Cat 6a, the maximum segment length is 100 meters (about 328 feet). This distance represents the attenuation point for each cable type. Cat 6 has a max distance of 55 meters (a bit more than 60 feet). Beyond these distances, a network repeater may be used to initialize a new cable segment, extending the attenuation point of the cable.

Cat 6a (Cat 6 augmented) is a version of a shielded TP that provides some additional protection for its transmission wires. As shown in Figure 3.1-3, its outside sheathing material is a low-smoke nontoxic material, with its internal wire pairs foil-wrapped and each wire protected as well.

Cross-Reference

To learn more about network devices used with Ethernet, see Domain 2.0, Objective 2.2.

Direct-Burial Underground Cable

Should it be necessary to cross an open space, you may be required to (or desire to) install a network cable underground. As it seems to be for all things cabling, three types of cabling can be placed underground: outdoor cable, underground burial cable, and direct-burial cable. The third one is the one included in the A+ Core 1 objectives.

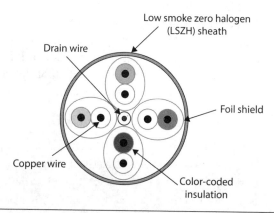

FIGURE 3.1-3   A cross-section of a Cat 6 cable showing its construction

There are no standards that specify the cable types or cable construction required to be designated as a burial-rated cable. However, in general, the cable industry agrees on the following:

- **Outdoor cable** This cable rating is high- and low-temperature and moisture resistant, and it holds up to tearing and abrasion damage. However, it is not a cable that should be directly buried underground in any conditions—hot, cold, rocky, sandy, wet, or dry.

- **Underground burial cable** This cable rating identifies media that can be installed underground, as long as it's placed inside some form of conduit. This type of cable has fillers as well as gel inside the external jacket to protect the internal wiring from moisture damage. However, moisture in the cable's installed environment can eventually degrade the outer jacket of the cable and allow moisture to corrode the core wiring. Damage to the core wires can alter the attenuation, conductivity, and other electrical properties of the cable.

- **Direct-burial cable** Cabling with this rating has passed some stringent water-absorption and crush-resistance testing that qualifies it to, like its name says, be buried directly underground without additional protection, such as a conduit. In addition, the cable must be UL (Underwriter's Laboratory) flame-resistant and qualify as a Power-Limited Tray Cable (PLTC). The term *tray cable* means that the cable can be placed in an open tray, trough, raceway, or conduit. The two primary types of direct-burial underground cable, in which each of the wires has a solid sheath that blocks out moisture and soil, are *underground service entrance (USE)* and *underground feeder (UF)* cable. USE cable is more commonly used by power utilities, and UF is common to residential use.

The bottom line on installing a cable outside and underground is that if you don't use conduit, you must be sure that the rating of the cable is specifically *direct-burial cable*.

Plenum

As mentioned, the most common cabling used for horizontal runs is Cat 5e or Cat 6 UTP. This cable is commonly installed in what is called *plenum space*, which includes spaces above ceilings, under floors, and inside walls. Plenum-rated UTP or STP cable has a coated sheathing that is fire-retardant, which allows it to be installed in a plenum space.

Plenum-rated cabling has a fire-retardant jacket that includes a Teflon layer that doesn't produce toxic fumes when it burns. The PVC (polyvinyl chloride) sheathing on a non-plenum or standard TP cable is flammable, easily burns, and produces dangerous fumes that can spread quickly through a plenum space.

 NOTE Horizontal cabling connects the devices on a single level, such as one floor of a building to connect end devices to a distribution device, such as a router or a switch. This cabling is commonly UTP. A vertical cabler runs from floor to floor to connect the individual floor distribution devices to the core system.

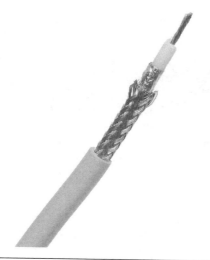

FIGURE 3.1-4   A stripped view of a typical coaxial cable

Coaxial

Coaxial cable, which is commonly called *coax,* consists of a core copper wire that is insulated, wrapped in a shield of braided cable (see Figure 3.1-4) to eliminate interference, and enclosed in a protective cover. Coaxial cable is rated using a Registered Guide (RG) scale. The first versions of Ethernet used coaxial cable, either 10Base5 or 10Base2, instead of UTP. Today, coax is mostly used for cable and satellite TV connections.

Fiber

Fiber optic cable uses either a laser light beam or a light-emitting diode (LED) to transmit Ethernet network frames, which makes it immune to electrical problems such as lightning, short circuits, and static. Fiber optic signals also travel 2000 meters (2 km) or more.

The fiber optic cabling used for data networks, among other applications, is either single mode or multimode. Over single-mode cables, lasers pulse single bursts of light over a core glass or plastic fiber. Multimode fiber carries multiple simultaneous LED signals, each traveling through the medium using a different reflection angle on the core. Because the reflection angles cause the light beam to weaken or disperse over long distances, multimode fiber is limited to relatively short transmission distances.

Most fiber optic Ethernet networks use 62.5/125 multimode cable. The numbers in the name of this cable represent the size of the core filament. The first number (62.5) represents the diameter of the raw core filament in microns, and the second number is the diameter, again in microns, of the core filament and its cladding (a reflective coating applied to the core filament to keep the light inside the strand). Fiber optics are half-duplex; data flows only one way, so fiber connections require two cables.

TABLE 3.1-3   A Comparison of Ethernet Cable Medium Standards

Ethernet Standard	Wiring	Cable Type(s)	Maximum Segment Length
1000BaseT	Four pairs UTP	Cat 5, 5e, and 6 UTP	100 meters
1000BaseCX	Two pairs STP	Cat 5, 5e, and 6 STP	25 meters
1000BaseSX	One pair multimode fiber optic	Multimode cable 770–860 nanometer diameter	550 meters
1000BaseLX	One pair single-mode or multimode fiber optic	Fiber optic cable 1270–1355 nanometer diameter	500 meters

 NOTE   A micron is one-millionth of a meter.

Using fiber optic cabling on a network requires a fiber optic switch and fiber optic network adapter cards. The transfer speed and attenuation distances are limited to that specified by the applicable Ethernet standard. Fiber optic cabling has extremely high transmission rates and distances, but when used for an Ethernet network, the distances can vary with the standard applied. Table 3.1-3 shows a comparison of the Gigabit Ethernet standards for UTP, STP, single-mode fiber, and multimode fiber.

Peripheral Cables

A peripheral device is any device connected internally or, more often, externally to a computer. For the most part, a peripheral device is used to enter, display, or transfer data. The connection from a peripheral device to a computer is a communication line between the two. There are three external peripheral device cable and connector types you should know for the A+ Core 1 exam: universal serial bus (USB), serial, and Thunderbolt. The following sections provide information on each of these.

USB

USB connectors are used to interface virtually any device to a PC or mobile device, including keyboards, mouse units, scanners, printers, audio devices, as well as gadgets not typically thought of as peripheral devices, such as lap warmers, cup heaters, personal fans, and more.

The core of USB is the USB host controller, an integrated circuit normally built into the chipset. It acts as the interface between the system and every USB device that connects to it. The USB root hub is the part of the host controller that makes the physical connection to the USB ports. A USB host controller is the boss (the master) of any device (the slave) that plugs

FIGURE 3.1-5   Typical USB hub (image courtesy of Targus Global)

into that host controller. The host controller performs two tasks: sending commands and providing power to connected USB devices. The host controller is upstream, controlling devices connected downstream to it. The host controller is shared by every device plugged into it, so speed and power are reduced with each new device.

You can add extra USB ports to a system using either a USB expansion card or a USB hub (see Figure 3.1-5). USB hubs come in powered and bus-powered varieties. Powered USB devices have their own power plug and bus-powered USB devices draw their power from the USB bus. Too many bus-powered devices on a bus-powered hub can cause problems, so it's best to use powered hubs in such situations.

 ADDITIONAL RESOURCES   For more information about USB, visit www
.usb.org.

USB devices are *hot-swappable,* which means you can connect or disconnect them at any time without powering down your computer. USB technology lets you use hubs to connect up to 127 devices to a single host controller on your computer.

 EXAM TIP   For the CompTIA A+ 220-1101 exam, you should expect one or more questions on the USB 2.0 and 3.x standards regarding their connectors and their maximum data speeds.

TABLE 3.1-4   USB Standards

Name	Standard	Maximum Speed	Cable Length
Hi-Speed USB	USB 2.0	480 Mbps	Up to 5 meters
SuperSpeed USB	USB 3.0/3.1 Gen 1	5 Gbps	Up to 3 meters
SuperSpeed USB 10 Gbps SuperSpeed+ USB	USB 3.1 Gen 2	10 Gbps	Up to 3 meters

There have been several generations of the USB standard, along with several connector types. Table 3.1-4 provides a quick reference to help you sort them out.

 NOTE USB 3.1 doesn't specify a limit, but interference can make longer cables slower.

Over the past two decades, there have been several types of USB connectors, which have been interchangeable for the most part. For example, Type-A USB plugs would fit USB 1.1 and 2.0 ports. However, the later USB versions, primarily the 3.x and 4 versions, have relatively unique connectors with clearly marked ports. USB 3.x suggests that ports should be blue to differentiate them from earlier versions with black or white ports. USB 3.x plugs are compatible with earlier USB standards, and vice versa. However, either way, new into old or old into new, the result is slower speeds.

Table 3.1-5 lists the common USB connectors and their purposes. Note that "keyed" means the plug fits into the socket in only one direction. Notice that the type of connector may be used in one or more of the standards.

TABLE 3.1-5   USB Connection Types

Connector	Plug Type	Plugs Into
Type-A	Keyed	Computers
USB 3.0/3.1 Standard-A	Keyed	Computers
USB 2.0 Type-B	Keyed	Larger peripherals
USB 2.0 Mini-B	Keyed	Smaller peripherals
USB 2.0 Micro-B	Keyed	Tiny peripherals
USB 3.0/3.1 Micro-B	Keyed	Tiny peripherals
USB Type-C	Reversible	Computers and peripherals

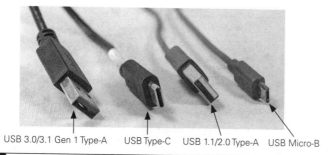

USB 3.0/3.1 Gen 1 Type-A   USB Type-C   USB 1.1/2.0 Type-A   USB Micro-B

FIGURE 3.1-6   USB Type-A, Type-C, and Micro-B cables

Figures 3.1-6 and 3.1-7 illustrate connector types listed in Table 3.1-5.

 EXAM TIP CompTIA uses the term *USB-C* for what others call USB Type-C. CompTIA also uses the term *micro-USB* for USB Micro-B and *mini-USB* for USB Mini-B. You might see either forms of the device names on the exam.

The USB Type-C connector is used on Android smartphones and tablets, Apple's iPad tablets, and many desktop and laptop computers. Newer Apple iPhones use a cable with a Lightning connector on one end and a USB-C on the other, both of which aren't keyed, so they're easier to use. USB-C is a form factor, not a specification. USB-C ports might run at USB 3.1 Gen 2, USB 3.1 Gen 1, or USB 2.0 speeds; check the device's specifications to find out.

 EXAM TIP You will likely see micro- and mini-USB, USB Type-C, and Lightning mobile device connection types on the exam. Know their characteristics and differences.

USB 1.1/2.0 Mini-B   USB 1.1/2.0 Type-B   USB 3.0/3.1 Gen 1 Micro-B   USB 3.0/3.1 Gen 1 Type-B

FIGURE 3.1-7   USB 2.0 and USB 3.0 Type-B and Micro-B cables

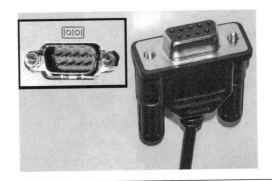

FIGURE 3.1-8   DB-9 serial port and connector

Serial Connector

On today's computers, most peripherals connect via a USB port, which is a form of a serial connector. However, some legacy desktop systems have one or more specific serial connectors, most likely to be a DB-9 connector. The DB-9 RS-232 connector supports a variety of low-speed peripherals, including dial-up modems, some early mouse units, and early printers. USB ports can be used to connect to serial devices through a USB DB-9 adapter. Figure 3.1-8 shows a DB-9 serial connector and port.

 EXAM TIP   Expect to see the DB-9 serial connector on the A+ Core 1 exam.

Thunderbolt

The *Thunderbolt* interface is a high-speed alternative to existing technologies, including USB and FireWire, for connecting peripherals using PCIe and DisplayPort technologies simultaneously, thus combining their capacity. Table 3.1-6 lists the characteristics for each of the versions of the Thunderbolt standard you may see on the exam.

As indicated in Table 3.1-6, the two standards that preceded Thunderbolt 3 were completely different from the USB Type-C connectors it uses. USB Type-C and Thunderbolt 3 are essentially interchangeable. This means that USB Type-C cables are compatible with Thunderbolt ports and that Thunderbolt cabling is compatible with USB Type-C ports. Figure 3.1-9 shows a Thunderbolt 3 port and connector.

TABLE 3.1-6   Thunderbolt Standards

Standard	Connector	Maximum Speed	Cable Length
Thunderbolt 1	Mini DisplayPort	10 Gbps	3 m (copper) / 60 m (fiber)
Thunderbolt 2	Mini DisplayPort	20 Gbps	3 m (copper) / 60 m (fiber)
Thunderbolt 3	USB Type-C	40 Gbps	3 m (copper) / 60 m (fiber)

Thunderbolt cables, which tend to be a bit more expensive than USB Type 3 cables, are made with either copper or fiber cores. The copper cables can run up to 3 meters (whether a single cable or chained). Optical runs extend much farther, up to 60 meters. Thunderbolt 3 is much faster than USB Type-C, with transfer speeds of 480 Mbps to 20 Gbps, but transfer rates of 40 Gbps are possible.

Video Cables and Connectors

Video cables connect displays, monitors, HDTVs, and projectors to your computer's video card or onboard video port. Table 3.1-7 provides an overview of the cables and connector types you should know for the A+ Core 1 exam.

TABLE 3.1-7   Video Cables

Video Cable Type	Standard Name	Reduced-Size Version	Signal Types Supported	Notes
VGA	Video Graphics Array	N/A	Analog video	VGA can be connected to HDMI, DVI-I, and DisplayPort ports with adapters.
HDMI	High-Definition Multimedia Interface	Mini-HDMI	HD video and HD audio	Video signal is compatible with DVI.
DVI	Digital Visual Interface	N/A	HD video	DVI-I (analog/digital) and DVI-D (digital) signals are compatible with HDMI.
DP	DisplayPort	Mini DisplayPort (mDP)	HD video and HD audio	Video signal is compatible with DVI and HDMI.

FIGURE 3.1-10 Typical HDMI, Mini-HDMI, DP, and mDP cables/connectors (left to right)

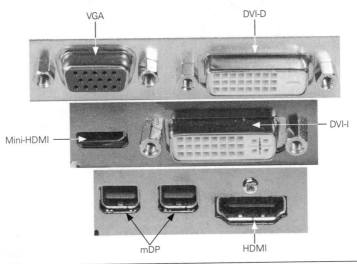

FIGURE 3.1-11 Typical video ports

Figure 3.1-10 illustrates some of these video cables, and Figure 3.1-11 illustrates most of these video ports.

Hard Drive Cables

Objective 3.1 of the CompTIA A+ 220-1101 exam refers to "hard drive cables," but it's important to know that this includes the cable types used with SSDs, optical drives, and tape drives. Different types of cables are used by the different types of hard drive and mass storage devices.

SATA and eSATA

Serial Advanced Technology Attachment (SATA) interfacing is commonly used for hard drives and optical drives. SATA creates a point-to-point connection (see Figure 3.1-12) between a SATA device, such as a hard drive or optical drive, and a SATA controller.

FIGURE 3.1-12   SATA power (wide) and data (narrow) cables and drive connectors

A SATA device's data stream traverses a thin seven-wire cable that can reach up to a meter in length. The SATA device's speed depends on the SATA standard in use. The SATA versions—1.0 (1.5 Gbps), 2.0 (3 Gbps), and 3.0 (6 Gbps)—have a maximum throughput of 150 MBps, 300 MBps, and 600 MBps, respectively. Notice that these speeds are in mega-*bytes* per second.

External SATA (eSATA) extends the SATA bus to external devices at the same speed as the internal SATA bus. The connector (see Figure 3.1-13) is like internal SATA but is keyed differently; it supports cables up to 2 meters outside the case and is hot-swappable.

 EXAM TIP   When you encounter the term *hot-swappable* on the exam, remember that a hot-swappable drive (or device) is immediately recognized by the system when it is connected, swapped, or replaced while the system is running.

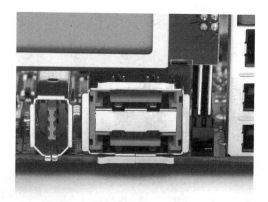

FIGURE 3.1-13   eSATA connectors (in center of photo)

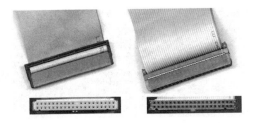

FIGURE 3.1-14 80-wire (left) and 40-wire (right) IDE cables

IDE

Integrated Drive Electronics (IDE) is the name used on the CompTIA A+ exam for what is also known as ATA and Parallel ATA (PATA) drives. These drives use a 40-wire flat ribbon cable to connect one or two drives to a host adapter built into a motherboard or an add-on card. IDE interfaces are found on legacy systems, although a few more-recent computers that use SATA for hard drives also use IDE for optical drives. Figure 3.1-14 shows an 80-wire IDE cable and an older, slower 40-wire IDE cable.

 EXAM TIP Although CompTIA uses the term *IDE* on the exam, the interface is more often referred to as *PATA* or *ATA/IDE* by the industry. They're the same thing, so be prepared!

SCSI

Small Computer System Interface (SCSI) refers to a large family of internal and external drive and device connectors. Internal SCSI devices such as tape drives and hard drives are used only by servers and connect via 50-wire or 68-wire flat cables that resemble wider versions of IDE cables. External SCSI devices use bulky round cables ranging from 25 pins to 68 pins. Each SCSI device is assigned an ID number, enabling multiple devices to be connected to a single host adapter using daisy-chaining. Unless you work with servers, it's unlikely you will encounter a SCSI host adapter or device in the field.

The SCSI interface has been largely replaced by *Serial Attached SCSI (SAS)* for servers and storage arrays. SAS 4, the latest version, runs at up to 22.5 Gbps. SAS also supports SATA drives. Another version of SCSI, *Internet SCSI (iSCSI)*, supports block-level I/O on storage devices through SCSI commands transmitted across a network.

Connectors

As you well know, storage and other types of peripheral devices must be attached to a computer using one form of a connector or another. Many device types use standard connectors, whereas others require a customized or proprietary connector. Connectors have names or designations, but most are referred to by an industry or application registration or a descriptive coding, such as RJ-45 or Mini SAS 4x.

Cable and connector standards are issued by a variety of national and international organizations. The most common of these organizations—and the one's you're likely to encounter on the exam—are the Institute of Electrical and Electronics Engineers (IEEE), USB Implementers Frontier (USB IF), Electronic Industry Association (EIA), Telecommunication Industry Association (TIA), Registered Jack (RJ), and International Electrotechnical Commission (IEC).

Connectors also have a gender that indicates which side of a connection a device constitutes. A "male" connector is the side with pins, blades, or spades. A "female" connector has the receptacle slots or pin holes that receive the connecting elements of the male side.

Let's look at the connectors you are likely to encounter on the A+ Core 1 exam.

Registered Jack Connectors

An RJ connector is a standard managed by the TIA for telecommunication network interfaces for data and voice services. The types of RJ connectors you will likely encounter on the exam are the RJ-11 and the RJ-45 and their configuration.

RJ-11

Dial-up and DSL modem ports look identical to traditional wired telephone jacks and use two-wire *RJ-11* telephone cables and connectors (see Figure 3.1-15). The locking clips on the male RJ-11 connectors secure the cable into the port. Most modems also have an output port for a telephone.

RJ-45

Network interfaces come in several varieties. Most network interface cards (NICs) and motherboards have an eight-wire RJ-45 port (see Figure 3.1-16). RJ-45 connectors look like wide RJ-11 telephone connectors and plug into the female RJ-45 ports in the same manner that RJ-11 telephone cables plug into a modem.

FIGURE 3.1-15   RJ-11 connectors on a modem

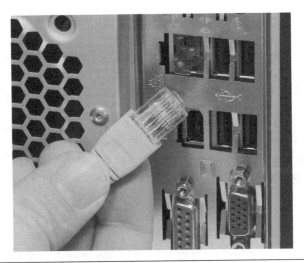

FIGURE 3.1-16   An RJ-45 connecter and port

T568A/B

The EIA/TIA T568A and T568B standards, while not specifically connectors, do specify the configuration of TP wiring and RJ-45 connectors. So, if you make up your own connectors, use either the T568A (commercial) or the T568B (residential) standard for their configuration. The wires in TP cable are color-coded (see Figure 3.1-17) and designated with a placement number, as listed in Table 3.1-8.

 EXAM TIP   It's a good idea to know the pin numbers of RJ-45 and their use in straight-through and crossover connectors.

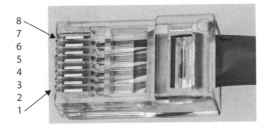

FIGURE 3.1-17   RJ-45 pin numbers using the T568A/T568B standards

TABLE 3.1-8   UTP Cabling Color Chart

Pin	T568A	T568B
1	White/Green	White/Orange
2	Green	Orange
3	White/Orange	White/Green
4	Blue	Blue
5	White/Blue	White/Blue
6	Orange	Green
7	White/Brown	White/Brown
8	Brown	Brown

FIGURE 3.1-18   A male F-type connector

Coaxial Cable Connector: F-Type

Coaxial cable connectors are based on the grade and purpose of the cable. The F-type connector is typically associated with terrestrial "over the air" and cable TV. It's also the most commonly used connector for coaxial cabling on Ethernet networks. F-type connectors are used to connect cable-based Internet services from a *point of presence (POP)* in a home or business to the *consumer premises equipment (CPE)*, such as a router or modem. Figure 3.1-18 shows an example of a male F-type connector.

EXAM TIP   For the A+ Core 1 exam, you should know the F-type coaxial cable connector.

Fiber Optic Cable Connectors

The A+ Core 1 objectives include three specific fiber optic cable connectors you could see on the exam: the straight tip (ST), the subscriber connector (SC), and the Lucent connector (LC), as shown in Figure 3.1-19. Some other fiber optic cable connectors you might see on the exam as wrong answers or distractors are FDDI, MT-RJ, and FC.

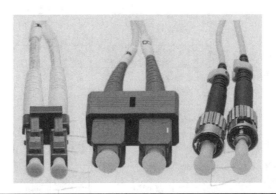

FIGURE 3.1-19   ST (left), SC (center), and LC (right) fiber connectors

Straight Tip

The straight tip (ST) fiber optic connector is a very commonly used connector for multimode networks, such as an industrial or academic campus and large buildings. The ST connector has a "push in and twist" locking mechanism that is also keyed. As shown in Figure 3.1-19, an ST connector uses a long cylindrical polymer or ceramic ferrule to hold the fiber cable.

Subscriber Connector

The subscriber connector (SC) is one of the most used fiber optic cable connectors, due to the facts that it's simple to install and inexpensive. An SC uses a push-pull function and a locking tab to secure the connection.

Lucent Connector

Like the subscriber connector, the Lucent connector uses a push-pull function, but the locking mechanism is a built-in latch. The LC is used when the space for the connection is limited. An LC is smaller (half the size of an SC or ST connector) and easier to install, which is why LCs are popular with single-mode fiber-in-the-home (FITH) services.

Punchdown Block

On the A+ Core 1 exam, this device is referred to as a *punchdown block*. However, it's also commonly called a *punch block*, a *quick connect block*, a *patch panel*, or a *terminating block,* among a few other terms. A punchdown block, so called because of the action used to install wiring and cabling into it, has a set of insulation displacement connectors (IDCs) into which cable wiring is inserted using a "punchdown" tool and action.

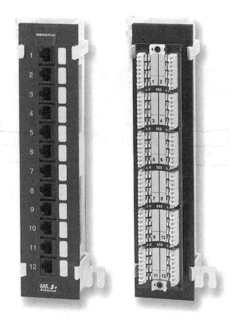

FIGURE 3.1-20   The RJ-45 (left) and punchdown (right) connections of a punchdown block

A punchdown block is commonly used as an interconnection device for incoming communication cables and wiring and the internal network as well as for centralizing and consolidating internal network wiring. Punchdown blocks are most commonly installed in a main communications facility that serves an entire building or a communication closet for an area of one or more floors of a building. Among the benefits of installing a punchdown block is that reconfiguring a network may only require moving RJ-45 connections from one port to another.

Two types of punchdown blocks are common in communication facilities: a 66 block and a 110 block. A 66 block is primarily used for voice system wiring. A 110 block, as used in a computer network, has IDCs on one side and RJ connections on the other (see Figure 3.1-20).

Molex and Berg

A Molex connector, which gets its name from its original developer, the Molex Connector Company, is a common two-part connection device used to provide DC power to internal components of a PC. Molex is the standard power connector for IDE (ATA, PATA) drives using the 4-pin Molex power connector, shown in Figure 3.1-21. Molex connectors can also be used with other internal DC-powered devices, such as case fans. Figure 3.1-21 shows a Molex power connector.

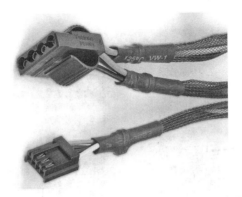

FIGURE 3.1-21   Molex (upper) and Berg (lower) power connectors

Another power connector commonly used to supply power to motherboards is the Berg connector. Named after its developer, Berg Electronics Company, it is more commonly referred to as a P7 or a mini-Molex connector. Figure 3.1-21 includes an example of a Berg connector.

Lightning Port

"Lightning" technology includes a bus and connector developed by Apple to connect its devices, including iPhones, iPads, and so on to computers, monitors, chargers, and more. The male lightning jack is symmetrical, which means that it's reversible and can be connected to a lightning port regardless of its orientation—unlike USB and other keyed connectors. While the primary use of a lightning cable, which typically has a lightning connector on one end and another standard connector (commonly a USB-A connector) on the other (see Figure 3.1-22), is to charge Apple devices. It can also be used to transfer digital files, such as photos and audio, between iOS devices and a computer.

FIGURE 3.1-22   A lightning cable with a USB jack

Adapters

Adapters and converters enable you to connect devices in interesting ways. You can use a cable with DVI on one end and HDMI on the other end, for example, to plug into a DVI port on the video card and the HDMI socket on the monitor. These devices fall into two broad categories based on the problems they solve: connecting one type of video cable or port to another and connecting almost anything to USB.

DVI to HDMI, DVI to VGA

Adapters and converters for video take two primary forms: relatively small devices that fit at one end of a cable, converting it to the desired interface, and cables with built-in converters that have different connectors on each end. The former is more flexible, but the latter is easier to use. Figure 3.1-23 illustrates a DVI-to-HDMI cable, and Figure 3.1-24 illustrates a DVI-to-VGA adapter.

FIGURE 3.1-23   A DVI-to-HDMI cable

FIGURE 3.1-24   A DVI-to-VGA adapter enables a DVI-I connection to work with VGA displays.

FIGURE 3.1-25   A USB-to-Ethernet adapter enables a USB port to connect to an Ethernet network.

USB to Ethernet

There are many USB adapters for different types of devices, but the most common one is the USB-to-Ethernet (RJ-45) adapter, as it enables computers without Ethernet ports to connect to a twisted-pair Ethernet network (see Figure 3.1-25).

 EXAM TIP   Other USB adapters you may encounter on the exam are USB-A to USB-B, USB to Bluetooth, and USB to Wi-Fi.

REVIEW

Objective 3.1: Explain basic cable types and their connectors, features, and purposes

- The most common types of network cable for Ethernet networks are Cat 5, 5e, 6, and 6a.
- Ethernet cabling uses RJ-45 connectors.
- Plenum-grade cables are designed for use in plenum (air spaces) and are fire-resistant.
- UTP cables are used in the vast majority of 10/100/1000BaseT networks.
- STP cables are shielded for use in areas of EMI and typically are used only in such environments.
- The T568A and T568B cable standards for UTP cable differ in their pattern and organization of white/green, green, orange, and white/orange wires.
- Coaxial cable is used for cable TV, LANs, and Internet.
- Fiber optic cabling can be used for Ethernet network, SAN, FTTN and FTTH.

3.1 QUESTIONS

1. Company A wants to eliminate separate speakers on desktops and use speakers built into monitors. Which of the following video card standards should be specified?

    A. DVI-I

    B. DVI-D

    C. VGA

    D. HDMI

2. Company B is planning to upgrade its Fast Ethernet network to Gigabit Ethernet. In checking existing cables, the network techs have discovered that some areas were wired with Cat 5, some with Cat 5e, and some with Cat 6. Which of the following should they do as part of the upgrade process?

    A. Replace all cables with Cat 6.

    B. Keep the same cables.

    C. Replace Cat 5 with Cat 5e or Cat 6.

    D. Replace all cables with Cat 5e.

3. Company C has purchased some new computers that have USB 3.0 ports as well as a USB-C port. It wants to use the USB-C port for very fast external SSD drives. What needs to be determined first?

    A. Are USB-C SSD drives available?

    B. How fast is the USB-C port?

    C. Can the USB-C port work with other form factors?

    D. Is USB-C always running at 10 Gbps?

4. Company D wants to run coaxial cable in its offices for use with HDTV. Which of the following cable types should the company specify?

    A. RG-6

    B. STP Cat 5e

    C. STP Cat 6

    D. RG-59

5. Company E wants to purchase SuperSpeed USB drives and card readers. However, all its techs can find are devices labeled with a USB version number. Which of the following USB versions does the company need?

    A. USB 3.1 Gen 2

    B. USB 3.0

    C. USB 1.1

    D. USB 2.0

3.1 ANSWERS

1. **D** HDMI carries HD audio and HD video signals.
2. **C** Cat 5e and Cat 6 support Gigabit Ethernet and either could replace Cat 5.
3. **B** USB-C supports USB 2.0, USB 3.0/USB 3.1 Gen 1, and USB 3.1 Gen 2 speeds.
4. **A** RG-6 is the standard for HD video.
5. **B** USB 3.0 (aka USB 3.1 Gen 1) is the version number for SuperSpeed USB.

 **Objective 3.2** Given a scenario, install the appropriate RAM

Many computer users mistakenly believe that programs run directly off the hard drive. This is rarely the case, because even the fastest hard drive can't keep up with the slowest CPU. Instead, programs must be transferred to a super-fast medium that can supply a CPU with the instructions and data it needs to run an application at the required speed. The medium capable of providing this support to the CPU is *random access memory*, or *RAM*. Launching an application loads the necessary files from the hard drive into RAM, where the CPU can access the data to run the program.

> **NOTE** Technically, you can use a hard drive or flash drive as virtual memory to expand the available RAM, but these devices are not nearly as fast as RAM, and it isn't quite the same as running a program from where it is stored on a hard drive.

RAM was once a precious commodity, and even a small upgrade cost hundreds of dollars. These days, it's not very expensive to add more RAM, and it is often the best upgrade for a sluggish system. This doesn't mean you can just grab any type of RAM; you've got to match the motherboard with the right type of RAM, running at the right speed. Manufacturers have produced RAM in many physical form factors (sometimes called *packages*) and technologies over the years. This section looks at the types of RAM included in Objective 3.2 of the CompTIA A+ Core 1 (220-1101) exam.

RAM Packages

For the A+ Core 1 exam, it's important you understand the form, fit, and function of the different types, configurations, and packaging of the various RAM technologies. Remember that the A+ exams are testing to see if you can apply your knowledge to a particular situation or scenario. The types of RAM you should know for the exam are discussed in the following subsections.

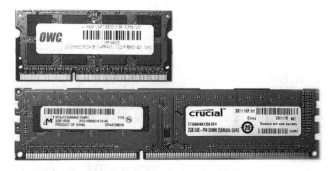

FIGURE 3.2-1 A DIMM (bottom) and a SO-DIMM (top)

Dual Inline Memory Modules

The memory modules found in virtually all desktop computers use an *inline memory module* form. Until 2000, *single inline memory module,* or *SIMM,* was the standard. This technology evolved to *dual inline memory module,* or *DIMM.* A DIMM is a circuit board on which dynamic RAM integrated circuits are mounted in series. The DIMM form factor is the dominate module for adding memory to personal computers, printers, or servers. There are standard and proprietary DIMMs, but the two most used are the 133.35-mm (millimeter) module used in desktop computers and other larger devices and the 67.6-mm small outline module, or SO-DIMM, used in laptop computers. Figure 3.2-1 shows examples of these two DIMMs.

Memory Architectures

Several memory architectures are used in computers. Dynamic RAM (DRAM) is the most-used basic memory architecture. Figure 3.2-2 illustrates how DRAM is the foundation for most other memory types.

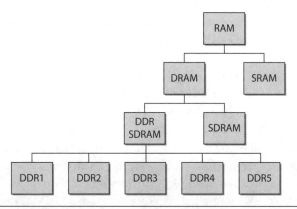

FIGURE 3.2-2 DRAM is the root of most RAM architectures.

The following are the memory architectures you can expect to find on the A+ Core 1 exam:

- **Dynamic RAM (DRAM)**   DRAM must be refreshed (recharged) every few milliseconds to retain its content. It is dynamic because the value it holds can be refreshed with a different value, as needed.
- **Synchronous DRAM (SDRAM)**   Most DRAM is asynchronous, meaning that it's not synchronized to the system clock. SDRAM is synchronized to the system clock, which means that it operates at higher transfer rates than basic DRAM. You may not see it specifically on the exam, but SDRAM is the type of DRAM memory that is the foundation architecture for the Double Data Rate (DDR) memory types.

Double Data Rate Memory

Basically, double data rate (DDR) memory's name comes from the fact that it transfers data in and out at twice the rate of single data rate (SDR) memory, specifically SDRAM. The "double" in DDR indicates that 2 bits are transferred in a single clock cycle from memory to an I/O register, an action called a "2-bit prefetch."

DDR memory has evolved from its original introduction in 2000 through five versions to today's DDR5. Each of the versions has added size, speed, and bandwidth to the prefetch function. The following briefly describes DDR3 through DDR5 (DDR1 and DDR2 are not referenced on the exam):

 NOTE   Prefetching decreases transfer times by buffering or caching a resource (such as a set of bits) before it is required.

- **DDR3**   DDR3 boasts higher speeds, more efficient architecture, and around 30 percent lower power consumption than DDR2. Desktop DDR3 uses a 240-pin DIMM. DDR3 doubles the size of the prefetch buffers from 4 bits to 8 bits, giving its bandwidth a huge boost when reading contiguous data. Many DDR3 systems support dual- and triple-channel memory configurations. Typical sizes of DDR3 DIMM sticks range from 1 GB up to 8 GB.
- **DDR4**   DDR4 provides higher speeds, more efficient architecture, and around 20 percent lower power consumption than DDR3. Desktop DDR4 uses a 288-pin DIMM that has a slight curve on both ends of its motherboard connector. Typical sizes of DDR4 DIMM sticks range from 4 GB up to 64 GB.
- **DDR5**   Introduced in 2021, DDR5 further improves channel efficiency, power management, and performance and is compatible with the multi-core architectures of emerging computer systems. DDR5 provides almost twice the bandwidth of DDR4 and nearly 50 percent more speed. Typical sizes of DDR5 DIMM sticks range from 8 GB up to 128 GB.

| **TABLE 3.2-1** | Comparison of DDR Memory Versions |

DDR Standard	Connection Pins	Prefetch Bits	Max Memory Size (GB)	Max Data Rate (Gbps)	Bandwidth (Gbps)	Voltage(V)
DDR3	240	8	8	1.6	17	1.3/1.5
DDR4	288	8	32	3.2	25.6	1.2
DDR5	288	16	128	6.4	32	1.1

Table 3.2-1 and Figure 3.2-3 provide features and a visual comparison of DDR3, DDR4, and DDR5 DIMMs.

 NOTE Both DDR4 and DDR5 have 288 pins on their edge connectors, but each uses a different pin arrangement.

 EXAM TIP You should be familiar with the various RAM sizes and speeds for DDR3, DDR4, and DDR5.

 ADDITIONAL RESOURCES To familiarize yourself with the many RAM standards and specifications for both desktops and laptops, visit www.crucial.com, paying attention to the characteristics, such as module size, package, and features.

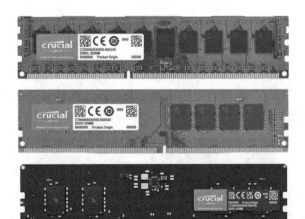

| **FIGURE 3.2-3** | DDR3 (top), DDR4 (center), and DDR5 (bottom) DIMMs compared (images courtesy of Micron Technologies, Inc.) |

Handling and Installing DIMM

Proper RAM handling and installation procedures prevent damage to your system. This section reviews the proper way to handle desktop RAM and how to install it.

RAM is extremely sensitive to electrostatic discharge (ESD). Therefore, you need to take precautions while transporting, handling, and installing it. Always store RAM in antistatic bags or sleeves when it's not installed on a computer, and keep it labeled with the type, size, and speed so that you can identify it later. Wear an antistatic wrist strap and ground yourself before working with RAM. Don't take a RAM stick out of its bag before you are ready to install it. Also, be sure to handle RAM by the edges of the module and avoid touching its contacts or circuits.

To install DIMMs, first power down the computer and unplug it from the AC outlet. DIMM sticks fit into their sockets vertically. Each of the memory slots/sockets on the motherboard will have a guide bar with which the guide notch on the DIMM is matched to ensure the DIMM is properly installed, as illustrated in Figure 3.2-4, and to prevent it from being inserted the wrong way. Make sure that the RAM retention clips at either end of the socket are pushed completely outward.

Hold the RAM stick by the edges, position it above the RAM socket, and press it straight down into the slot with gentle pressure (see Figure 3.2-5). When the RAM is fully inserted, the retention clips will rotate into the retention notches on each end of the stick. Snap the clips firmly into place, and you're done.

Barring ESD, not a lot can go wrong. The main thing to look for is improper seating. If the retention clip doesn't engage fully, your RAM stick isn't inserted completely. DDR3 sockets typically use a retention clip on both ends. DDR4 sockets use a retention clip on one end and a fixed guide rail on the other end, and DDR5 sticks will only fit into DDR5 slots on a DDR5 motherboard. If, for any reason, the DDR stick doesn't easily fit, it's not in the right position or it's the wrong memory.

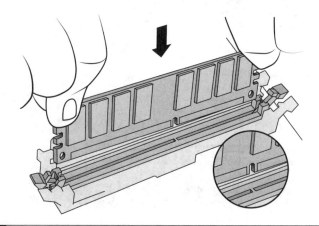

FIGURE 3.2-4   Match the guide slot on the DIMM with the guide bar in the memory socket.

Properly seating a DIMM

To remove a DIMM, push the retention clip(s) on the socket outward. These clips act as levers to eject the stick partially so that you can then pull it all the way out.

Laptop RAM

Laptops, notebooks, some all-in-one computers, and other small form factor PCs all use DDR RAM, just as desktops do. However, due to the space limitations of these devices, RAM, including DDR RAM, is packaged as *small outline dual inline memory modules* (*SO-DIMMs,* shown in Figure 3.2-6). Although it should be obvious, you should know that DIMMs and SO-DIMMs are not interchangeable.

The performance characteristics of a SO-DIMM are essentially the same as a similar DIMM with the same technology. The information in Table 3.2-1 applies to both DIMMs and SO-DIMMs. A SO-DIMM is installed in the same way a DIMM stick is installed in a larger unit. The key thing in either case is to use the alignment notch on the card to position the module into the mounting slot.

There are SO-DIMMs for each of the DDR versions, including DDR5. There are also low-voltage versions of the DDR3 SO-DIMMs, identified as DDR3L modules. The low-voltage versions and the standard voltage versions aren't necessarily compatible, so be sure you know with which type you're working. A DDR5 SO-DIMM requires 1.1 V (volts), which is 0.1 V lower than that of the DDR4.

- **DDR3 SO-DIMM**   DDR3 SO-DIMM is packaged in a 204-pin module, such as the one shown in Figure 3.2-6. Note that some DDR3 SO-DIMMs use low-voltage DDR3 memory. These modules are called DDR3L SO-DIMM. Check the specifications for a specific device to determine if it uses standard voltage (DDR3) or low-voltage (DDR3L) memory.

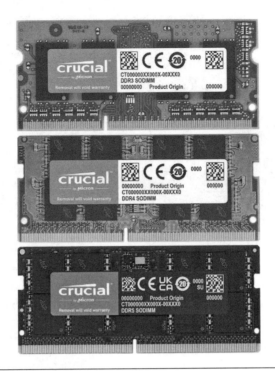

FIGURE 3.2-6   DDR3 (top), DDR4 (center), and DDR5 (bottom) SO-DIMMs compared (images courtesy of Micron Technologies, Inc.)

- **DDR4 SO-DIMM**   DDR4 SO-DIMM is packaged in a 260-pin module, such as that shown in Figure 3.2-6. A DDR4 SO-DIMM is slightly wider than previous SO-DIMM types.
- **DDR5 SO-DIMM**   This module is a 262-pin SO-DIMM with two independent I/O channels for increased bandwidth, the efficiency of fly-by topology, and a standardized sideband bus. Figure 3.2-6 shows an image of a DDR5 SO-DIMM.

EXAM TIP   You should be able to differentiate the DIMM and SO-DIMM form factors and the number of pins in the edge connectors of each for the A+ Core 1 exam.

Handling and Installing SO-DIMM Sticks

Just like with a desktop, protect yourself and the portable device by removing all power and protect the SO-DIMMs by using proper ESD avoidance techniques. With portables, removing power includes disconnecting removable batteries. If it has built-in batteries, consult the manufacturer's resources to check if and how you can safely work on it.

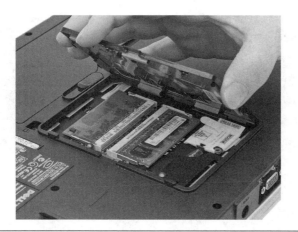

FIGURE 3.2-7   Removing a RAM panel

 NOTE   Some portables have both built-in and removable batteries.

Once you know you can work safely, confirm what kind of RAM you need by checking the manufacturer's website or manual. Next, check the existing RAM configuration to confirm what you need to buy. To go from 4 GB to 8 GB, you need to know if the portable has one 4-GB module or two 2-GB modules.

Next, locate the RAM slots. They're often behind a panel on the bottom of the portable, as shown in Figure 3.2-7, but sometimes they're separated.

Then you press out on the retaining clips, and the RAM stick pops up (see Figure 3.2-8). Gently remove the old stick of RAM and insert the new one by reversing the steps.

FIGURE 3.2-8   Releasing the RAM

FIGURE 3.2-9   Confirming RAM installation by checking total memory in UEFI BIOS Utility

Confirming RAM Installation

Once you've installed RAM, confirm that the computer recognizes it by booting up and checking the RAM count message or by looking in the UEFI/BIOS setup utility (see Figure 3.2-9). Modern systems automatically detect the RAM size and configure the system accordingly. You rarely need to reconfigure these RAM settings. You can also verify the amount of installed RAM from within the operating system—for example, in any version of Windows, simultaneously press the WINDOWS and PAUSE keys to bring up the System Properties applet.

Performance Configurations for Desktop and Laptop

Current desktop and laptop motherboards use multichannel memory configurations to increase memory performance. With a 64-bit data bus, DIMMs deliver 64 bits of data at a time on a *single memory channel*. A *dual-channel* memory architecture doubles the number of data bits from 64 to 128, which also doubles the available bandwidth. Since memory modules are 64-bit devices, two memory modules are required to be installed in parallel to achieve a dual-channel architecture. A *triple-channel* memory architecture requires three memory modules be installed in series (on memory slots of the same color) to create a 192-bit data bus. To achieve a *quad-channel* memory architecture—you guessed it—four memory modules are installed to create a 256-bit memory data bus. Use identical RAM sticks to populate a bank for multichannel memory modes. Always check the motherboard or system documentation for details.

Each of the multiple-channel memory architectures requires a memory controller that supports its number of channels. Dual-channel memory controllers support two channels simultaneously, and triple-channel and quad-channel configurations require memory controllers that support three and four channels, respectively. Motherboards that support a multichannel mode can also run in lesser-channel modes, but the best performance is provided by the highest mode the motherboard supports.

 EXAM TIP Know the differences and configurations of single-, dual-, triple-, and quad-channel memory.

Error-Correcting Memory

High-end, mission-critical systems often use special *error-correction code (ECC)* RAM that uses special circuitry to detect and correct errors in data. ECC RAM contains circuitry that not only detects errors but corrects them on the fly without interrupting system processes. ECC RAM is common on performance-enhanced workstations and servers.

Virtual Memory

It may seem like everything is or could be virtual on a computer these days. One virtual component is available on "virtually" any system with an OS, which of course is all of them. Virtual memory or *virtual RAM* is only virtual in the sense that it's not actually a physical part of a system's main memory (RAM). Instead, it's a partition of secondary storage, usually a hard disk, set aside as logical memory.

Virtual memory is controlled by a memory management unit (MMU) of the operating system. The virtual memory area is commonly referred to as *swap space* or a *swap file* because it's used to temporarily store idle or low-priority pages of memory content and free up memory space for an active process.

The amount of virtual memory to configure on a system varies with the operating system, the applications running on the machine, and a few other factors. You can have too much virtual memory, in which case the MMU is constantly *thrashing*, or moving pages in and out of memory and to and from virtual memory. Common errors associated with virtual memory issues can be out of memory and thrashing, both of which can be caused by the amount of memory allocated to the swap space.

REVIEW

Objective 3.2: Given a scenario, install the appropriate RAM

- Desktop RAM uses the DIMM form factor, which is available in DDR3, DDR4, and DDR5 forms.
- DIMMs are installed by lining up the module with the appropriate RAM slot and pressing the DIMM down until it locks into place.
- Laptop, notebooks, and other small form factor computers use the SO-DIMM form factor for RAM. It is available in the same forms as DIMMs.
- SO-DIMMs are installed by lining up the module with the appropriate RAM slot at an angle, pushing the module into the slot, and pivoting the top of the module until it locks into place.
- Single-channel memory accesses a single DIMM as a channel.
- Dual-channel memory accesses two DIMMs as a channel for greater bandwidth.
- Triple-channel memory accesses three DIMMs as a channel for even greater bandwidth.
- Quad-channel memory accesses four DIMMs as a channel for still greater bandwidth.
- DIMM slots on multichannel systems for a given bank are typically the same color. Use identical RAM sticks to populate a bank for multichannel memory modes.
- Error-correction code (ECC) RAM contains circuitry that not only detects errors but corrects them on the fly without interrupting system processes.
- Virtual memory is an area on secondary storage used to provide additional backup space to the MMU.

3.2 QUESTIONS

1. How many pins does a module of DDR4 DIMM RAM use?
   A. 108 pins
   B. 186 pins
   C. 205 pins
   D. 288 pins

2. What is stored in RAM?
   A. Currently running programs
   B. Programs that aren't running
   C. Nothing
   D. Hardware information

3. How many DIMM cards are required to achieve a 256-pin architecture?

    A. One

    B. Two

    C. Three

    D. Four

4. You are adding RAM to a dual-channel system that has one 4-GB module to upgrade it to 8 GB. Which of the following do you need to confirm before you buy more RAM?

    A. The current stick's brand of RAM

    B. The current stick's speed of RAM

    C. The current stick's type of RAM

    D. All of the above

5. You are purchasing 288-pin RAM to upgrade computers in your organization. What type of RAM are you purchasing?

    A. DDR5 SO-DIMM

    B. DDR4 SO-DIMM

    C. DDR4 DIMM

    D. DDR5 DIMM

3.2 ANSWERS

1. **D**   DDR4 DIMM memory uses a 288-pin connector.

2. **A**   RAM is the workspace used by programs as they are running. Programs that are not running are located on a local or network storage device.

3. **D**   Quad-channel memory with four DIMMs creates a 256-bit memory architecture.

4. **D**   To run the computer in dual-channel mode for better speed, the new module must be identical to the old, so all of these factors must be matched.

5. **D**   Standard DDR5 DIMMs have 288 pins. A DDR5 SO-DIMM has only 262 pins.

Objective 3.3 # Given a scenario, select and install storage devices

The large-volume data storage industry is in a definite period of massive transformation, with flash memory and storage media technologies rapidly replacing magnetic and optical media. Nevertheless, you should expect to encounter magnetic, solid-state, optical, and flash media in your work as a tech, and all four types are important parts of this objective.

Hard Drives

Traditional *hard disk drives (HDDs)* store data magnetically on spinning platters, using fast-moving actuator arms with read/write heads that are controlled by a servo motor (see Figure 3.3-1). The important properties are physical size, storage capacity, spindle speed, cache size, and interface.

Most modern HDDs are 2.5 or 3.5 inches wide and have storage capacities measured in gigabytes (GB, billions of bytes), terabytes (TB, trillions of bytes), or petabytes (PB, 1024 terabytes). The 2.5-inch HDD is primarily used in laptops and external USB or Thunderbolt storage peripherals. The 3.5-inch HDD is common to desktop and server computers and external AC adapter powered storage peripherals. Currently, 2.5-inch HDDs have a storage capacity of 4 TB, and 3.5-inch drives store up to 20 TB.

 EXAM TIP   Know the HDD 2.5- and 3.5-inch form factors and spindle speeds as well as the drive categories represented.

| **FIGURE 3.3-1** | Inside a hard drive |

| TABLE 3.3-1 | Typical HDD Spindle Speeds |

Spindle Speed	Typical Purpose	Drive Interface
5400 RPM	Standard for portable computers	Serial ATA (SATA), Integrated Development Environment (IDE)
7200 RPM	Standard for desktop computers	SATA, IDE
10,000 RPM	Enthusiast and server computers	Small Computer System Interface (SCSI), Serial Attached SCSI (SAS)
15,000 RPM	Enterprise servers	SAS

Hard disk drives with higher spindle speeds seek, write, and read faster, but in doing so, they consume more power and generate higher heat and noise. Table 3.3-1 shows common HDD spindle speeds with typical uses. Cache size, measured in megabytes (MB), affects the drive's sustained throughput.

Solid-State Drives

Solid-state drives (SSDs) use flash memory chips to store data. SSDs weigh less, have no moving parts, seek faster, have higher throughput, consume less power, produce less heat, have better shock resistance, and last longer than HDDs. The only downside is that HDDs have the advantage in cost.

Most consumer SSDs use a SATA 2.5-inch hard drive format or an M.2 flash drive format. An M.2 SSD is a small form factor SSD that uses two different internal data bus designs: *serial ATA (SATA)* and *Non-Volatile Memory Express (NVMe)*. The original form factor for SSDs is SATA 2.5 inch. Figure 3.3-2 compares a SATA 2.5-inch drive with an M.2 drive.

| FIGURE 3.3-2 | SATA (top) and M.2 (bottom) SSDs |

NOTE Confused by all the *xx*D acronyms yet? *Hard drive* and *hard disk* were traditional synonyms, but in this book, we use *hard drive* as an umbrella term, including HDD and SSD.

NVMe

Non-Volatile Memory Express (NVMe) is a protocol that uses the PCI Express (PCIe) bus to allow computers to connect to SSD devices. NVMe is used by SATA and standard M.2 SSDs. NVMe drives transfer data at 2.5 to 3 times the speeds of SATA and standard M.2 SSDs.

SATA

The *serial ATA (SATA)* hardware interface is primarily used for connecting HDD storage devices to a computer. SATA is a faster version of the legacy parallel ATA (PATA) interface, both of which are IDE devices, which have the device controllers in the drive. SATA drives include SATA SSD, M.2 SSD, mSATA SSD, and several others.

 EXAM TIP The M.2 form factor supports both NVMe and SATA SSDs. You might encounter a question that asks about the differences, so keep in mind that NVMe is faster but doesn't work in all M.2 slots.

mSATA

The name *mSATA* refers to *mini-SATA*, which is a standard developed by the SATA International Organization for an ultra-thin, low-power storage device. The form factor of mSATA is smaller than that of most SATA SSDs. Despite its smaller size, an mSATA device can store up to 1 TB. Figure 3.3-3 shows an example of an mSATA drive.

FIGURE 3.3-3 An mSATA drive (image courtesy of Micron Technologies, Inc.)

| FIGURE 3.3-4 | M.2 modules: M.2 NVMe (top) and M.2 SATA (bottom) (image courtesy of Samsung) |

M.2 SSD

An *M.2 SSD* is even smaller than an mSATA SSD, which makes it popular for tablet computers and ultra-thin notebooks and the like. An M.2 SSD module has a capacity of up to 2 TB and is inserted into an interface circuit board using mating connections that are either B key sockets or M key sockets. These modules are available as M.2 SATA and M.2 NVMe (see Figure 3.3-4).

Flash Memory

Flash memory, which uses solid-state technology like that found in SSDs, is rapidly displacing other data storage technologies. For the exam, you need to know the two flash memory families: flash drives (aka, thumb drives) and memory cards.

Flash Drives

Flash drives connect to a computer through a standard USB connection. Flash drives and memory cards have very different usages: flash drives have effectively replaced most of the legacy removable storage, such as floppy disks, CD-RW, and the like. Generally, a flash drive is connected to a computing device through either a USB Type-A or Type-C. The capacity of flash drives continues to increase with advances in flash memory, with these drives having storage capacities up to 2 TB.

Memory Cards

Memory card is a generic term for different small insertion cards commonly used in portable devices, such as notebooks, cameras, tablets, and other small and mobile devices. Memory cards vary in type, storage capacities, and form factors. The most common forms used with computing equipment are Secure Digital (SD), microSD, and CFexpress.

| FIGURE 3.3-5 | Assortment of SD memory cards |

SD Card

Although it's considered to have been replaced by later memory card types, SD cards (examples of which are shown in Figure 3.3-5) remain relevant in computing. Smaller form factor versions, such as miniSD and microSD, share a general format, although the smaller types may require a converter to fit into the larger SD slot. SD cards have storage capacities up to 2 TB.

ADDITIONAL RESOURCES To learn more about the different form factors, speeds, and capacities of SD and CF cards, see www.sdcard.org and https://compactflash.org/.

EXAM TIP Be familiar with the differences between USB flash drives and memory cards, including capacities and uses.

Installing Storage Devices

Three types of interfaces are used for internal storage devices on recent systems: IDE, SATA, and M.2. This section explains how to install devices that use these interfaces.

Installing SATA Drives

There used to be a few catches when installing SATA drives; these days, just connect the power, plug in the controller cable (see Figure 3.3-6), and wait for the OS to automatically detect the drive. The keying on SATA controller and power cables makes it impossible to install incorrectly.

FIGURE 3.3-6   Properly connected SATA cables

Since motherboards come with many SATA connectors, how does the system find the right hard drive to boot up to? That's where the BIOS/UEFI settings come into play. By default, boot order and drive letter priorities are based on SATA controller IDs: SATA 0 is C:, SATA 1 is D:, and so on.

 EXAM TIP   BIOS/UEFI setup utilities enable you to change boot order easily, which is great for multi-OS computers.

When installing optical drives, you might also need to install movie playback apps supplied with some drives. The SATA interface works the same way with any type of SATA drive.

Installing IDE Drives

If you need to install an IDE drive, each drive on the cable (which supports up to two drives) must be configured via a jumper block, which is a small plastic electronic connector that ties together two (or more) pins in a configuration block to set a configuration type.

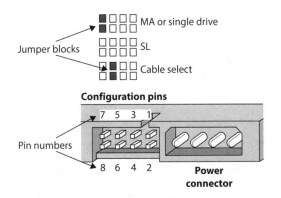

The jumper settings for an IDE device

The configuration block on an IDE drive is located next to the Molex power connector on the back of the drive. As illustrated in Figure 3.3-7, the two pins on which the jumper block is placed (an action referred to as *jumpering*) set the role of the drive. All drives connected to an 80-wire cable are set as CS (cable select). When two IDE drives are connected to a legacy 40-wire cable, one drive is jumpered as MA and the other as SL. The jumpering for a single device on a 40-wire cable varies, so you should see the drive's documentation for its settings.

Installing M.2 Drives

With any type of M.2 device, including standard SSDs, NVMe SSDs, and other types of M.2 devices used in laptops, the selection and installation processes have these steps:

1. Select a device that fits into the slot.

2. Secure the device with a mounting screw.

All M.2 cards are 22 mm wide, with lengths varying from 30 mm to as much as 110 mm. The most common size, however, is 2280 (22 mm wide, 80 mm long), as illustrated in Figure 3.3-8.

An M.2 2280 SSD installed and secured into an M.2 slot

RAID

A *redundant array of independent* (or *inexpensive*) *disks (RAID)* uses multiple hard drives to increase performance and protect data. Motherboards with built-in RAID controllers may have a BIOS/UEFI setting to enable or disable RAID (see Figure 3.3-9). The following list describes each of the RAID level you should know for the Core 1 exam.

 EXAM TIP   A RAID array collects two or more hard drives into a logical unit. CompTIA expects you to know RAID levels 0, 1, 5, and 10.

- **RAID 0: Disk striping**   Disk striping requires at least two drives. It increases performance by splitting work over multiple drives, but it does not provide redundancy to data. If any drive fails, all data is lost.
- **RAID 1: Disk mirroring/duplexing**   RAID 1 arrays require at least two hard drives, although they also work with any even number of drives. RAID 1 *mirrors* data across multiple drives, providing safety at the cost of storage space (since data is duplicated; you need two 2-TB drives to store 2 TB of data).

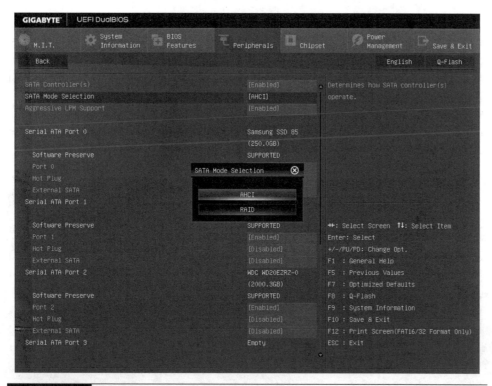

FIGURE 3.3-9   BIOS/UEFI settings for RAID

- **RAID 5: Disk striping with distributed parity**   RAID 5 distributes data and parity information evenly across all drives. This is the fastest way to provide data redundancy. RAID 5 arrays effectively use one drive's worth of space for parity, requiring a minimum of three drives. In RAID 5, three 2-TB drives provide a capacity of 4 TB, while four 2-TB drives provide a capacity of 6 GB.

- **RAID 10: Nested, striped mirrors**   RAID 10 takes two mirrored pairs of drives and stripes them together. This creates an array with excellent speed and redundancy, though it takes four drives as a minimum. RAID 10 is not one of the original RAID levels but is fairly common today. RAID 10 combines RAID levels 0 and 1 to create a RAID configuration that mirrors two striped-drive pairs (RAID 0+1) and stripes two mirrored-drive pairs (RAID 1+0 or RAID 10). Arrays that combine single standard RAID types are *multiple RAID* solutions or *nested RAID*.

 EXAM TIP   Be sure you know and understand the RAID 0, 1, 5, and 10 (1+0) configurations for the A+ Core 1 exam, especially the minimum number of disks required for each and the basic method(s) each implements, such as mirroring, striping, redundancy, and so on. You will encounter at least one of these on the test.

Optical Drives

Compact disc (CD), *digital versatile disc (DVD)*, and *Blu-ray Disc (BD)* drives use lasers to read (and sometimes to write or burn) data on *optical discs*. These devices have been and still are used to back up and archive data. Internal optical drives use the SATA interface and external optical drives typically connected to USB ports.

All three of these optical media are available in three types: read-only(R), write-once (W), and rewritable (RW). Optical *combo drives* read and write to the different optical media types. However, you should always check compatibility, especially with older drives.

 NOTE   Optical discs use a unique Compact Disc File System (CDFS), more accurately called the ISO 9660 file system.

CDs have a capacity of either 650 MB or 700 MB. DVD and Blu-ray media have several combinations of media types and either single or dual layering, which translate to different storage capacities. Table 3.3-2 shows DVD and Blu-ray Disc capacities.

TABLE 3.3-2	Common DVD/Blu-ray Disc Capacities in DVD-Industry Gigabytes	
	Single Layer	**Dual Layer**
Single-sided DVD	4.7 GB	8.5 GB
Double-sided DVD	9.4 GB	17.1 GB
Blu-ray Disc	25 GB	50 GB
Mini Blu-ray Disc	7.8 GB	15.6 GB

REVIEW

Objective 3.3: Given a scenario, select and install storage devices

- SATA HDD, SSD, and optical drives are installed using a SATA data cable and a SATA power cable.
- M.2 drives are available in conventional (SATA SSD speed) and NVMe (2.5 to 3 times faster) types.
- HDDs are available in 2.5-inch and 3.5-inch form factors.
- HDDs have spindle speeds of 5400 RPM, 7200 RPM, 10,000 RPM, and 15,000 RPM.
- 3.5-inch drives are used in AC-powered enclosures as well as desktops and servers.
- 2.5-inch drives are used in USB-powered enclosures and laptops.
- NVMe uses the PCIe bus to connect to SSD devices.
- mSATA refers to mini-SATA (an ultra-thin, low-power storage device). The form factor of mSATA is smaller than that of most SATA SSDs.
- The most common family of flash memory cards is SD, including miniSD and the very popular microSD.
- RAID 0 is faster than other RAID types because data is striped across two drives; it has no redundancy.
- RAID 1 mirrors the contents of one drive to the other; RAID 5 uses at least three drives and distributes data and recovery (parity) information across all drives; RAID 10 or RAID 1+0 combines striping and mirroring, which requires four drives.
- Optical discs are available in CD, DVD, and BD (Blu-ray) types.

3.3 QUESTIONS

1. Your client is planning to replace 500-GB hard disks with similarly sized SSDs. Assuming compatibility, which of the following would provide the best performance?

   A. NVMe 2.5-inch

   B. NVMe M.2

   C. SATA M.2

   D. SATA 2.5-inch

2. Which of the following is not an interface type used for internal storage devices on newer systems?

   A. IDE

   B. SATA

   C. M.2

   D. Serial

3. Your client wants to add an NVMe drive to their desktop systems to boost performance, but the M.2 slots in these systems don't support NVMe drives. Which of the following interfaces can be used instead?

   A. SATA

   B. PCIe

   C. SATA

   D. ISO 9660

4. Your client wants to choose a RAID array type that offers excellent speed and reliability. Which of the following is the best match for this requirement?

   A. RAID 10

   B. RAID 1

   C. RAID 5

   D. RAID 0

5. Your client accidentally purchased a microSD card for their digital camera instead of an SD card. Which of the following is the best way to use the card?

   A. Copy the data from an existing card to the new card.

   B. Return the card to the store for the correct type.

   C. Use an adapter with the card.

   D. Buy a new camera that uses microSD cards.

3.3 ANSWERS

1. **B** The NVMe M.2 SSD is the fastest type of SSD.

2. **D** IDE, SATA, and M.2 are internal storage device interfaces. Serial is not used internally in a system.

3. **B** NVMe drives are available in PCIe cards; NVMe uses the PCIe bus for extra speed over SATA.

4. **A** RAID 10 combines mirroring for data protection and striping for speed.

5. **C** SD adapters for microSD cards are very common and often bundled with microSD cards.

Objective 3.4   # Given a scenario, install and configure motherboards, central processing units (CPUs), and add-on cards

Custom PC configurations and upgrades rely on a tech's ability to integrate off-the-shelf components from various sources into a working system. In this objective, you learn how to choose, install, and configure compatible motherboards, CPUs, and add-on cards.

Motherboard Form Factor

A *form factor* defines the motherboard's size, shape, orientation, how it's mounted in the computer case, the location of onboard sockets and expansion slots, and more. Essentially, the form factor of a motherboard determines how a computer performs. It sets which components are compatible and can be connected to the motherboard as well as sets operating aspects such as power supply requirements, the size and shape of the case, and to a certain extent what you can do on the computer.

The most common form factors for PC motherboards are ATX and ITX, which stand for *Advanced Technology eXtended* and *Information Technology eXtended,* respectively. Each of these form factors has variations, and there are proprietary versions as well. For the most part, form factors are not interchangeable, especially ATX and ITX. These two form factors define separate designs and orientations for not only their motherboards but for all compatible supporting components as well. This means that, for example, ATX motherboards fit into ATX cases, and ITX motherboards fit into ITX cases.

ATX

The ATX motherboard form factor (see Figure 3.4-1) was developed to replace the legacy AT form factor. The ATX form factor rearranged the placement of expansion slots, CPU, and RAM for easier access and enhanced performance. The ATX design also corrected a design problem of the AT motherboards that caused some longer expansion cards to contact the CPU. The ATX standards have changed with advancements in technology, including revisions for new power connectors, power supply fans, and airflow and enhanced cooling.

The ATX motherboard design collects its onboard I/O ports in a *port cluster* panel that can be accessed on the back of an ATX case. Figure 3.4-2 illustrates a port cluster on an ATX motherboard and case.

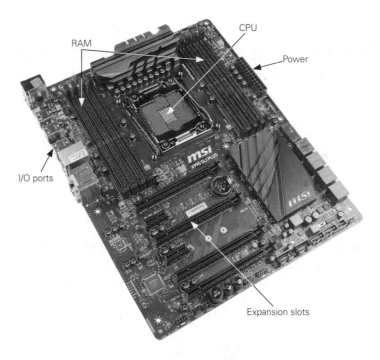

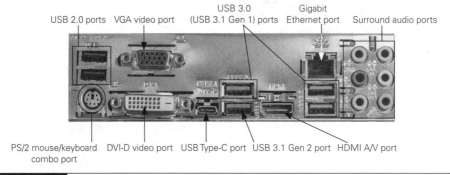

The ATX form factor has several variations, including the following two, which are shown on the left side of Figure 3.4-3:

- **Standard (full-sized) ATX** The standard or full-sized ATX (most referred to as the ATX form factor) is 12 inches by 9.6 inches. It supports the latest video and graphic cards, provides seven expansions slots, and fits into a full-size ATX case.

| Standard-ATX | Mico-ATX | Mini-ITX | Nano-ITX | Pico-ITX |

FIGURE 3.4-3   Examples of ATX and ITX form factor motherboards (image courtesy of VIA Labs, Inc.)

- **Micro-ATX**   Also referred to as mATX, the micro-ATX motherboard is 9.6 inches by 9.6 inches square and uses the same basic motherboard layout and power connectors as the full-sized ATX. The micro-ATX is scaled down to fit into smaller computer cases. While an ATX motherboard won't fit into a micro-ATX, the smaller form factor can be installed in an ATX case.

EXAM TIP   Know the differences between the ATX and the ITX motherboard/ system board form factors.

ITX

The ITX form factor is the most common of the *small form factor (SFF)* motherboards. Originally, the ITX form factor was for a full-sized motherboard, but it never took hold. However, smaller versions of the form factor have fared much better, specifically the mini-, nano-, and pico-ITX form factors, all shown on the right side of Figure 3.4-3.

Of the three ITX versions, the *mini-ITX* (or *mITX*) is the largest at 6.7 inches square. The mini-ITX competes with the larger micro-ATX. The *nano-ITX* motherboard, at 4.7 inches square, and the *pico-ITX* motherboard, at 3.8 inches by 2.8 inches, are smaller yet. These much smaller motherboard form factors are used for embedded systems and specialized devices such as routers.

Motherboard Connector Types

A motherboard is more than a large circuit board on which RAM and CPUs are installed. Storage, video, I/O, and other devices are also installed or connected to a motherboard. In the subsections that follow, you learn about the devices that mount on a motherboard or interconnect to each other using the slots, jacks, wires, and support chips that are a part of a motherboard's design and form factor and collectively known as an *expansion bus*.

Expansion Bus Architectures

When a device in a computer needs to communicate data or instructions with another device on that computer, it "takes a bus." In the context of computer technology, a *bus* is communication line built into or added to a motherboard that allows devices to communicate. A bus is a path created by embedded wiring to which devices are or can be connected. Expansion cards are installed on a motherboard through its expansion bus.

The expansion bus on a motherboard has the primary purpose of providing a standardized access point for adding devices to a computer. The expansion bus allows the motherboard (and through it, the computer) to be customized to the requirements of the user.

Over the years, many expansion bus architectures have been and, in some cases, are still used, including the following:

- Peripheral Component Interconnect (PCI)
- PCI Express (PCIe)
- Small Computer Systems Interface (SCSI)

Although there have been a few others that were specialized to memory cards, video, graphics, and more, the A+ Core 1 exam's focus is on the PCI and PCIe architectures.

PCI

The *Peripheral Component Interconnect (PCI)* expansion bus architecture was released to the public domain in the 1990s by the Intel Corporation with hopes of attracting motherboard manufacturers to incorporate it into their designs. Compared to the expansion buses it hoped to replace, PCI was wider at 32 bits, faster at 33 MHz, and more flexible. PCI was also self-configuring, a feature that would lead to the Plug and Play (PnP) standard. The lack a cost for this exceptional technology led manufacturers to incorporate PCI into their products to replace earlier bus structures.

PCIe

PCI Express (PCIe) is an updated version of PCI. However, PCIe uses a point-to-point serial connection instead of PCI's shared parallel connections to communicate. The serial interface reduces overhead and supports higher transfer speeds without interference from other connected devices. A PCIe device's point-to-point (direct) connection to the northbridge component of the chipset allows it to transfer data without the need to wait for other devices.

A *PCIe lane* consists of a single wire on which data is sent and received. However, a PCIe device can use 1, 2, 4, 8, 12, 16, or 32 lanes with corresponding slots referred to as ×1 (by one), ×4 (by four), ×8 (by eight), and so on. Each direction of a lane transfers at a speed that depends on the PCIe version of the expansion card, the PCIe device, and the motherboard. If there is a conflict of PCIe versions between a slot and a card, the slower version is supported.

TABLE 3.4-1   Data Transfer Speeds of the PCIe Versions

PCIe Version	Bus Transfer Rate (Giga-Transfers per Second, GTps)	Throughput Speed (GBps)			
		×1	×4	×8	×16
PCIe 1.0	2.5	0.25	1.0	2.0	4.0
PCIe 2.0	5	0.50	2.0	4.0	8.0
PCIe 3.0	8	1.0	4.0	8.0	16.0
PCIe 4.0	16	2.0	8.0	16.0	32.0
PCIe 5.0	32	4.0	16.0	32.0	63.0
PCIe 6.0	64	8.0	32.0	63.0	126.0

Some PCIe configurations have special purposes:

- **PCIe ×32**   Because of its large size and the fact that there really aren't many devices readily available that use it, this PCIe version is rarely used.
- **PCIe ×12**   This PCIe version is rarely included on consumer-market PCs but is commonly found on server motherboards.
- **PCIe ×2**   This PCIe version is used for internal connections but not for expansion slots.

Table 3.4-1 lists the transfer speeds of the various PCIe versions.

 NOTE   A lot of laptop computers offer an internal PCIe expansion slot called PCI Express Mini Card, or Mini PCIe. It works like any PCIe expansion slot, although it's not compatible with full-sized cards.

The most common PCIe slot is the 16-lane (×16) version most video cards use, while ×1 and ×4 are the most common general-purpose PCIe slots. The first PCIe motherboards used a single PCIe ×16 slot and several standard PCI slots. Figure 3.4-4 compares PCIe and PCI slots on a typical late-model motherboard.

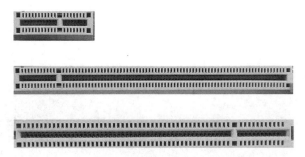

FIGURE 3.4-4   PCIe ×16 (bottom), PCI (middle), and PCIe ×1 (top) slots

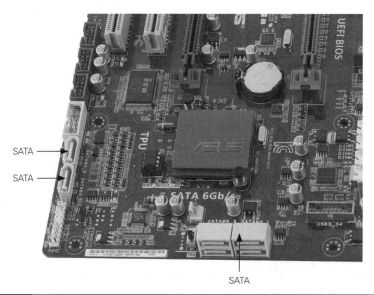

SATA

SATA

SATA

FIGURE 3.4-5 Front-mounted and top-mounted SATA ports on a typical motherboard

 EXAM TIP Given a scenario, be able to identify the various PCI and PCIe slots.

SATA

SATA connectors on motherboards might face upward or be positioned along the front edge to face forward. Some motherboards feature ports in both positions (see Figure 3.4-5).

eSATA

eSATA is an external (that's what the *e* stands for) interface for SATA devices that competes with USB 3.0 for connecting external storage devices. eSATA is essentially a SATA connector accessible from outside a computer for attaching a storage device, which could be a SATA disk drive, an eSATA flash drive, or even a USB 3.0 flash drive. However, eSATA, because it doesn't supply power, is giving way to the eSATAp (power over eSATA or the eSATA/USB hybrid port) connection standard (see Figure 3.4-6).

Motherboard Headers

A *header* is a set of pins in a socket on a motherboard that is used to add more connection ports to a computer. The primary two types of headers commonly found on PC motherboards

FIGURE 3.4-6   An eSATAp + USB port

are 1394 (Firewire) and USB, which are not cross-compatible. For example, a USB port panel add-on can be installed in a PC case drive bay and connected to the motherboard using the USB header, like those shown in Figure 3.4-7.

A motherboard may also include several other types of headers, including audio, game port, network adapter, and serial and parallel ports.

M.2 Interface

Originally called the Next Generation Form Factor (NGFF), the M.2 interface was developed to overcome the limitations the mSATA to support SFF devices, such as SSD. The M.2 standard supplies better performance and capacity in a smaller package. M.2 supports both

FIGURE 3.4-7   USB headers on a motherboard

FIGURE 3.4-8   An M.2 interface connector

SATA and PCIe but can be used in only one at a time. Figure 3.4-8 shows the two sides of an M.2 interface.

Motherboard Compatibility

Adding a component such as a CPU, memory, or cooling device to a motherboard depends on its compatibility with any other particular component you wish to add. The following subsections list the criteria to determine a component's compatibility with a certain motherboard.

 NOTE   A motherboard is also referred to as a *system board* in the product literature of some components.

CPU Compatibility

You should consider the following criteria when determining whether a CPU is compatible with a motherboard:

- **Manufacturer**   The two primary CPU manufacturers are Intel and Advanced Micro Devices (AMD). The CPUs of these manufacturers require different motherboards and are not compatible to each other.
- **CPU socket type**   Each CPU socket is specifically designed to mount a specific CPU or series of CPUs. The CPU socket must be compatible with the CPU to be mounted on a motherboard. For example, Figure 3.4-9 shows an AMD A4 CPU socket.
- **Memory compatibility**   There are four criteria for determining the compatibility between a motherboard and the memory modules to be used:

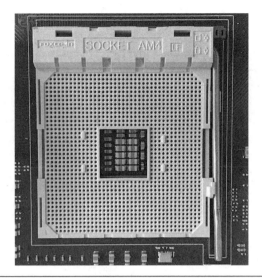

FIGURE 3.4-9   An AMD A4 CPU socket

- **Form factor**   What memory slots are available (DIMM or SO-DIMM)? What DDR generation is supported? Older motherboards typically support DDR3, and newer motherboards support DDR4 or DDR5.

- **Capacity**   The limit on the amount of memory a system supports is determined primarily by the CPU. For example, a motherboard that supports 128 GB may actually be limited to 4 GB by a 32-bit processor. Therefore, be sure to match the memory capacity to the motherboard and CPU.

 NOTE   To find the memory capacity on a Windows PC, enter the command **wmic memphysical get maxcapacity** at a command prompt and divide the result by 1,048,576. The result is the maximum memory capacity in gigabytes.

- **Chipset**   Different CPUs support different chipsets. Some chipsets support overclocking and others don't. A low-performance chipset can restrict the operations of a high-performance CPU, and a fully featured chipset may be wasted on a low-performance CPU. Check with the CPU manufacturer to determine the capability of a motherboard's chipset with a CPU.

- **BIOS/UEFI**   For a system to function properly, the motherboard, CPU, chipset, and the system BIOS must all be compatible. The motherboard manufacturer's website should list the compatibility information for the motherboard and the BIOS. A new motherboard should be good to go, but a CPU upgrade may require a BIOS update—before you install the new CPU.

- **Fit** Some RAM modules require large heat sinks that may obstruct other components, such as the CPU cooling devices. Check that the height and position of the memory modules and the size and position of the CPU cooling devices are able to fit together and function properly.

System Compatibility Issues

Depending on the use or purpose of a system, relatively unique compatibility issues may exist. Servers, desktops, and mobile PCs all have vital considerations when you're determining the compatibility of a motherboard and other components.

Servers

Like all systems, a motherboard in a server computer must be capable of supporting the demand to be placed on it. However, the two primary considerations for a server motherboard choice are the chipset and the compatibility of the CPU and memory modules. The chipset controls the overall functionality of the motherboard. Also, as discussed earlier, the motherboard, CPU, and memory must all be matched to each other as well as the workload of the server.

Desktops

The compatibility issues of a desktop computer are those described earlier in this section, but like all systems, the key issue is how it will be used. The motherboard, CPU, and memory must all be properly sized and configured to handle the role and purpose of the system. An engineering workstation requires more capabilities than a computer used strictly for records retrieval.

Mobile

Laptops and notebooks are the mobile devices that are capable of major upgrades, but they may not be conducive to upgrading the motherboard, CPU, or memory. The options for upgrades to these components are more limited than those in a server or desktop system. Check the manufacturer's guidelines on upgrading a mobile device and the compatibility of the devices that can be upgraded.

Multisocket Motherboards

Motherboards with two or more CPUs are generally used by high-end or enterprise systems. Dual-processor motherboards are readily available from the major motherboard manufacturers, but anything beyond that (this is, three, four, or more processors) is less common and typically must be customized. Figure 3.4-10 shows an example of a dual-socket motherboard.

On a multi-CPU system, based on a multiple-socket motherboard, if one processor becomes overloaded, its load is shared with another processor, which makes the entire system more

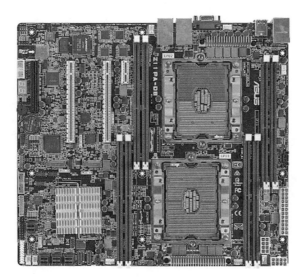

FIGURE 3.4-10 A dual-socket motherboard (image courtesy of ASUSTeK Computer Inc.)

efficient and faster. Compatibility issues mainly involve the CPUs supported and especially the chipset. These elements must be matched to achieve optimal performance of the system. See the motherboard manufacturer for information on what components are compatible and supported.

BIOS/UEFI Settings

The configuration setup utility stored in the system ROM enables you to configure important system settings stored in CMOS. These settings include CPU setup, boot sequence, power management, and several others, which are described next.

CMOS stands for *complementary metal-oxide semiconductor,* which is the material used to make the chip. CMOS has a very small amount of storage in which the configuration settings for a system are stored, and it requires a power source to retain the data it holds, which is provided by a battery on the motherboard. The term *CMOS* is most commonly used to refer to the data stored on the chip rather than its material.

 NOTE CMOS is an algorithm commonly associated with BIOS and the system configuration of a computer.

BIOS/UEFI

The *Basic Input/Output System (BIOS)* is stored on a *read-only memory (ROM)* chip, which also stores the BIOS system and configuration setup utilities. These BIOS utilities are examples of firmware. The system ROM is typically labeled with the BIOS maker's name but can

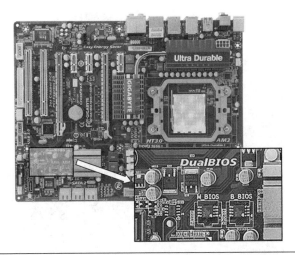

FIGURE 3.4-11   The inset shows a magnification of the M_BIOS and B_BIOS chips.

also be a tiny chip (or a set of two tiny chips) on the motherboard. Some motherboards have two BIOS chips: an *M_BIOS* and a *B_BIOS* (see Figure 3.4-11). An M_BIOS is the main or primary BIOS chip, and it's used during system startup. The B_BIOS is a backup or reserve to the M_BIOS, and it overwrites the M_BIOS chip should it become corrupted.

There's a big difference between system ROM chips and RAM: RAM is called *volatile* because it stores data only while it's powered. ROM is *nonvolatile* and retains data even when the system isn't powered. Except for replacing the CMOS battery (described in the next section) if it dies, system ROM requires no specific maintenance.

The firmware on modern systems is the *Unified Extensible Firmware Interface (UEFI)*. Here are the essentials:

- UEFI is often accessed through a graphical system setup utility. Most laptops, notebooks, and desktop PCs also have a text-mode utility for both BIOS and UEFI.
- UEFI supports booting to partitions larger than 2.2 TB.
- The UEFI setup utility can be opened from within the OS, which is something that cannot be done with BIOS.
- UEFI supports a security feature called Secure Boot that ensures a device boots using only trusted software.

 NOTE   Although it may sound as if BIOS and UEFI are perhaps mutually exclusive, most of the currently available operating systems versions support BIOS and UEFI together.

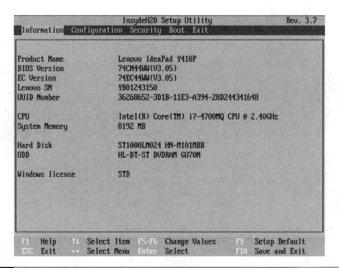

InsydeH20 Setup Utility   Rev. 3.7

Information Configuration Security Boot Exit

Product Name	Lenovo IdeaPad Y410P
BIOS Version	74CN44WW(V3.05)
EC Version	74EC44WW(V3.05)
Lenovo SN	YB01243150
UUID Number	36268652-3D1B-11E3-A394-28D244341648
CPU	Intel(R) Core(TM) i7-4700MQ CPU @ 2.40GHz
System Memory	8192 MB
Hard Disk	ST1000LM024 HN-M101MBB
ODD	HL-DT-ST DVDRAM GU70N
Windows license	STD

F1 Help   ↑↓ Select Item F5/F6 Change Values   F9   Setup Default
ESC Exit   ↔   Select Menu Enter Select   F10 Save and Exit

FIGURE 3.4-12   The main menu of a text-based BIOS configuration utility

The BIOS Setup Utility

As stated earlier, the traditional BIOS CMOS configuration setup utility cannot be accessed once a device is fully started and running an OS. Accessing the BIOS configuration utility must be done near the beginning of the system boot process. Depending on the device manufacturer and the BIOS type in use, the method used varies. At one time, a prompt was displayed to let you know which key you needed to press to access the BIOS utility. However, many newer systems no longer do so. The instructions for entering the BIOS configuration utility can be found in the documentation of the motherboard.

Figure 3.4-12 shows an example of the main (opening) tab of a BIOS configuration setup utility. The information displayed by this utility reflects the current configuration of the software and hardware of the system. Most of these settings can be changed and stored to the CMOS and remain in effect unless modified in the future.

Today, most configuration setup utilities are graphical user interfaces and mouse-friendly, like the one shown at the top of Figure 3.4-13, rather than the text-mode utilities you must navigate with a keyboard, like the one shown at the bottom of Figure 3.4-13. In either case, both the text and the GUI styles open to a main screen with a good overview of your CPU, RAM, hard drives, and optical drive settings, along with either a series of menu choices or tabs on which specific configuration settings can be accessed, reviewed, and modified.

Navigating the CMOS Setup Utility

Although the items listed on the main menu of a text-based utility or the tabs on a GUI utility may not be exactly the same from vendor to vendor, the configuration settings and hardware designations are virtually always the same.

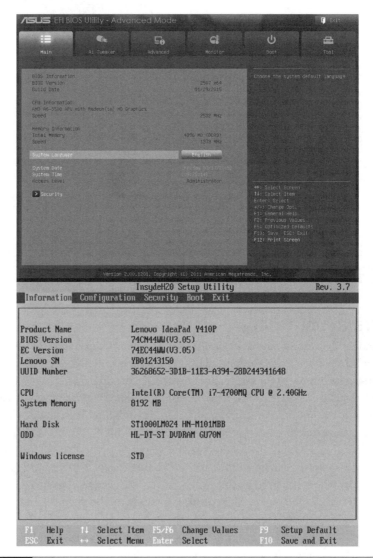

System information screen in graphical (top) and text-mode (bottom) setup utilities

When you're accessing and working with the configuration utilities, there are two navigation features to keep in mind before you exit a system configuration setup utility, especially if you changed any of the settings:

- **Save & Exit Setup**   To avoid accidents, *only* use this option when you intend to make a change and you're certain what the effect will be. Typically, selecting this option brings up a confirmation prompt such as "Are you sure you want to make these changes? Y/N."

• **Exit Without Saving**   This option discards your changes. Choosing this option brings up another "Are you sure? Y/N" confirmation prompt. Press Y to take your leave of CMOS setup without doing any damage.

 NOTE   There's enough variety in how tabs, menus, and options are labeled in different setup utilities that you'll inevitably find yourself hunting for what you need.

Boot Options

The boot options (see Figure 3.4-14 for an example) hold one of the most frequently changed settings in the setup utility: the boot sequence. This setting decides which devices your system attempts to boot from and in what order. Other options you're likely to find here dictate whether the system boots from USB devices or network locations, displays detailed POST (power-on self-test) information, displays the key combination to reach the setup utility, and so on.

FIGURE 3.4-14   Boot tab in graphical setup utility

EXAM TIP The boot sequence is the first place to check if you have a computer that attempts to boot to an incorrect device or gives an "invalid boot device" error. If you have a USB thumb drive inserted and this setting has removable devices ahead of hard drives in the boot order, the computer will dutifully try to boot from the thumb drive.

USB Permissions

In a variety of situations, it may be necessary to disable access to USB ports to prevent the damage or loss of sensitive data or the introduction of malware through the actions of unauthorized employees or intruders. There are four basic ways to disable USB ports:

- **Disabling USB ports in BIOS** USB ports can be disabled for any operating system. Open the BIOS, access the Integrated Peripherals tab, and change the status of the USB controller to Disabled. If you wish to enable the USB ports later, just change the setting to Enabled.

- **Disabling USB ports in the Device Manager** You can use the Device Manager to disable the USB port on your Windows device by selecting the Universal Serial Bus Controller option in the Windows Device Manager, right-clicking the USB device you want to disable, and choosing Disable Device from the pop-up list, as shown in Figure 3.4-15. Another option is to uninstall the device from the Device Manager completely.

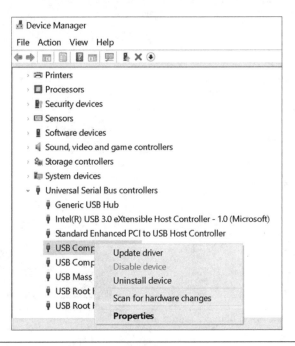

FIGURE 3.4-15 Disabling a USB device on the Device Manager

- **Disconnecting the USB** This process should be your last resort, unless you want to permanently disable a USB port on a system. While you can't disable all of the USB devices this way, you can remove one USB port simply by unplugging it from the motherboard.

- **Locking USB ports with Registry entries** You can disable a USB port using the regedit utility to change its settings in the Windows Registry. In the left pane of the regedit window, navigate to HKEY_LOCAL_MACHINE\SYSTEM\CurrentControlSet\Services\USBSTOR. For this key, double-click the Start option in the right pane. In the Start box, change the value to 4 (Disable). A value of 3 enables the port. Save the entry and exit regedit.

Trusted Platform Module

The *Trusted Platform Module (TPM)* is a secure microchip that acts as a crypto-processor to provide hardware-based security features. TPM is resistant to malware attempting to alter its security features. TPM creates, stores, and controls cryptographic keys, provides device authentication using a burned-in RSA key, and manages system security metrics and measurements.

During the boot process, TPM "measures" the firmware and OS code and stores the measurements. The TPM measurements benchmark how the system started up and verifies that a TPM-generated key was used in the boot process. TPM keys are used in a variety of ways, including the following:

- **Attack mitigation** TPM can be configured so that the TPM key is not available outside TPM, which can be used to mitigate malware and phishing attacks.

- **Authorization** TPM can be configured to require an authentication/authorization code before the TPM keys can be used. Too many bad guesses initiates protection against what TPM sees as a dictionary attack.

- **Confidentiality** TPM can be configured to protect any data identified by a user.

CompTIA wants you to know about the security options you might find in the BIOS/UEFI setup utility, whether collected on a single tab (see Figure 3.4-16) or scattered about other menus:

- **Passwords** When a user's BIOS/UEFI password is set, the system won't boot without the correct password. An administrator's BIOS/UEFI password restricts access to the BIOS/UEFI utility itself.

 EXAM TIP Remember that BIOS/UEFI configuration settings—including passwords—can be wiped by using the CMOS clear jumper or button or by removing and replacing the CMOS battery.

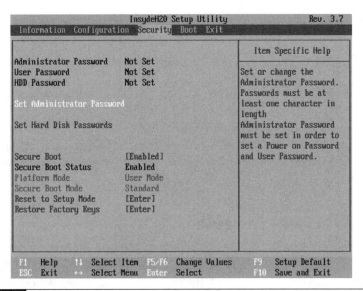

FIGURE 3.4-16 Security tab in text-mode setup utility

- **Secure Boot** This UEFI protocol protects the system from some low-level malware and other exploits by refusing to load driver or OS software that hasn't been properly signed by a trusted party. Secure Boot requires an Intel CPU, a UEFI BIOS, and an operating system designed for it.

Cross-Reference

More information on TPM is included later in this objective in the section "Encryption."

Fan Controls

There is a direct relationship between the proper adjustments of the cooling system inside a computer case and the reliable operation of the CPU, motherboard, and all the other internal components of a PC. The operational settings of a PC's cooling system and case fan(s) are a necessity not only for the immediate operation of the computer but also for its service life.

There are essentially three ways to set the cooling and fan controls on a computer:

- **Manufacturer-supplied software** Quality cooling system components and case and CPU fans come with software provided by the manufacturer that is specific to the device or component. Since it is specific to a particular device or brand, this software is without compatibility problems and is simple to use.
- **BIOS/UEFI settings** Virtually all BIOS and UEFI systems provide you with the capability to view and set fan speeds, cooling system temperature targets, and other operational settings.

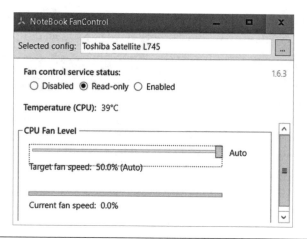

FIGURE 3.4-17   The main page of the NoteBook FanControl software

- **Third-party software**   Third-party system monitoring software, including fan control and monitoring software, can typically be configured to a long list of PC hardware and multiple operating systems. Several third-party fan control and cooling system monitoring packages are available as freeware, demoware, or licensed. Figure 3.4-17 shows the basic user interface for the NoteBook FanControl software.

ADDITIONAL RESOURCES   For more information on the popular fan control and monitoring software packages available, navigate to the article "The Ultimate Guide to CPU Temperature" by Miodrag Matović (https://www.thetechlounge .com/cpu-temperature/).

Secure Boot

Secure Boot is a security standard that helps to ensure a device only starts up with firmware and software that the device or operating system manufacturers trust and have approved. Under the Secure Boot process, when the device starts up, firmware verifies the signature of each of the software elements involved in the boot process—including all UEFI and Option ROM firmware and drivers, the operating system, and Extensible Firmware Interface (EFI) drivers—for validity before passing control to the operating system to complete the startup.

There are three levels to a Secure Boot on a Windows system:

- **Secure Boot**   PCs with both UEFI firmware and a TPM can boot using only trusted boot software.
- **Trusted boot**   A Windows PC's system verifies the validity of each of the startup components before loading it.

- **Measured boot** As the boot process progresses, its actions are logged. The log of the complete boot process can then be forwarded to a trusted device for an objective analysis of the PC's health.

Boot Password

A *boot password,* also commonly referred to as a *BIOS password,* when configured, controls the access to the CMOS-stored information used by the CPU to start up a computer. In a sense, a boot password serves as an authentication of just who is starting up the system, which in some highly secured areas could be very important.

The downside to configuring a boot password on a system's BIOS is that forgetting it means no bootup, which can be a real hassle. Some help is available, though: the BIOS provider can expose a backdoor BIOS password, which may require that the firmware be flashed immediately after gaining access. Also, user-created boot passwords can commonly be reset by removing the CMOS battery or by software specifically designed for this purpose.

Encryption

Essentially, *encryption* is the process used to convert readable cleartext data into garbled, unreadable, undecipherable data. The purpose of this conversion is to ensure that only those authorized to access, read, or use the data are the ones who do so. Of course, this is a simplification, but not by much. Encrypted data is stored, transmitted, and, if unencrypted, used.

The process of encryption takes in plaintext data and encrypts it using an encryption algorithm and an encryption key to produce ciphertext. Ciphertext requires a specific decryption key before it can be viewed or used. There are two basic types of ciphertext: symmetric (private key), which uses the same key for encryption and decryption, and asymmetric (public key), which uses a private (secret) key to encrypt the data and a public key (not secret) to decrypt it.

Using TPM

The use of TPM, also referred to as ISO/IEC 11889, improves the general security of a PC. On a computer, TPM securely creates and stores encryption keys and verifies that the operating system and firmware are valid and have not been damaged or tampered with. Essentially, TPM is used by an operating system to safeguard the user to verify and authenticate the startup and operations of a PC. Windows, Linux, and macOS all implement TPM functions in their security processes.

TPM is a chip installed on a PC motherboard, plugged into the motherboard using a small card, or integrated into the microprocessor on AMD and Intel CPUs. The current version is TPM 2.0, but TPM has been available to PCs since 2005. Any PC manufactured after 2016 is likely to have TPM as a part of its system.

FIGURE 3.4-18   A rackmount HSM

NOTE   You can check to see if a Windows 10 PC has TPM. If there is a Security Processor section on the Settings | Update and Security | Windows Security | Device Security page, TPM is available on the system. If Security Processor information is not displayed, check your motherboard or CPU manufacturer's website for information.

A TPM chip interacts with the security systems on a PC to provide input to the allow/disallow decision. Each time a user logs in to a system, TPM initiates an encryption key to be associated with the user's session if no problems are detected. However, if a threat, either real or suspected, is detected, the system is locked down as a preventive measure. The security functions of TPM include the creation and storage of encryption keys and device authentication.

Hardware Security Module

A hardware security module (HSM) is used for basically the same function as a TPM. However, the two devices have one major difference: an HSM is a standalone or expansion card insert hardware device (see Figure 3.4-18) instead of a chip on the motherboard. HSMs are intrusion- and tamper-resistant. This makes them an excellent choice for protecting and storing encryption keys that can be securely accessed by authorized users. An HSM controls access and limits the risk of threats to private encryption keys.

HSM is used to secure digital keys and signatures and to encrypt and decrypt documents. HSM can be used for personal security, but it is mostly used in banking, healthcare, and purchase card systems.

CPU Features

CPUs have a variety of features that distinguish them from each other, including the instruction set in use, number of cores, hardware virtualization, encryption, multithreading, and other architecture features, each of which is briefly explained in the following subsections.

x64 and x86 Architectures

Although the terms x86 and x64 are considered by many to be form factors, bus widths, or other technology or design elements of a CPU, they are, in fact, identifiers for *instruction set architectures (ISAs)*. The *x* in either term represents an ISA version. Both ISAs were developed by the Intel Corporation for its CPUs.

x64 Architecture

The x64 ISA, also referred to as *x86-64* or the *x86-based 64-bit ISA,* is actually a family of ISAs for computer processors. Several manufacturers have developed proprietary 64-bit ISAs. Intel and AMD support Intel 64 and AMD 64, respectively. The x64 ISA has a virtual address space of around 256 tebibytes (TiB, the binary value equivalent of a terabyte) and relative addressing in memory.

Here's a list of some of the primary features of the x64 ISA:

- A 64-bit integer capability that supports a value range of approximately plus or minus 9 quintillion, or $\pm 2^{63}$
- An approximate 256-TiB virtual address space

 NOTE   A *virtual address space (VAS),* also known as a *logical address space,* is a range of virtual memory addresses allocated to a process by the operating system. It represents areas of physical memory and their addresses that are referenced in a relative way by a process.

- A very large file mapping in a process's address space
- A large physical address space in RAM of up to 256 TiB

Applications of the x64 ISA include the following:

- Mobile processors
- Supercomputers
- Current operating systems
- Video games consoles
- Virtualization technologies

x86 Architecture

The x86 ISA defines how a processor manages and executes various instructions from an operating system and application programs. The x86 ISA is based on Intel's 8086 and 8088 microprocessors and grew from a 16-bit instruction set (for the 16-bit processors) to a 32-bit instruction set. The x86 ISA is based on the *complex instruction set computing (CISC)* architecture.

Complex instructions are executed one at a time and nearly all take more than one cycle to complete. The x86 ISA has been adopted by various microprocessor manufacturers because of its compatibility with PCs to Supercomputers.

The following lists some of the primary features of the x86 ISA:

- Uses CISC computing architecture
- Optimizes system performance using a hardware approach
- Uses more registers and less memory for operations
- Designed for complex addresses

Some applications of the x86 ISA are:

- Mobile devices and PCs
- Gaming consoles
- Workstations running specific processing-intensive applications (intensive workstations)
- Cloud computing segments

Advanced RISC Machine

A *reduced instruction set computer (RISC)* uses a smaller, optimized instruction set, as opposed to a CISC. Of the two, RISC is the more efficient and is used by many of the current CPUs. However, when a need arose for a low-cost, efficient 32-bit RISC CPU that could be used in embedded control systems, digital signal processors (DSPs), and portable multimedia devices, the condensed *Advanced RISC Machine (ARM)* instruction set was developed. ARM is *orthogonal,* meaning that all instructions are in a standard format and use the same addressing scheme for all addressable registers and resources, which is a feature of all RISC CPUs. ARM processors are common to smartphones, tablets, and other handheld computing and communication devices.

Single Core and Multicore

Originally, all CPUs had only one processor core. In fact, it wasn't even called a core. However, when CPU clock speeds hit the practical limit of roughly 4 GHz, CPU producers combined two or more CPUs (cores) onto a single processor die to create *multicore* CPUs. The first multicore processors combined two CPU cores onto one microprocessor integrated circuit (IC) in a *dual-core* architecture. When combined onto a multicore microprocessor, each discrete core has its own resources.

 EXAM TIP   For the A+ Core 1 exam, know the basic differences between a single-core CPU and a multicore CPU.

ADDITIONAL RESOURCES To access information on the microprocessor (and much more) in a computer, you can use the CPU-Z utility (https://www.cpuid.com/softwares/cpu-z.html).

Multithreading

Virtually all of the multicore CPUs process multiple threads, which is called *multithreading* (the execution of more than one thread simultaneously). A thread is essentially a basic unit of a process, and a process is a running program that can have multiple threads.

There are basically two types of threads execution:

- **Concurrent execution** The processor allocates and switches resources from one thread of a multithreaded process to another, as needed.
- **Parallel execution** The separate threads of a process run on different processors in parallel.

Multithreaded processes can use one of three types of process approaches:

- **Many to many** Multiple threads interact with an equal or lesser number of threads.
- **Many to one** Multiple threads are linked to a single thread.
- **One to one** With this approach, one thread is linked to just one other thread.

Hardware Virtualization

Intel and AMD have built-in support for *hardware virtualization*: Intel's Virtual Technology Extensions (VT-X) and AMD's AMD-V and Secure Virtual Machine (SVM). Although supported on different CPUs, these extensions essentially work the same.

Hardware virtualization (also called *hardware-assisted virtualization* or *native virtualization*) is enabled by an expanded instruction set on the Intel and AMD processors. The processor provides a logical structure for defining a virtual environment on a computer. Hardware virtualization is enabled through BIOS/UEFI firmware.

Enabling Hardware Virtualization

If hardware virtualization is not enabled on a PC, one or both of the following conditions or messages will appear:

- The PC doesn't have either VT-x or AMD-V hardware acceleration, or it is not available on the system.
- This computer doesn't have VT-x/AMD-V enabled.

Should one of these or a similar message appear, provided your system has one of the hardware virtualization technologies available (we discuss how you can check this next), you can use one of the following processes (whichever is appropriate) to find and enable hardware virtualization:

- Boot the PC into its BIOS or UEFI setup configuration utility.
- Locate the Virtualization settings (often located under System Configuration).
- Enable the Hardware Virtualization and the save and exit.

Verifying Hardware Virtualization Is Enabled on a Windows System

On a Windows system, you can check if hardware virtualization is enabled using a variety of methods. Here are two you can use on a Windows system:

- **systeminfo** At a command prompt, enter the command **systeminfo**. Toward the bottom of the information displayed, find the section labeled "Hyper-V Requirements" (see Figure 3.4-19). If the "Virtualization Enabled in Firmware:" is "No," access the BIOS/UEFI settings to enable this feature.
- **Task Manager** Open the Task Manager from Power User menu or use CTRL-ALT-DEL and choose Task Manager. Click the Performance tab. In the lower-right corner of the Performance windows, the status of Virtualization is shown.

Verifying Hardware Virtualization Is Enabled on a Linux System

To check the status of hardware virtualization on a Linux system, use the following series of commands at the command prompt:

1. Install the cpu-checker utility:

```
$ sudo apt-get update
$ sudo apt-get install cpu-checker
```

2. Check the hardware virtualization status:

```
$ kvm-ok
```

```
                              Status:          Media disconnected
Hyper-V Requirements:      VM Monitor Mode Extensions: Yes
                           Virtualization Enabled In Firmware: Yes
                           Second Level Address Translation: Yes
                           Data Execution Prevention Available: Yes
```

FIGURE 3.4-19 The Hyper-V Requirements section of a systeminfo command's output

If the PC has hardware virtualization enabled, a message to the effect that it exists or can be used is displayed.

Cross-Reference

For a comprehensive overview of virtualization, see Domain 4.0 in this book.

Expansion Cards

Although most current motherboards and systems include many built-in ports, there are still some functions and features that can be added to a computer to improve them over the standard defaults available. For example, audio/visual functions are commonly upgraded with expansion cards. The A+ Core 1 exam focuses on expansion cards in Windows systems, although expansion cards are supported by macOS and Linux systems as well.

Video Cards

A *video card* (or *display adapter*) handles the video chores within computing devices by processing information from the CPU and sending it to the display. It is configured the same way whether it is an onboard *graphics processing unit (GPU)* that is a part of the CPU or an expansion card.

Onboard

An *onboard* video card uses a GPU commonly integrated onto CPUs. Almost all laptops and thick and thin client desktops use onboard graphics support. Desktop computers with onboard GPUs typically have one or more video ports available, as shown earlier in Figure 3.4-2.

Add-on Card

A video/graphics card that inserts into a PCIe slot is one type of what CompTIA refers to as an *add-on card*. Video cards typically require additional power over what the expansion slot provides. A midrange PCIe video cards uses a 6-pin PCIe power connector commonly located at the top-front edge of the card (the end pointing away from the card bracket). High-end cards use an 8-pin version or, in some cases, two PCIe cables. Figure 3.4-20 illustrates a PCIe video card with a 6-pin power connector and a 6/8-pin PCIe power cable.

The main parts of a video card are the video RAM and video processor. The video processor takes information from the video RAM and shoots it out to the monitor. Early video processors were little more than an intermediary between the CPU and video RAM, but powerful modern video cards need fans to cool their video processors (see Figure 3.4-21).

When installing a video card into a Windows system, you must also install video device drivers and use the Device Manager to confirm that it works. The next step is to configure the video card in the Display Control Panel applet or using first-party software included with the card.

FIGURE 3.4-20   Connecting a PCIe power cable to a PCIe video card

FIGURE 3.4-21   Video card with a cooling fan

Sound Cards

For the most part, computers use sound chips built into the motherboard that aren't necessarily of the highest technology or quality. In fact, embedded sound production devices may have an audible hum or buzz caused by external interference or interference from other devices on the motherboard, especially when heard through headphones. A sound card that produces

FIGURE 3.4-22   Klipsch 2.1 speaker set

a higher sound quality is a frequent addition to a computer to improve its sound production with audio speaker sets like those shown in Figure 3.4-22.

> **NOTE**   The numbers used to describe speaker sets, such as 2.1, 5.1, and 7.1, define the number of satellite speakers and a subwoofer. A 2.1 system, for example, means two satellites and a subwoofer. A 5.1 set, in contrast, has two front satellites, two rear satellites (for surround sound), a center channel speaker, and a subwoofer. A 7.1 set adds two additional rear satellites for sound effects to the speaker configuration used for 5.1 surround sound.

Install a sound card like you would any expansion card. Plug audio cables into the correct ports, and they should work fine. If you don't see errors but get no sound, check the Sound applet in the Windows Control Panel to confirm that the correct devices are working, connected, and set to their defaults and that the playback indicator shows activity on the correct device.

The 3.4-mm audio ports on the motherboard port cluster or sound card bracket aren't the only audio output. The ports you might find include S/PDIF (Sony/Philips Digital Interface) optical or digital ports, HDMI (High-Definition Multimedia Interface), and DisplayPort HD video ports, which also output HD audio.

Capture Card

A *capture card* is either an internal expansion card or a peripheral device that records (captures) the display images and content and then formats them for playback as a livestream

FIGURE 3.4-23   A PCIe capture card (top) and a Thunderbolt video capture device (bottom)

or a high-resolution video file. Capture cards are classified as input devices, despite the fact they are, as the name states, capture devices. A common use is to capture the video from video game consoles as well as computer video and camera images.

External capture cards are connected to a computer through USB and USB-C or Thunderbolt. A capture card expansion module is inserted into a PCIe slot. Figure 3.4-23 shows examples of capture card devices.

Network Interface Card

The *network interface card (NIC)*, also called a *network adapter*, links a device to a network infrastructure. Virtually all current PCs and network-capable devices have an onboard port for a network connection. However, some devices, such as tablets and other handheld devices, can use a peripheral device to connect and interact with an Ethernet network. Notebook and desktop computers can also use peripheral network connections, but for other reasons, such as support for faster speeds or to connect to a fiber optic network.

A Windows system will automatically detect and configure a NIC. On some Windows systems and on Linux and macOS systems, you may need to install and configure an expansion card NIC, following the manufacturer's instructions.

Cross-Reference

To learn more about NIC configuration, see Domain 2.0, Objective 2.2.

FIGURE 3.4-24 An Ethernet RJ-45 port with LED status lights

Technically, a computing device or a network-enabled device doesn't communicate directly with the network. The networked device interacts with the NIC, and the NIC places network messages on the network medium. To read the message, the receiving node interacts with its NIC.

Ethernet NICs have LED *status indicators* (also called *link lights*) used to display the condition of the link or to confirm a connection. Most NICs have two LEDs, but some can have three: a link or connection light, an activity light, and possibly a speed light if there are three LEDs on the NIC, as detailed in the following list:

- **Link light** This indicates whether a network connection has been established between the NIC and the network. If the link light is showing green, all is well. However, if the LED is unlit, there is a connection problem.
- **Activity light** This LED indicates an interaction between the NIC and the network by flickering or flashing intermittently. If this indicator is flashing too fast, there could be a problem with the connection or something on the network.
- **Speed light** If present, this light indicates the transmission speed of the connection. This LED is found on some 10/100 Mbps Ethernet NICs.

Also, some NICs use two- or three-color LEDs (green, red, and amber) to combine the status lights and other legacy cards (mostly PCMCIA) that have no LEDs at all. Most of the LEDs are integrated into the RJ-45 port, as shown in Figure 3.4-24. There aren't any real standards for this, but one LED lit up usually indicates the connection status, and all lights shining bright likely means there's no physical connection. To be sure, consult the motherboard or NIC manual.

Cooling Mechanism

CPUs have no moving parts, at least none you can see with your naked eye, but even so, they generate a considerable amount of heat. Extreme heat is a big problem to a CPU and many other of a PC's components. Excessive heat causes system instability, lockups, and even dead CPUs. For the most part, CPU packages are made from high-tech thermal plastics and

FIGURE 3.4-25   Top of retail heat sink (left) and bottom of fan assembly (right) for an Intel CPU

ceramics that dissipate heat, but additional cooling is needed from what is called *active cooling*. Active cooling has several forms, but the most common are a combination of a *heat sink and fan assembly* (see Figure 3.4-25) and a *liquid cooling system*.

Heat Sink and Cooling Fans

Unlike the CPU socket, mounting heat sink and fan assemblies properly takes more force than you'd expect! A small flathead screwdriver will help.

 EXAM TIP   Some systems are *fanless* or use *passive cooling*. Smartphones and tablets are the passively cooled devices you're most likely familiar with. Passive CPU heat sinks may still rely on other fans to create good airflow in the case.

Heat sink and fan assemblies for CPUs usually come as a unit; if not, attach the fan to the heat sink before installing both onto the CPU. Again, different CPUs, socket designs, and heat sinks require different installation procedures, so be sure to read the CPU or motherboard documentation before removing cooling devices from or installing them on the CPU or motherboard. Perhaps the most important operational maintenance components in a PC are the parts that make up the direct cooling system of its CPU. The basic parts in the CPU cooling assembly are a heat sink, a cooling fan, and a paste or sealant material to hold the assembly together. Let's look at each of these components.

Heat Sinks

A *heat sink* is essentially the cooling device for the CPU and the component that directly impacts the running temperature of the CPU. Table 3.4-2 compares the various operating temperatures of AMD and Intel CPUs. For each of the CPUs included in the table, the running temperatures are a range of values that represent the temperature of the CPU under light to heavy loads. The maximum temperature is the threshold beyond which the CPU could be damaged.

TABLE 3.4-2   Comparison of CPU Temperatures

CPU	Running Temperature	Maximum Temperature
AMD A6	122–145° F	158° F
AMD A10	120–140° F	162° F
Intel i5	113–149° F	212° F
Intel i7	104–140° F	162° F

 NOTE   The temperatures for any give CPU version can vary based on its build and included technologies. The values shown in Table 3.4-2 are averages for the CPU families given.

A CPU heatsink is generally an engineered aluminum or copper block with fins that serves to draw heat up and away from the CPU and dissipate it into the air flowing to and around the fins. Figure 3.4-26 shows a sampling of various types of CPU heatsinks. In each of the heatsinks shown in this figure, notice the fins and the air gaps between them.

There are three primary types of heatsinks used with CPUs, each with some advantages and disadvantages, depending on how and where they are used:

- **Active heatsink**   This type of heatsink has a fan or blower incorporated into it. The assemblies shown in Figure 3.4-25 are examples of active heatsinks.

FIGURE 3.4-26   Heatsinks are available in a variety of designs, shapes, and sizes.

- **Passive heatsink** This type of heatsink has no moving parts and uses convection to dissipate heat. The samples shown in Figure 3.4-26 are passive heatsinks.
- **Hybrid heatsink** As you might guess, a hybrid heatsink combines the capabilities of active and passive heatsinks.

On today's PCs, in order for any heatsink to be an effective cooling device for a CPU, it must be combined with a cooling fan. Active heatsinks include a fan by definition, but passive and hybrid heatsinks must be combined with a fan to reduce the heat they absorb. However, the heatsink is also assisted in its heat dissipation through the use of a thermal conductor, which is typically either thermal paste or a thermal pad.

Thermal Conductors

The primary purpose of thermal conductors is to remove any air gaps between the heatsink and the cooling fan. Two types of thermal conductors are predominantly used: thermal conductive paste and thermal gap pads, which provide thermal conductivity and thermal impedance, respectively. *Conductivity* is the transference of heat, and *impedance* is the efficiency with which the heat is transferred. Thermal conductor materials are generally grouped together as *thermal interface material (TIM)*.

Thermal Pads Officially known as *thermal gap pads, thermal pads* conform to the space between the heatsink and the cooling fan to fill any gaps. The pads are typically fiberglass and aluminum, with a thickness of between 0.01 and 0.2 inches. Thermal pads are easily installed and don't require adhesive or thermal paste. In addition to being used as a part of a CPU cooling assembly, thermal pads can also be used to dissipate heat from chips and other components mounted on the motherboard, as illustrated in Figure 3.4-27. Manufacturers of active heatsinks, which include the heatsink and a cooling fan, include a thermal pad because they don't need adhesion and stay in place without it.

FIGURE 3.4-27 A CPU heatsink with a thermal pad

NOTE Thermal pads are definitely one-time use.

Thermal Paste Officially *thermal conductive paste, thermal paste* is used for the same purpose as a thermal pad, but because it is basically a liquid, it works differently. Thermal paste is a conductive material that is used to fill the extremely small gaps, often microscopic in size, between a CPU or a graphics processing unit (GPU) and a cooling assembly. The purpose of the thermal paste is to prevent air, which is a conductor of heat, from being trapped and reducing the effectiveness of the cooling system. Thermal paste is typically silicon-, ceramics-, or metal-based.

Thermal paste is applied from an injector (see Figure 3.4-28) to the surfaces to be sealed before they are combined. The application process is a bit different for circular and squarish cooling devices being attached to the CPU or a GPU. For a circular assembly, a small dot of thermal paste is applied in the center of the base of the cooling device. The amount of paste should be about the size of a grain of rice. Anything more may result in paste getting on the motherboard. For the squarish assembly, the most effective method is to place a small amount of thermal paste on the base of the cooling assembly and use a plastic bag or finger cover to spread the paste evenly across the base of the cooler. In either case, be sure that the area that will be in contact with the CPU is evenly covered. The rule of thumb is that the paste should barely cover the area to be sealed.

FIGURE 3.4-28 A small amount of thermal paste applied to a CPU cooling assembly

A few other TIMs are available for sealing the CPU and cooling system, including thermal grease, thermal adhesive, thermal gap filler, thermal tape, phase-change materials, and liquid metals. Each of these materials has its advantages and disadvantages, but they all fulfill essentially the same purpose as thermal paste and thermal pads.

Liquid Cooling System

As discussed earlier, there is a maximum temperature that a CPU can reach before it may be damaged by that heat. Most systems implement what is called *thermal throttling,* which means the processor reduces its performance to prevent excessive overheating. An alternative cooling method that helps to prevent both the damage and the reduction of performance is *liquid cooling.*

Your car has a liquid cooling system, and the ones installed in computers work essentially the same. A liquid is circulated through a heatsink attached to the CPU. The cooler liquid passing through the heatsink, absorbs the heat, and the now hot liquid flows to a radiator. The radiator transfers the heat from the liquid to outside the case, thus cooling the liquid, which then flows back through the system.

Two types of liquid cooling systems are popular for PCs: all-in-one (AIO) coolers and custom loop coolers. AIO cooling systems are the most common of the two and the most likely type you will encounter on the A+ Core 1 exam. An AIO system includes a block that has a pump that attaches to the CPU. From this assembly, two tubes attach to a radiator that has a fan to cool the liquid. Figure 3.4-29 illustrates the major parts of a liquid cooling system in a PC.

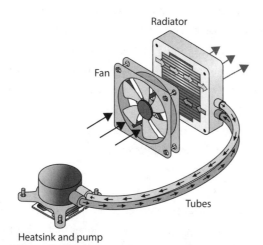

FIGURE 3.4-29 The components of a PC liquid cooling system (image courtesy of Intel Corporation)

REVIEW

Objective 3.4: Given a scenario, install and configure motherboards, central processing units (CPUs), and add-on cards

- Motherboards have port clusters at the rear for USB ports, audio jacks, network ports, and other built-in ports.
- PCI slots have been for the most part replaced by PCIe slots that use ×1 to ×16 lanes.
- Intel and AMD CPUs are not interchangeable.
- Most hard drives and optical drives connect to SATA ports.
- A motherboard header is a motherboard socket for adding connection ports.
- The M.2 standard supports both SATA and PCIe but can be used in only one at a time.
- CPU/motherboard compatibility elements are manufacturer, CPU socket type, memory compatibility and capacity, form factor, and chipset.
- Dual-processor motherboards are generally used by high-end or enterprise systems.
- The BIOS/UEFI utilities are firmware, and the configuration settings are stored on CMOS.
- USB ports may be disabled to protect sensitive information.
- TPM creates, stores, and controls encryption keys as well as manages system security metrics.
- Secure Boot ensures a device starts up with trusted firmware and software.
- A boot password controls access to CMOS-stored information.
- Encryption converts cleartext into undecipherable data to ensure only authorized access.
- HSM is a hardware device for protecting and storing encryption keys.
- The x64 and x86 ISAs are 64- and 32-bit processor and PC architectures, respectively.
- A RISC is an optimized instruction set, and an ARM has a standardized instruction set.
- Intel VT-x and AMD-V provide hardware virtualization support.
- Video cards use faster RAM than motherboards, and most have cooling fans.
- Most video cards require extra power from a PCIe power connector.
- Sound cards and onboard sound chips support stereo or surround audio.
- HDMI and DisplayPort output digital audio.
- NICs have status lights to indicate connection and speed.
- USB expansion cards and header cables enable you to add more USB ports.
- A heatsink is a cooling device of aluminum or copper that draws heat away from a CPU.
- The two types of thermal conductors are thermal conductive paste and thermal gap pads.
- Liquid cooling circulates liquid to cool CPUs.

3.4 QUESTIONS

1. You have been tasked with reviewing motherboard form factors for a project. The number-one requirement is that the motherboard be as small as possible. Which of these motherboards is the smallest?

   A. Micro-ATX

   B. Mini-ITX

   C. ITX

   D. ATX

2. Your client has selected PCIe version 3.0 graphics cards to refresh the organization's video editing workstations. However, the systems support PCIe version 2.0. Which of the following statements is true?

   A. The cards will run at PCIe 3.0 speeds.

   B. The motherboards must be replaced with PCIe 3.0–compatible versions.

   C. The cards cannot be used.

   D. The cards will run at PCIe 2.0 speeds.

3. You are upgrading your personal system with USB 3.0 (USB 3.1 Gen 1) devices but have run out of external ports. You need two more ports. Which of the following would provide these ports?

   A. USB 2.0 header cable

   B. USB-C header cable

   C. USB 3.0 header cable

   D. SATA-to-USB conversion cable

4. You are creating documentation for other technicians to use as they configure the UEFI firmware on new systems. Which of the following statements should not be in the documentation because it is incorrect?

   A. SATA drives cannot be configured as hot-swappable.

   B. USB ports can be disabled.

   C. The boot sequence can be changed.

   D. You can exit UEFI/BIOS setup without saving changes.

5. Which of the following is not a material used to seal a CPU cooling system?

   A. Thermal paste

   B. Thermal pad

   C. Liquid metal

   D. Thermal foam

3.4 ANSWERS

1. **B** The Mini-ITX (mITX) is the smallest motherboard listed.

2. **D** When two different PCIe versions are present (slot and card), the slower version is used.

3. **C** A USB 3.0 header cable provides two USB 3.0 ports; however, not all motherboards with USB 3.0 have headers.

4. **A** SATA drives are hot-swappable when configured as AHCI in the UEFI/BIOS firmware.

5. **D** Thermal paste, thermal pads, liquid metal are all materials that can be used to seal gaps in a CPU cooling system. Thermal foam is not developed for this purpose.

Objective 3.5 # Given a scenario, install or replace the appropriate power supply

Power supply units (PSUs) provide the electricity that enables computers to run. PSUs are a common reason for PC failures, yet they are often neglected and not included in preventive maintenance programs. As port-powered peripherals such as universal serial bus (USB) devices become more numerous and CPUs and GPUs require more power, PSUs with larger wattage ratings are more in demand.

Input: 110–120 VAC vs. 220–240 VAC

A desktop computer includes a PSU (see Figure 3.5-1) that converts high-voltage *AC (alternating current)* power to the low-voltage *DC (direct current)* power for the computer's motherboard and devices. Its internal fan also helps cool the components and drives. When connected to a properly grounded outlet, the power supply also provides grounding for all the other equipment inside the case.

The standard AC voltage in the U.S., Canada, Mexico, and 34 other nations is between 110 volts (V) and 120 V, which is commonly referred to in the U.S. as ~115 volts AC (VAC). In the remaining 175 or so countries of the world, the standard AC voltage ranges from 220 VAC to 240 VAC. Because of the difference in the standard voltages, many power supplies include the capability to use a dual-voltage switch to select the voltage appropriate to a certain location. The red slide switch on the back of the PSU shown in Figure 3.5-1 is a dual-voltage selector.

Dual-voltage
switch

FIGURE 3.5-1   An ATX 500-watt power supply

CAUTION   Even if the plug pattern and the outlet are compatible, plugging a 110-V device into a 220-V outlet would cause the device to run up to about twice its designed operations and burn out fairly quickly. On the other hand, if you were to plug a 220-V device into a 110-V outlet, the device may run for a while but will eventually stop.

EXAM TIP   For the A+ Core 1 exam, you should know that a PSU can be switched between the two primary electrical voltage range services.

PSU Terminology

The terminology used to describe the electrical capabilities of a PC PSU can be confusing. A PSU can be fixed input, switching dual-output, fixed output, or multiple output voltage devices. Typically, a standard desktop computer includes a *fixed input/fixed output* PSU. This means that the power supply will produce a single voltage that won't change—it is fixed at that voltage. Like the one shown in Figure 3.5-1, a PSU that can be switched between voltage inputs is known as a *switched input* device. However, it can be confusing that a switched input PSU can also be a fixed input PSU, because once a single voltage service input is selected, the PSU is a fixed input device.

Most current power supplies are *auto-switching*, meaning that they will detect the incoming voltage and configure themselves accordingly. You can use an auto-switching power supply anywhere in the world, from the 110–120 VAC in New York City to the 220–240 VAC in Hong Kong. This is especially important with portable computers!

CAUTION   If you are using a fixed input power supply connected to a 220–240 VAC power line, don't turn it on if the voltage selector switch is set to 115 VAC. That's a sure way to kill the power supply and possibly other components as well!

EXAM TIP   The power connector for the AC plug on the back of a power supply is called an IEC-320 connector, and you should expect to see a question on the CompTIA A+ Core 1 exam that refers to the power supply unit as a PSU.

Output: +3.3 V, +5 V, and +12 V

PC PSUs vary in their output, efficiency, and the number of +12-V *rails* used. A *power supply rail* is a path on a PSU's printed circuit board (PCB). A PSU rail inputs AC power from an external source and transforms it into DC power that is output to cables connected to internally powered devices.

In virtually all PSUs, there are rails for +3.3 V, +5 V, and +12 V. Three different voltages are needed because not all PC hardware devices require the same power to operate. For example, the USB ports operate on 5 V, DDR4 RAM requires only between +1.2 and +1.35 V, and the case fan runs on +12 V, as does the CPU. The job of the PSU is to provide the appropriate power levels required by each of the PC's components.

Regardless of whether the incoming power is at 120 VAC or 220 VAC, it must be converted to both direct current (DC) and, initially, +12 V, which is the standard voltage with which a PSU works. This conversion is performed by the *AC/DC converter* in the PSU. A portion of the +12-V power flows to +3.3-V and +5-V converters, completing the conversion of the AC power source into the three rails of the PSU. Earlier it was mentioned that DDR RAM needs only +1.2 V or +1.35 V of power, but the lowest voltage produced by the PSU is +3.3 V. To deal with this, most motherboards, especially the newest models, have power regulators as well as converters to refine the power to the needs of the components mounted on them.

The +12-V rail is the source of power to the CPU and possibly the GPU. It's common in recent PSUs that the +12-V rail is divided into two or more rails to reduce the amperage (amps) each carries for safety reasons. A *single-rail* power supply is usually enough for an average desktop computer, but a high-end system may require a *multi-rail* power supply. In practice, avoid running too many devices off one rail in a multi-rail power supply.

EXAM TIP   Make sure you know the voltage ranges of input (110–120 VAC and 220–240 VAC) and output (+3.3 V, +5 V, and +12 V) supported by power supplies.

ADDITIONAL RESOURCES   To learn more about the internal components and the operations of a PSU, read the article "Anatomy of a Power Supply Unit (PSU)" at https://www.techspot.com/article/1967-anatomy-psu/.

Output: +5 V and +12 V Connectors

As described earlier, a PSU converts high-voltage AC to low-voltage DC in order to provide the appropriate power levels for the motors on hard drives and optical drives (+12 V) and onboard electronics (+5 V) via the device cables that are integrated into the PSU.

The device cables and connectors common to most PSUs are *serial ATA (SATA)* and *Molex*, as shown in Figure 3.5-2. Higher-end power supplies have a dedicated 6- or 8-wire *PCIe* connector for PCI Express video cards (see Figure 3.5-3).

Power supplies connect to the motherboard with either a 20-pin or 24-pin *P1* connector on the primary power circuit and then a 4-wire *P4* secondary power connector or an 8-wire EPS12V power connector to supply power to the CPU (see Figure 3.5-4). The EPS12V connectors use one 4-pin (P4) connector on motherboards that use a 4-pin ATX12V connector and use both on motherboards that use an 8-pin EPS12V connector.

FIGURE 3.5-2   Molex (left) and SATA (right) power connectors

FIGURE 3.5-3   PCIe power connector

FIGURE 3.5-4 EPS12V/ATX12V connectors (left) and P1 connector (right)

 EXAM TIP The +5-V orange (sometimes gray) wire on the P1 connector is called *power good* and is used in the initial boot sequence.

Many modern ATX motherboards use an 8-pin CPU power connector, variously referred to as EPS12V, EATX12V, or ATX12V 2×4. Half of this connector will be pin-compatible with the P4 power connector; the other half may be under a protective cap. On any computer, check the motherboard's installation manual for when to use the full 8 pins. For backward compatibility, some power supplies provide an 8-pin power connector that can split into two 4-pin sets, one of which is the P4 connector (refer to Figure 3.5-4). Although they look similar, the 8-pin CPU power connector is not compatible with the 8-pin PCIe power connector. Table 3.5-1 lists

TABLE 3.5-1 Power Connectors and Voltages

Connector	Voltages	Common Use
Molex	5 V (red), 12 V (yellow)	Legacy storage and optical drives, some PCIe video cards and motherboards, and case fans
SATA	5 V, 12 V (3.3 V orange optional)	SATA drives
PCIe	12 V	PCIe video cards
P1 (20-wire)	3.3 V, 5 V, 12 V	Primary power for older ATX motherboards
P1 (24-wire)	3.3 V, 5 V, 12 V	Primary power for current ATX motherboards
P4 and 8-pin CPU power connector	12 V	Secondary power for current ATX motherboards
AUX	3.3 V, 5 V, 12 V	Auxiliary power for old motherboards
Ground wire	Black	Used by all connector types

the common connectors of the ATX12V power supplies—the current standard—with their voltages and uses.

 CAUTION   Power connectors are keyed so that you can't easily plug them in backward, but some older designs can be forced. Reversing the power on a device will fry it. Don't force a power connector.

24-Pin Motherboard Adapter

To enable the same power supply model to work with older 20-pin ATX motherboards and modern motherboards that use 24-pin connectors, some vendors provide 24-pin motherboard adapters.

Redundant Power Supplies

The name *redundant power supply* may seem like this device isn't really necessary, which is ironic because its purpose is just the opposite. A redundant power supply configuration involves a single device, almost always a rack-mounted device, that operates with two PSUs. The two PSUs are both fully capable of powering the device. In normal operation, each of the power supplies provides an equal portion of the power to a connected device. In most cases, there are two devices sharing the load and providing the redundancy, but more PSUs can be interconnected in the redundant grouping. Figure 3.5-5 shows a dual-PSU redundant power supply.

Staying with the set of two PSUs, if one of the PSUs is turned off or fails for any reason, the other PSU is powered and connected to provide full power on demand. This redundancy avoids downtime for the powered device.

FIGURE 3.5-5   A redundant power supply unit (image courtesy of Hewlett-Packard Enterprises)

| FIGURE 3.5-6 | A fully modular power supply with two examples of its cabling (image courtesy of Micro-Star International) |

Modular Power Supply

A standard (typically ATX) PSU will almost always have a few extra unused cables hanging about inside the system case. All of these cables are integrated into the PSU circuitry and cannot be eliminated without damaging them. A module power supply eliminates this problem by providing outlets that are used only if needed. Plus, there are a few other advantages to using modular power supplies, which we'll get to later.

The two types of modular PSUs are the fully modular and the semi-modular units. Essentially, the difference between them is that every cable that plugs into the fully modular unit can also be removed. A fully modular PSU, like the one shown in Figure 3.5-6, has a series of standard outlets, typically arranged by the output power voltages, into which an adapter cable can be plugged and used to connect to a powered device.

Whereas the fully modular PSU has no permanently attached cables. a semi-modular PSU has integrated cables for the devices that are common to virtually all PCs, such as a 24-pin ATX, 4/8-pin CPU, and maybe PCIe for the motherboard, CPU, and memory. Other cables may or may not be needed for a particular PC, such as cables with SATA, PCIe, or Molex connectors.

Wattage Rating

You may run into questions on the A+ Core 1 exam regarding the differences among volts, amps, and watts. Therefore, you should have some understanding of each and how it relates to the others. To that end, here is a basic description of these terms:

- **Volts**   Voltage (V) measures the electrical pressure of the charge on a medium. It's something like the pressure of water in a hose.
- **Amps**   Amperage (A) measures the amount of electricity flowing through the medium. Sticking with the water hose example, an amp is like the gallons per minute (gpm) pressure of the water in the hose.
- **Watts**   Wattage (W) measures the amount of electricity needed to operate or power an electrical device. Watts are calculated as $A \times V = W$. To complete the water analogy, watts would measure the force of the water required to fill a water balloon.

Power supplies provide a certain *wattage* that the motherboard, drives, and fans draw on to run. That's the desired output. Power supplies also produce *harmonics* (the hum you hear when the power supply runs), which can cause problems with the power supply and other electrical devices on the circuit if not controlled.

> **EXAM TIP**   Wattage is the amount of amperage flowing at a specific voltage, usually written as $W = V \times A$.

A computer requires sufficient wattage to run properly. Every device in the system also requires a certain wattage to function. For example, a typical magnetic hard drive draws 15 W of power when accessed (SSDs use less), whereas a quad-core Intel i9-9900K CPU draws a whopping 162 W at peak usage—with average usage around 92 W. The total combined wattage needs of all devices is the minimum you need the power supply to provide.

If the power supply can't produce the wattage needed by a system, that computer won't work properly. Because most devices in the system require maximum wattage when starting, the typical outcome of insufficient wattage is a paperweight that looks like a computer. The only fix for this situation is to remove the device or get a power supply with more wattage. Today's systems require at least 500-plus-watt power supplies to function.

Good computer power supplies come with *active power factor correction (active PFC),* which is extra circuitry that evens out high-voltage AC power before passing it to the main power supply circuits, thus eliminating harmonics. Avoid any old and poor power supplies without this circuitry.

Number of Devices/Types of Devices to Be Powered

It's essential to know the number and types of devices that require power and the electrical properties needed before installing a new power supply in a PC. Power supplies vary in the number of Molex, SATA, and mini (Berg) connectors provided. In fact, some PSUs support only a single PCIe power connector. Molex connectors are no longer used for drives but are used for case fans when there aren't sufficient fan ports on the motherboard. Molex connectors can also be adapted to run SATA drives or devices that use mini (Berg) connectors.

Avoid using splitters to run more devices than can be connected directly to a power supply. Cheap splitters that use thin wires can overheat, and even the best-quality splitters can introduce points of potential failure into a system.

Power Supply Installation Notes

Be careful when you work with power supplies or inside a computer. Here's why: an ATX power supply never turns off. If an ATX power supply is connected to AC power, the PSU feeds 5 VDC to the motherboard. Installing cards, chips, or memory modules to a motherboard

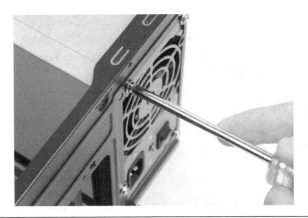

FIGURE 3.5-7   Power supply secured in the case

while power is flowing could damage those components. Remember to always unplug the power supply and wait about ten seconds before you work inside the computer or disconnect the power supply for replacement!

Before you connect the power supply, you'll need to mount it inside the case with four standard case screws (see Figure 3.5-7). The only exceptions are some small or proprietary cases.

REVIEW

Objective 3.5: Given a scenario, install or replace the appropriate power supply

- Power supplies support 110–120 VAC and 220–240 VAC, either through a sliding switch or with internal auto-switching.
- The IEC-320 connector is used for the AC plug on the rear of the power supply.
- Power supplies generally provide +3.3-V, +5-V, or +12-V power to peripherals via the SATA and Molex power leads. PCIe power leads provide +12-V power to PCIe cards.
- P1 provides power to the motherboard using a 24-pin (newer) or 20-pin (older) keyed connector.
- Redundant power supplies provide an automatic power supply replacement should one PSU fail.
- Fully modular PSUs have no integrated cabling and provide plugs for a variety of standard adapters, and semi-modular PSUs have the basic power cables, for the motherboard and CPU, plus adapters for other connector types.
- Older motherboards use the P4 4-pin 12-V connector to provide power to the CPU (the power is stepped down by the motherboard); newer motherboards use the EPS12V 8-pin connector for this job.

- Higher wattage ratings in power supplies are needed when the power draw of installed and onboard devices approaches or exceeds the output of the current power supply.
- Active PFC helps eliminate harmonics for better-quality power.
- Power supplies are typically mounted using four screws on the rear that fasten through the case wall.

3.5 QUESTIONS

1. Your client's 20-pin ATX power supply has failed. Which of the following can be used to enable a modern power supply to be used as a replacement?

   A. ATX12V adapter

   B. 24-pin motherboard adapter

   C. EPS12V adapter

   D. Aux adapter

2. Your data center supports several applications that users must have access to at all times with no downtime acceptable. What type of power supply configuration should be installed for the servers running these applications?

   A. Semi-modular PSU

   B. Fully modular PSU

   C. Redundant PSU

   D. Higher wattage PSU

3. What are the most common power source input and output voltage ranges associated with a PC PSU?

   A. Input: 110–120 VAC / Output: ±12 V

   B. Input: 220–240 VAC / Output: 110–120 VAC

   C. Input: 110–120 VAC / Output: +3.3 V, +5 V, +12 V

   D. Input: 110–120 VAC / Output: +3.3 V and +5 V

4. You have received a frantic call at home from a fellow gamer who has swapped her old PCIe video card for a new one and can't plug the original PCIe power cable into the new card. Which of the following is the best solution?

   A. Look for an 8-pin PCIe lead.

   B. Use the 8-pin EPSV12 lead.

   C. Cut off some power supply cables and splice in a new header.

   D. Put the old card back in because the new one can't be used.

5. Power supplies can connect to the motherboard with which of the following connectors? (Choose all that apply.)

   A. A 20-pin P1

   B. A 24-pin P1

   C. 4-wire P4

   D. 8-wire EPS12V

   E. 4-pin ATX12V

   F. All of the above

3.5 ANSWERS

1. **B** A 24-pin motherboard adapter enables a modern 24-pin power supply to work with an older system and get the benefits of potentially higher wattage.

2. **C** A redundant PSU configuration will provide power automatically should one PSU fail.

3. **C** PC PSUs commonly use inputs of 110–120 VAC and convert it to +3.3 VDC, +5 VDC, or +12 VDC.

4. **A** Many (but not all) power supplies have both 6-pin and 8-pin PCIe power leads.

5. **F** All of the connector types are used to connect a PSU to a motherboard.

Objective 3.6 Given a scenario, deploy and configure multifunction devices/printers and settings

One of the more common activities an A+ Certified Service Technician performs is initial setup and configuration of multifunction devices (MFDs) and printers. Objective 3.6 of the A+ Core 1 exam details the essential steps required to successfully install and configure these devices. An MFD, as its name implies, offers multiple operations, which typically include built-in devices for printing, faxing, scanning, copying, and, in some models, interacting with the Web. Instead of a separate device to perform each of these actions, an MFD combines them into a single multifunction device.

EXAM TIP Make sure you know the steps required to install printers and their drivers.

Keep in mind that not all MFDs are printers, but most are. Therefore, when the term *printer* is used in the discussion of this objective, remember that most of this material also applies to MFDs.

Unboxing, Placing, and Configuring an MFD

 NOTE The following discussion on the initial setup and the configuration of an MFD is based on the installation guide of a Xerox MFD. The installation guide books that ship with most devices are proprietary, but, for the most part, the tasks and objectives are the same.

Obviously the first action you take to begin the installation and configuration of a *multi-function device (MFD)* is to remove it and its materials from the box or packaging. It's best to unpack the device near to where it is to be placed. This will save you steps and help you avoid the possible loss of needed components. Typically, an installation and configuration guide is packaged with the device, along with an operations manual, toner, an installation media, a features guide, and perhaps a quick overview of each of the functions supported by the MFD.

Initial Configuration

Most of the better MFDs are configured for operation *out of the box (OOTB)*. However, some configuration steps are required to localize and verify the operation of the device. The following is a generic list of the tasks typically performed (in the listed sequence) to set the initial configuration of an MFD:

1. Connect the MFD to the nearest AC power source available. If the AC outlet causes the power cord to create a hazard, relocate the device to remove the safety risk.

2. Connect the printer's network adapter to the network medium as required for wired or wireless networks.

3. Confirm that the printer is recognized by the network. The printer should be configured for the network by the Dynamic Host Configuration Protocol (DHCP) and be able to communicate over the network. To test this, use the setup menu on the printer to verify the IP address assigned. If the IP address function times out, there are connection issues, but they may or may not be caused by the onboard network interface card (NIC).

4. If communications are functional with the network, power-cycle (restart) the printer. Most MFDs start up in a setup/configuration wizard mode that guides you through the settings needed. These commonly include location, time zone, and date and time, and sometimes a couple of proprietary preferences.

5. Follow the instruction in the documentation for the printer to install the appropriate print medium (ink jet, toner, and so on) and print a test page.

6. If provided as an option, print a summary of the device's configuration settings.

7. Test each of the embedded functions of the printer:

   a. From a browser, attempt to reach the IP address assigned to the printer.

   b. If available, scan a document and e-mail it to yourself or to the customer.

   c. If available, copy a document and e-mail it to yourself or to the customer.

   d. The fax function is still available on some MDFs, but it's beginning to disappear. If it's present, repeat the test used for the scanner and the copier.

   e. Be sure that the function testing performed verifies the functions that will be used the most.

Follow the instructions in the printer's installation and operations manuals to complete the appropriate settings.

Device Drivers

Before the printer or any of its functions can be tested from a network client or host computer, the device driver(s) appropriate to the server's or node's operating system must be installed and configured.

Windows

Most printers and MFDs are plug-and-play devices on Windows systems, and once a connection is established, Windows automatically detects and installs the appropriate drivers. If the system doesn't detect the device, you need to install the printer and the device drivers manually. You have a couple of options available to add a printer to a Windows system. One way is using the Devices and Printers option on the Control Panel and its Add a Device app. The second way is using the Printers & Scanners option of the Settings app (see Figure 3.6-1). You should also follow the installation and configuration instructions provided with the device.

macOS

The macOS connects automatically with AirPrint-compatible printers. On other compatible printers, macOS installs the device drivers automatically. If the printer is connected via USB, verify that the macOS installation is up to date so that the latest printer drivers are available. If you are installing a Wi-Fi printer on macOS, an AirPrint-compatible Wi-Fi printer is configured automatically, but noncompatible printers may need to be connected via USB temporarily for configuration.

FIGURE 3.6-1   The Printers & Scanners page in the Windows Settings app

Linux

Linux printer installation varies with the operating system distro and the drivers available. Many HP and Brother printers can use manufacturer-provided Linux drivers. To install other printers using a typical Linux graphical user interface (GUI), use the Printers or System | Printers option in your desktop environment to select a printer and use the drivers provided with the GUI. The Common Unix Printer Service (CUPS) is used if printer configuration software is not provided; install it using your Linux distribution's package manager.

PostScript and PCL

The CompTIA A+ Core 1 exam objectives list *PostScript* (PScript or PS) and *Printer Control Language (PCL)* under the objective "Use appropriate drivers for a given OS." However, each of these printer "drivers" was developed for use by or with a specific manufacturer's products: PostScript by Adobe Systems and PCL by Hewlett Packard. Each of these drivers is classified as a page description language that provides a digital image layout in text and binary to a printer and provides an appearance map of a page.

PostScript

PostScript was originally developed by Adobe for its desktop publishing products as a dynamic programming language. Most PostScript-compatible printers have an interpreter that, like an interpretive programming language, translates the PostScript commands into the pixels

```
%!
/Times-Roman findfont 18 scalefont setfont
%save before using translate
gsave

%This cordinates places the images on the page
105 210 translate

%————-The page image begins————————
76.8 86.4 scale
40 45 1 [ 40 0 0 -45 0 45 ]
{ <
57 65 20 74 68 65 20 50 65 6f 70 6c 65 20 6f 66 20 74 68 65 20 55 6e 69 74 65 64 20 53 74 61
74 65 73 2c 20 69 6e 20 4f 72 64 65 72 20 74 6f 20 66 6f 72 6d 20 61 20 6d 6f 72 65 20 70 65 72
66 65 63 74 20 55 6e 69 6f 6e 2c 20 65 73 74 61 62 6c 69 73 68 20 4a 75 73 74 69 63 65 2c 20
69 6e 73 75 72 65 20 64 6f 6d 65 73 74 69 63 20 54 72 61 6e 71 75 69 6c 69 74 79 2c 20 70 72 6f
76 69 64 65 20 66 6f 72 20 74 68 65 20 63 6f 6d 6d 6f 6e 20 64 65 66 65 6e 63 65 2c 20 70 72 6f
6d 6f 74 65 20 74 68 65 20 67 65 6e 65 72 61 6c 20 57 65 6c 66 61 72 65 2c 20 61 6e 64 20 73 65
63 75 72 65 20 74 68 65 20 42 6c 65 73 73 69 6e 67 73 20 6f 66 20 4c 69 62 65 72 74 79 20 74
6f 20 6f 75 72 73 65 6c 76 65 73 20 61 6e 64 20 6f 75 72 20 50 6f 73 74 65 72 69 74 79 2c 20 64
6f 20 6f 72 64 61 69 6e 65 20 61 6e 64 20 65 73 74 61 62 6c 69 73 68 20 74 68 69 73 20 43 6f 6e 73
74 69 74 75 74 69 6f 6e 20 66 6f 72 20 74 68 65 20 55 6e 69 74 65 64 20 53 74 61 74 65 73 20 6f
66 20 41 6d 65 72 69 63 61 2e > } image
%————-The page image ends —————————

%Restore settings from before interpretation
grestore
```

FIGURE 3.6-2   An example of PostScript page commands

(dots) that create the printed page on a particular printer. Figure 3.6-2 shows an example of PostScript commands, and Figure 3.6-3 shows the page produced from the code.

NOTE   Some printers refer to PostScript interpreters as *raster image processors (RIPs).*

PostScript commands allow laser printers to produce high-resolution graphics and text on the same printed page. PostScript 3 is the latest, current, and most likely last version for PostScript. Adobe forecasts that the Portable Document File (PDF) format will soon become the document and graphics publishing standard. PostScript images and command files can be saved as *Encapsulated PostScript (.eps)* files.

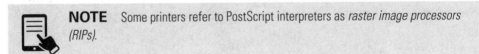

We the People of the United States, in Order to form a more perfect Union, establish Justice, insure domestic Tranquility, provide for the common defence, promote the general Welfare, and secure the Blessings of Liberty to ourselves and our Posterity, do ordain and establish this Constitution for the United States of America.

FIGURE 3.6-3   The results printed from the PostScript example in Figure 3.6-2

Printer Control Language

Printer *Control* Language (PCL) is often confused with Printer *Command* Language, which is an alias of the Page Description Language, which is confusingly also PCL. The PCL you need to know about (that is, the Printer Control Language) was developed by Hewlett-Packard as a printer control protocol for its line of laser and inkjet printers. However, it has been adapted to many other types of printers, including thermal and impact.

The current version of PCL is version 6, which has been the standard since the middle 1990s. PCL 6 consists of three parts:

- **PCL 6 Enhanced**   Also known as PCL XL, this standard provides support for printing from GUI-based systems such as Windows.
- **PCL 6 Standard**   This is the backward-compatible standard equivalent to PCL 5.
- **Font synthesis**   This standard supports scalable fonts and print structure designed to be future-proof.

The basic difference between PostScript and PCL is that the former is a page description language developed for desktop publishing and the latter is a page description language developed as a printer control protocol. A page description language describes the layout and appearance of the page to be printed. Is either a device driver? Technically no, but they are printer device command sets.

 EXAM TIP   PCL is commonly used for basic office document and letter printing, whereas PostScript is more often used for detailed graphics printing.

Device Connectivity

There are several ways to connect a printer to a computer, but the best way to connect any particular printer is often limited to the one or two methods available on the printer itself. The most common way to connect a printer to a PC is with a USB connector. Other methods that are not nearly as popular include wireless, peer-to-peer sharing, and, even more rare, a parallel connection. On a LAN, printers are also shared on the network.

Wireless-enabled printers are gaining popularity and are being used in standalone PANs and shared LANs, However, wireless printers, like a directly connected printer, require a print app or client to be installed on the connecting PC. The newest printers, especially those connecting to a Windows system with a USB connection, are *Plug and Play (PnP),* which means Windows establishes the configuration and creates the linkage. However, regardless of the connection type, on all operating systems (Windows, macOS, and Linux), a device driver may be required and is normally provided with the printer. Windows and macOS include a variety of standard printer interfaces and drivers as well.

FIGURE 3.6-4 A Type-B (left) to Type-AB (right) USB printer cable

USB Connections

Virtually all PC-compatible printers provide USB connection capability, but the USB connection for a printer is usually specifically configured. A USB-enabled printer commonly has a Type-B connector on its rear panel very near an RJ-45 connector, if one is included. The printer cable then has a Type-B connector at one end and, depending on the device to which the printer is being connected, a Type-AB (see Figure 3.6-4) or perhaps even a Type-C connector.

Ethernet Connections

If a printer is directly connected to a PC, no network, Ethernet, or anything is necessary. However, if the printer to be connected is a node on an Ethernet network, some configuration is necessary on the PC. Most of the major printer manufacturers, such as HP, Zebra, Canon, Lexmark, and others, provide either media with installation or configuration apps or a website that guides users through the process. However, some printers do require configuration to the network and then to a PC.

Connecting a network-capable printer to an Ethernet network is a relatively simple process. Physically, a network cable is used to connect the printer to a router, switch, or hub that is active on a network. On the printer itself, a built-in configuration or setup function will automatically configure the printer to the network or guide the user through a step-by-step setup. However, connecting to the now-networked printer is different in each operating system.

EXAM TIP Both Ethernet and wireless are listed separately in Objective 3.6 for Domain 3 of the A+ Core 1 exam. You may assume that should the exam reference Ethernet, it's referring to a wired network. This is probably a safe assumption, but be careful with that.

Add an Ethernet Printer to a Windows System

The process for adding a connection to a network printer from a Windows 10/11 system, and most of the previous versions, includes the following steps:

1. On the Start menu, open the Settings app and access Printers & Scanners from the Devices option (refer back to Figure 3.6-1).

2. Click the plus sign icon to add a printer or scanner.

3. Windows searches its local and network connections for a printer(s) available to be added.

4. Select the device to be added and click Add Device to have the system add the appropriate drivers to the system.

5. If the printer is not found, the message "The printer I want isn't listed" displays. Click the message to open an Add Printer dialog box that supports locating or adding a printer manually.

Add an Ethernet Printer to a macOS System

The latest versions of macOS include the capability to search for and install most network printers, much like Windows 10/11. Any adjustments needed to the automatic configuration or the capability to add a printer manually can be done in the Print & Fax section of the System Preferences function.

Add an Ethernet Printer to a Linux System

The most popular Linux distros include a service to detect and add network printers, much like Windows and macOS. On a GUI desktop such as GNOME or KDE, select either the Settings or All Settings option to display the settings options. Click the Printers icon to initiate a search and install a service that will automatically link to the printer. If no printers are found, use the *Common Unix Printing System (CUPS),* which is a web-based utility for managing all things printing.

Wireless Printers

The most common way to add any printer to a network, regardless of it being wireless or not, is to install it as a standalone device on the network that can be reached and used by authorized workstations on the network. Obviously, on a wireless network, any printer added would be a wireless device, which means it has a built-in wireless network adapter. For the most part, the installation and configuration software for any particular printer would be supplied by its manufacturer.

Once a wireless (or Wi-Fi) printer is configured on a LAN, the process for enabling each workstation is essentially the same as that used for connecting to a wired printer. The same utilities and apps are used, with the only exceptions concerning print characteristics and settings.

Device Sharing

Unless multiple users in an office print documents frequently, there's little need for each user to have an individual printer. There are numerous ways to share printers, and the ones you should know are in this section.

Wired

The same ports built into a typical printer for directly connecting the printer to a single computer can also be used to share the printer. The following are three of the more commonly used methods for sharing a printer among devices:

- Use a *USB* hub to share a printer between two nearby computers. This method eliminates the need for the computers to be connected to a network.
- On a network, a printer attached directly to a node can be shared, provided the host computer is running and *File and Print Sharing Services* is activated.
- Another approach for sharing a printer on a network is to establish the printer as an addressable Ethernet network node.

Wireless

Most of today's printers come ready to connect wirelessly to local computers and networks. Here are the most common wireless connections used to provide connectivity to a printer:

- A printer with *Bluetooth* is ready to connect to any computer or mobile device using Bluetooth. The devices must be in range (~10 meters), the devices must establish pairing, and a suitable printing app must be installed on the mobile devices.
- It's also common for a printer to have *Wi-Fi (802.11x)* onboard, which allows it to readily join a wireless network using its own IP address and be ready to print after installation and configuration. Perhaps the hardest part of connecting a printer to a wireless network is setting the wireless configuration (SSID, password, and encryption key) using the printer's control panel.

Public and Shared Printers

A *public printer* is a network node to which a user or group is granted access. For example, a public printer in a college library may require a login either to a network or possibly the printer itself, and it may require a fee. Another example is a publicly accessible printer on a customer-oriented coffee shop's network that allows virtually anyone to e-mail documents to be printed to it. In other works, a public printer is available to the public. However, who is included in "public" may be defined differently by each network.

A *shared printer* is a private printer whose owner controls access to it by granting permission to selected users. Figure 3.6-5 shows the Windows 11 Control Panel's Network and

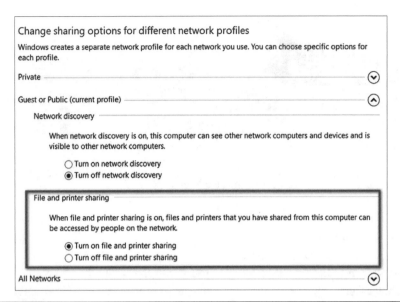

Change sharing options for different network profiles

Windows creates a separate network profile for each network you use. You can choose specific options for each profile.

Private

Guest or Public (current profile)

Network discovery

When network discovery is on, this computer can see other network computers and devices and is visible to other network computers.

○ Turn on network discovery
◉ Turn off network discovery

File and printer sharing

When file and printer sharing is on, files and printers that you have shared from this computer can be accessed by people on the network.

◉ Turn on file and printer sharing
○ Turn off file and printer sharing

All Networks

FIGURE 3.6-5 The Windows Change Sharing Options for Different Network Profiles dialog box

Sharing Center's Change Sharing Options for Different Network Profiles dialog box on which the settings in the highlighted area can be used to share a printer.

Print Server

Although today's printers have way more capabilities than those of the past, many lack processing power. A printer performs much better when some of its processing and management tasks are handled by a *print server*. There is a major difference between a network printer and a print server on a network. A network-capable printer can be added to a network as an addressable node that other nodes in the same broadcast domain can access and use. A print server works more like a router for print jobs, and, in fact, some routers also function as *integrated print servers*.

A print server can be in one of three forms: a special-purpose network hardware device, a function built into a printer, or software running on a network server, such as a file server. Figure 3.6-6 illustrates the first two of these forms. A hardware-based print server (also known as an *external print server*) is essentially a computing device dedicated to providing print queue management and, if two or more printers are connected to the device, load balancing when necessary. A network printer can also provide print server functions (commonly referred to as an *internal print server*) such as queue management and control. Third-party software running on network server hardware can manage all queue, load balancing, and print services and control functions for a network.

 NOTE Some external print server devices don't provide support for all MFD functions.

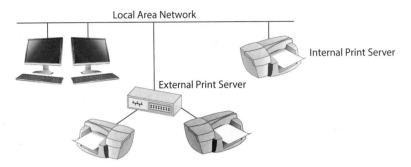

| **FIGURE 3.6-6** | An illustration of external and internal print servers |

Cloud Printing

A variety of *cloud printing* applications, such as Google's Cloud Print, Microsoft's Universal Print, and UniPrint's InfinityCloud, provide users with the ability to print a document on a remote printer from virtually any location where an Internet connection is available. A cloud printing app encapsulates a document into a file and then sends it to a cloud-based print server. The cloud server routes the print file to a real printer for printing.

Cloud printing allows you to print from any device, including mobile devices, connected to a network. A cloud printing service creates a connection between a source device and an Internet-connected printer selected by the user. Cloud printing avoids the device driver, font and image compatibility, and print queue issues associated with traditional directly connected or LAN-based printing.

Remote Printing

Remote printing is something like cloud printing, but without the cloud. Essentially, remote printing replaces fax machines for sending documents from one location on a network to a printing device on the same network, regardless of whether it's wired or wireless or on a LAN, proprietary WAN, or the Internet. Remote printing provides local or remote users with the capability to retrieve a document from a remote location and print that document on either a local or remote printer.

Configuration Settings

After you have installed a printer on a system, the next step is to review and possibly modify its configuration, which determines how the printer is to perform. On a Windows system, find the newly installed printer in the Devices and Printers on the Control Panel or Printers & Scanners in Settings and then right-click its icon and select Printing Preferences. To configure a printer in macOS, open the Print dialog box, select the printer, click Show Details, and choose the options desired. To configure a printer in Linux, see the documentation for your GUI or distro.

Options vary by device and features, but here are the ones you need to know for the A+ Core 1 exam:

- **Duplex**   The duplex setting specifies whether and how to use each side of a printed page. Simple duplexing uses the front and back of each sheet in sequence, but advanced options can reorient the print to account for binding on any given edge as well as reorder pages to support folded booklet layouts.
- **Collate**   Enabling the collate option prints a full copy of a multipage document before starting the next copy. When this option is disabled, the printer prints all copies of a page before moving to the next page.
- **Quality**   The quality settings enable you to manage the tradeoffs between quality and speed, ink use, and memory use:
  - The most obvious of these, *resolution,* specifies what DPI the document should be printed at.
  - Some printers may let you choose some mode or quality presets that optimize printing for graphics or text or choose to manually configure your own advanced settings.
  - Some printers may have settings that reduce ink or toner used, for economic and environmental reasons.
- **Orientation**   Virtually all printers commonly used in SOHO environments have the capability of printing a page in either portrait (8.5" by 11") or landscape (11" by 8.5"). Plus, on many you can print a variety of different standard or customized page sizes, such as A3. On larger print systems, you might find a few other orientation settings.
- **Tray settings**   Generally, the tray settings for a printer define the size of the paper in a paper tray, which paper tray is active (selected) when there are more than one, the type of paper in the tray (such as preformatted for checks and forms), and perhaps the thickness of the page.

 NOTE   The names and descriptions of settings that influence quality might discuss quality itself, ink or toner use, environmental friendliness, or even cost savings. As a result, quality-reducing settings may be scattered around multiple menus.

 EXAM TIP   Make sure you know the configuration settings for printers covered in this section.

Device Sharing

Unless multiple users in an office print documents frequently, there's no need to have a printer for every computer. There are a variety of ways to share printers, as you will see in this section.

Wired

The ports that are built into a typical printer, which are provided primarily for directly connecting to a single device, are the same ports used for device sharing, as follows:

- Use a *USB* switch to share a printer between two nearby computers without the need for networking; if the computer is on a network, you can share the printer as long as the host computer is running. (Don't forget to install file and print sharing services!)
- Use the *Ethernet* port to plug the printer into a wired network. It will have its own IP address.

Wireless

Many printers today are ready to connect wirelessly to other computers or networks.

- A printer with *Bluetooth* is ready to connect to any computer or mobile device with Bluetooth after pairing (just make sure you have a suitable printing app for the mobile device).
- A printer with *Wi-Fi* onboard (802.11 a, b, g, n, ac, or ax) is ready to join your wireless network, have its own IP address, and be ready to receive print jobs after configuration. The hardest part of the process may be entering the SSID and encryption key using the printer's control panel.
- *Infrastructure* is a long name for the way that normal Wi-Fi networks work: every devices, including the printer, use an SSID to connect to an access point (AP) or router.
- *Ad hoc*, on the other hand, allows for direct connection between any two Wi-Fi devices without going through a router or AP. Windows does not officially support ad hoc connections, but you can find a variety of methods online for setting up an ad hoc connection to your printer.

Security

Protecting access to a printer and allowing its use to only authenticated and authorized users can be a high-priority issue in any security policy and plan. Printers aren't always considered to be elements of risk, but there are a variety of threats to their security. Some of these areas—especially the ones that follow because you'll likely see them on the A+ Core 1 exam—are discussed in the following sections.

User Authentication

A lot of sensitive information gets printed, especially in places like schools and hospitals, where strict privacy regulations apply. Therefore, safeguards need to be in place to make sure this information isn't leaking out. With some types of network printers, the user must authenticate on the device after sending the print job before the job is printed. This can be done with a user code that is stored in the printer's address book or by using various authentication servers.

Badging

Some networks include resources, data, and other assets to which access must be restricted due to security, privacy, or unauthorized use. For example, a small company may have a 3D printer on its network but wants its use restricted to only those employees who are qualified to operate it properly. This can be done through a concept called *badging,* which is a digital indicator that a certain user account has attained a certain security clearance or access permission. Although this is a logical process, it is essentially the same as a physical clearance to access restricted assets or facilities.

Audit Logs

In case you're wondering what badging and audit logs have to do with multifunction printing, the short answer is security. The primary purpose of audit logs in any system is to be able to provide an event trail should there be a system security or function issue. This applies to printer events as well.

On a Windows system, the entries in the various audit log files can be viewed using the *Event Viewer,* a sample of which is shown in Figure 3.6-7. On a macOS system, the system logs can be displayed using the View Systems Logs option on the *Console* app. Linux systems store audit logs in the /var/log/audit directory and can be viewed using the *aureport* command tool.

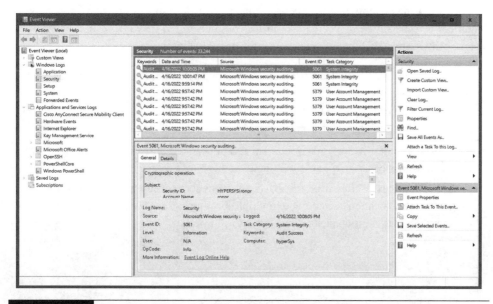

FIGURE 3.6-7   The Event Viewer is used to analyze the Windows audit logs.

Secure Print

Many of the latest model printers include the ability to prevent confidential, sensitive, or classified documents from being printed. The control panel for each printer offering this feature requires a four- to ten-digit password to be entered before the document will be printed. Each printer manufacturer approaches this control a bit differently, but the process is essentially the same for all of them.

Other forms of secure printing controls offered on current printers, typically the higher-end printers and MFDs, include the following:

- **Image overwrite**   If desired, a document image kept in the printer's storage can be digitally shred.
- **Data encryption**   Data in motion to and from the printer can be encrypted using SSL/TLS or IPSec.
- **Unauthorized remote access**   Data stored on the print device is secured against outside access while in the process of being printed.

Some print systems also offer badging and limited access levels to restrict access.

Network Scan Services

Printers and MFDs that provide *network scanning* give you the ability to scan a document and save the scanned image file where you wish. This allows you to scan an important, confidential, or sensitive document and store the resulting image file in one or more locations. Some network scanning systems require the use of user-defined templates on where and how the document is to be stored if specified. Features common to the network scan services of the various printer and MFD manufacturers include the following:

- **Server Message Block (SMB)/Common Internet File System (CIFS) file share**   This is a repository of files shared over a network.
- **HTTP/FTP file share**   Similar to an SMB file share, this file share provides access to documents uploaded via HTTP or FTP.
- **Scan to e-mail**   An original document can be scanned into an e-mail message format for transmission.
- **Cloud services**   Often used for sharing documents to group members in scattered geographical locations, scanning to multiple locations, storage in the cloud with multiple access, and other group facilitation services.

Automatic Document Feeder

An automatic document feeder (ADF) supplies one document at a time from a tray in conjunction with the document functions of an MFD (scanner, copier, printer, photo processing, and fax). The speed of an ADF is rated in *pages per minute (ppm)*. An ADF provides a productive means of loading multiple pages to an MFD. However, it may also be a major roadblock should it fail to operate properly.

A key feature of an ADF is the capability to feed (scan) each side of a two-sided document as separate sheets, a feature called *duplexing,* to an ADF function. The two types of ADF duplexing are *Reversing ADF (RADF)* and *Duplexing ADF (DADF)*. As its name implies, an RADF first scans one side of a document and then reverses (flips) the document to scan the second side. A DAFD scans both sides of a document in one pass, which requires two scanners, making it obviously the more expensive of the two feed methods. Both duplexing methods are rated in *images per minute (ipm)*.

REVIEW

Objective 3.6: Given a scenario, deploy and configure multifunction devices/printers and settings

- Most MFDs are preconfigured but may require localization and verification of device settings.
- Windows and macOS automatically install the appropriate drivers for a device added to a system.
- PostScript and PCL provide a digital image layout in text and binary to a printer.
- A printer or MFD can be configured as a private, shared, or public printer.
- Network printers are addressable nodes on a network.
- A print server can be an external, internal, or embedded device.
- Printer and MFD options can include duplexing, collation, page properties, and quality and tray settings.
- Printers can be shared using USB hubs, Ethernet switches, or wireless access ports.
- Wireless printers can connect to source devices via Bluetooth or IEEE 802.11x media.
- Print security can be enhanced though user authentication, badging, and audit logs, among other methods that limit access and to create a record of use.
- The secure print feature can prevent confidential, sensitive, or classified documents from being printed.
- Network scanning provides the capability to scan a document and save the image file wherever you wish.
- Most MFDs include automatic document feeders and flatbed scanners.

3.6 QUESTIONS

1. Total Seminars has purchased a new MFD to be added to its LAN. Which of the following can it use to connect the MFD to the network?

    A. USB

    B. Serial

    C. RJ-45

    D. IEEE 802.11

    E. Any of the above

    F. None of the above

2. You suspect that an attempt to gain unauthorized access to a network printer was made recently, and you want to investigate this security event. Which of the following would you use to scan the audit logs on a Windows system?

    A. File Explorer

    B. Microsoft Edge

    C. Event Viewer

    D. Telemetry Log for Office

3. You need to share a printer between two computers that, for security reasons, should not be networked. Which of the following is the best solution?

    A. USB print server

    B. KVM

    C. Ad hoc wireless

    D. USB switch

4. A user in your department is unable to print to a Bluetooth printer, even though Bluetooth is enabled on the printer and her computer. Which of the following is the most probable cause?

    A. The Bluetooth devices are not paired.

    B. There's no Bluetooth router.

    C. The Bluetooth cable is loose.

    D. The firewall setup.

5. After a new departmental MFD is installed, users must enter an assigned code to access and print classified documents. This is an example of which of the following options? (Choose two.)

    A. Secure printing

    B. Remote printing

    C. Badging

    D. Network printing

3.6 ANSWERS

1. **E**   Any one of these options (A through D) could be used. However, RJ-45 and IEEE 802.11 are the most commonly used means for network printing.

2. **C**   The Event Viewer supports the viewing, selecting, and reporting of system, security, and application events on a Windows computer.

3. **D**   A USB switch enables the USB device (such as an MFD or printer) to be shared without networking.

4. **A**   A Bluetooth printer (or another Bluetooth device) must be paired with a computer or mobile device before it can be used.

5. **A C**   Both secure printing and badging are forms of user authentication, which is required to gain access to the MFD and other resources.

Objective 3.7 **Given a scenario, install and replace printer consumables**

U sers interact with computers through their senses and the primary medium of this inter- action is sight via displays and printers. The consumable "supply" necessary for a display is electricity. However, a printer, in addition to electrical power, uses other supplies and con- sumables to produce its visual response.

A printer's supplies and consumables, with the exception of paper of different types, are unique to the printer and its print mechanism. Some printers use heat or electrical charges to form their output images; others use inked ribbons, wax, or sublimates. Regardless of how the printer, well, prints, it involves a consumable element. In this objective, we look at various types of printers and their components, operations, and the supplies and consumables each requires. But before we get into the particulars of each printer, we'll talk a bit about calibration.

> **EXAM TIP**   The A+ Core 1 exam's objectives cover the gamut of printer technologies, but its coverage focuses primarily on laser printers and inkjet printers.

Calibration

Every type of printer has some form of calibration procedure. The purpose for calibrating any printer is to ensure that the text and images it produces are legible, in alignment, and, especially on color printers, that the colors are true and don't bleed over into one another.

Color printers, regardless of their type, should be calibrated following the manufacturer's prescribed method (usually in the installation or user manual) out of the box and whenever major maintenance or repair is performed. Laser printers and 3-D printers especially should have a calibration step included in their periodic or preventive maintenance programs. Most home and small office printers have a calibration or print test page built into their installation or configuration menus.

Laser Printers

The technology used to print a document on a laser printer defines the consumables and supplies required and used by that printer. The print function of laser printers use the same process:

1. A cylindrical drum has an image projected onto it by an infrared laser and photoconductivity.

2. Toner is attracted to the charged areas of the drum (those not charged by the laser).

3. The toner particles are directly transferred onto paper, and heat is applied to fuse the toner onto the paper.

Not every one of these steps has a consumable element (other than electricity, that is), but obviously there are parts of the process that do.

Laser Printer Imaging Process

The imaging process of a laser print involves seven phases, each of which deals with a specific part of transferring a digital image into a visual print:

- **Processing**   When the print command is entered, clicked, or tapped, the document or image to be printed is translated into a language such as PostScript or PCL, which is converted by a raster image processor into a bitmap image of the document that defines each line to be printed.

- **Charging**   Also known as the *conditioning* step. After receiving the image of what is to be printed, the printer's processor charges the photosensitive imaging drum with an AC charge from a primary charge roller to erase any residual charge left from a previous print image. A DC charge is then uniformly applied to ready the imaging drum for receiving the print image.

- **Exposing**   After the imaging drum is charged, a laser applies a positive charge to the areas on the drum that represent the image of each line to be printed. A monochrome laser printer has only one drum, which prints one darker color (such as black). Some color laser printers, especially MFD printers, may have four drums, one each for cyan, magenta, yellow, and black (CMYK). The laser doesn't actually contact the imaging drum, but its beam is reflected unto the drum via one or more mirrors.

4. **Developing**   With the print image represented on the drum electrostatically, toner is applied to the drum by an adjacent roller, which uses an electric charge to pull toner from its reservoir. The developing roller and the lower-charge portions of the imaging drum have a lower charge to that applied by the laser, and toner is attracted to areas of the drum with a higher voltage. The toner is negatively charged in the tone reservoir. As the toner is applied, it is attracted to those areas with a weaker negative charge (which works in effect like a positive charge) to provide the structure of the image to be printed.

5. **Transferring**   After the print image is set on the imaging drum, a sheet of paper is fed into the imaging process by the transfer belt, a transfer roller, or pad. A positive charge is placed on paper's surface that is opposite the charge of the drum. As the paper moves over the drum, the image is transferred onto the paper.

6. **Fusing**   After the toner is transferred to the paper, the paper passes through extremely hot fusing rollers and pressure rollers that first melt the toner onto the surface of the paper and then apply pressure to further set (fuse) the melted toner onto the page. The paper is then moved to the output tray or sorter.

7. **Cleaning**   This phase is also referred to as the "cleaning and recharging" phase. Before the process can repeat for the next page to be printed, any residual toner is removed from the imaging drum by a neutrally charged cleaning blade that wipes the surface of the drum. A charging roller then applies a uniform negative charge to the imaging drum to remove any lingering charge (and image) from it. The process can then repeat.

 EXAM TIP   For sure, know the seven phases of the laser imaging process for the A+ Core 1 exam.

Laser Printer Components

The major components of a laser printer are the same regardless of manufacturer and model, with only some minor differences. In addition to the components previously explained in the laser printing process, the other parts and assemblies of a laser printer you should know about are described in the following list. These components include the imaging drum, fuser assembly, transfer belt, transfer roller, pickup rollers, separation pads, and the duplexing assembly. At least have some knowledge of what they are, what they do, and how they fit into the overall laser printing process for the A+ Core 1 exam. Figure 3.7-1 illustrates the major components of a typical laser printer.

 EXAM TIP   For the A+ Core 1 exam and the questions on Domain 3.0, know the key printer components described in this section.

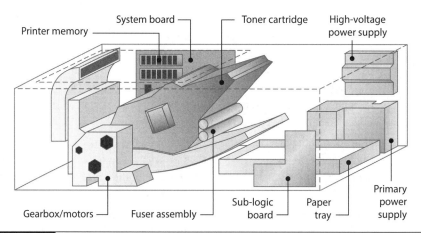

Printer memory — System board — Toner cartridge — High-voltage power supply

Gearbox/motors — Fuser assembly — Sub-logic board — Paper tray — Primary power supply

FIGURE 3.7-1   Components inside a laser printer

- **Imaging drum**   The imaging drum is a grounded cylinder with an ungrounded coat of photosensitive compounds. When light, from a laser, hits these particles, their electrical charge "drains" out through the grounded cylinder. It's common on most newer model laser printers that the toner cartridge or fuser assembly also contains the imaging drum (along with other components of the imaging process), which can become worn out about the time the toner supply runs out. Figure 3.7-2 shows an example of a toner cartridge.

- **Fuser assembly**   The fuser assembly is usually near the bottom of (but not included with) the toner cartridge and usually has two rollers (a pressure roller and a heated roller)

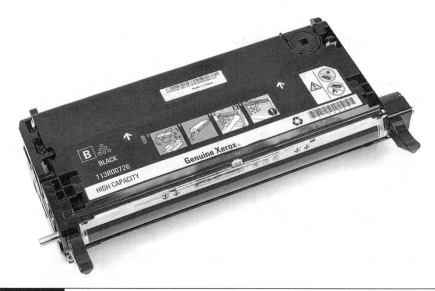

FIGURE 3.7-2   A laser printer toner cartridge may contain the imaging drum.

to permanently fuse the toner to the paper. The heated roller has a nonstick coating such as Teflon to prevent toner from sticking.

- **Transfer belt** The transfer belt is a larger rotating belt in color laser printers. It works like a conveyor belt to transfer color toners to the imaging process. The transfer belt passes each of the CMYK reservoirs and collects the correct amount of each color to produce an image. On single-pass color laser printers, the transfer belt places all of the CMYK colors on the page at the same time.

- **Transfer roller** On monochrome laser printers, toner is pulled from its reservoir and onto the paper by a transfer roller. The transfer roller applies a positive charge to the paper, which attracts the paper to the negatively charged imaging drum and causes the toner particles to be transferred to the page. A static charge eliminator then removes the charge to keep the paper from wrapping around the drum.

- **Pickup roller and separation pad** These components work in tandem to feed sheets of paper to the print process. The rubber pickup roller has a rough surface that pulls a sheet forward from the paper tray. The separation pad, which is tensioned with a spring, applies pressure on the pickup roller to grab one sheet. If a printer begins having paper jams frequently, these two items and the spring could be the problem.

- **Duplexing assembly** Most SOHO and MFD laser printers are simplex (or single-sided) printers. Many newer and all high-end laser printers offer duplex (or two-sided) printing. In order to print on both sides of a sheet, a laser printer requires a *duplexing assembly*. At the end of the imaging process, the duplexing assembly pulls the sheet with one side printed back into the printer and flips the page to repeat the imaging process on the reverse side.

 EXAM TIP Be familiar with the general purpose and function of each of the laser printer components discussed.

Laser Printer Maintenance

Maintenance doesn't always mean repair. Maintenance also includes preventive measures such as cleaning, replacing, and calibrating. How frequently routine maintenance is performed on a laser printer depends on a variety of factors, but typically a printed page count is set to trigger a warning message that the maintenance should be performed. Most of the major laser printer brands provide or recommend maintenance kits (or service kits) that contain the supplies and parts used for the maintenance actions. Maintenance kits aren't generally available for home or small office units and are intended primarily for the larger laser printers, copiers, or multi-function devices.

Maintenance kits, while extending the life of a laser printer, can't prevent the general wear and tear on the printer. Instead, they are intended to help extend the longevity of the printer; they cannot overcome age and use.

EXAM TIP Know the contents of a maintenance kit and the elements of a maintenance program: replacing the toner or toner cartridge, applying a maintenance kit, calibrating the imaging components, and cleaning the printer.

Maintenance Kit Contents

The contents of a manufacturer's laser printer maintenance kit can vary with different models, but in general they commonly include the following replacement parts or assemblies:

- Transfer, pickup, and feeder rollers
- Fusing assembly
- Separation pad
- Transfer rollers, belts, and pads
- Feeding unit
- Cooling fan

The maintenance kit may also include miscellaneous tools and cleaning materials appropriate to its model.

Cleaning a Laser Printer

A clean laser printer produces excellent documents clear of smudges, paper jams, and muddled print. However, cleaning a laser printer on a regular basis is also very important to the lifespan of the printer.

Cleaning Supplies

The supplies used to clean a laser printer are readily available on the market. However, some of the items are special to their purpose for what they do or don't do. The list for the supplies used to clean a laser printer includes the following:

- **Protective gear**   You should absolutely wear gloves (rubber or micro-foam nitrile) and a protective dust particle mask. As described earlier, toner is nasty stuff, with fine sharp-edged particles that you really don't want to breathe in or get on dry skin.
- **Toner vacuum**   A regular vacuum cleaner, meaning the type you'd use to clean the floor or to dust the woodwork, shouldn't be used on electronic equipment, such as inside the case of a computer or around the imaging drum or toner cartridge of a laser printer, for two primary reasons. One, a standard vacuum cleaner generates a great amount of static electricity at the nozzle; two, any toner drawn into the vacuum may end up in its exhaust and be blown out into the air.

- **Activated toner cloths** These disposable (single-use) wipes attract and hold toner particles that remain on the non-electrically charged areas of the printer after it has been vacuumed.

- **Alcohol** Never, repeat, *never* use rubbing alcohol or any product containing high amounts of alcohol of any type. Standard strength isopropyl alcohol can be used to clean the areas inside a laser printer. The cleaning products used on CDs, tape drives, and other electronic elements that include a 99 percent isopropyl solution are good to use.

- **Brushes and swabs** Soft-bristle narrow brushes, like specially made electronics cleaning brushes or paint brushes, can be used to dust the print drum. Hard or stiff bristle brushes can cause toner to go airborne and may scratch the drum.

Cleaning Steps

Before beginning the actual cleaning process on a laser printer, you should ensure the safety of yourself and the printer. Two very important actions that should be taken before you open the printer for cleaning are (1) powering off and cooling down the printer and (2) gloving and masking up for protection.

About one hour before beginning to clean the inside of a printer, you should turn it off, unplug the power cord from the power source, and allow the printer to cool down in terms of both temperature and static electricity. As suggested in the previous section, you should wear gloves and a mask when working with toner and toner cartridges. You don't need to wear a hazmat suit; just protect your hands and lungs.

To clean a laser printer, the following generic steps are typically used:

1. *Open the printer.* Refer to the printer documentation to be sure of the method used to open the printer for cleaning.

2. *Identify and extract removable components.* Again, refer to the printer's documentation to find and remove all of the detached components of the printer. This is typically the toner cartridge, tone reservoir (tank, supply, bottle), and the print drum. Take care not to spill the toner and not to touch the surface of the print drum. Place the photo-sensitive print drum in a darkened area.

3. *Clean the toner cartridge.* Set one end of the toner cartridge on an activated toner cloth and use another cloth to remove any excess toner from its surface. Set the cartridge aside, covered and protected by activated or static-free cloths.

4. *Use the toner vacuum to clean the printer.* Using a toner vacuum, slowly and gently remove any toner that may have been spilled into the inside of the printer case. Be very careful not to let the vacuum contact any inside surfaces of the printer case.

5. *Brush excess toner from hard-to-reach areas.* Use a soft brush or cotton swab to move any toner from the nooks and crannies of the printer case and then use the vacuum to remove it from the case.

6. *Clean the transfer rollers and charge rollers.* Wet a cotton swab with isopropyl alcohol and gently wipe the rollers on both the top and bottom surfaces.

7. *Clean the feed rollers.* Using one or more cotton swabs and isopropyl alcohol, wash the paper feed roller to remove any toner residual that may have built up.

8. *Reassemble the printer.* Using the printer's documentation, reinsert the components removed earlier using the same care used to remove them.

9. *Clean the outside of the case.* If needed, clean the outside of the printer's case using activated toner cloths and some isopropyl alcohol.

10. *Restart the printer.* Reconnect the printer to a power source, power it on, and use its built-in test procedure or one of your own to verify the reassembly is correct.

 EXAM TIP It's doubtful that you will encounter a question that requires you to sequence the maintenance and cleaning steps for a laser printer. However, you should have a general understanding of the actions performed and why each step is included.

Inkjet Printers

Where laser printers are common to higher-end and high-volume printing situations, *inkjet printers* are the most common printer type overall, and especially in homes and small offices. Among the most apparent advantages an inkjet has over a laser printer is that its ink and print mechanisms are contained in sealed drop-in cartridges that are replaced when its ink supply is gone. Another advantage, which may actually be its best, is that inkjet printers are much less expensive than laser printers.

Inkjet Printing and Components

An inkjet printer, which is the most popular general-purpose and SOHO printer in use, prints documents and images by spraying ink on sheets of paper with a resolution of at least 300 dots per inch (dpi). In some cases, an inkjet printer can produce images in full-color and in resolutions of 600 dpi and higher. If that's not enough, an inkjet can be the print component of a multifunction device that can make copies, send and receive fax documents, as well as scan text and images.

The characters and images printed by an inkjet are made up of small dots that are sprayed onto the surface of a page as its print head moves side to side to produce one print line at a time. However, before we look at the print process of an inkjet printer in detail, let's first cover the components of the inkjet and the role each plays in printing a document.

 EXAM TIP For the Core 1 exam, be sure you know the components of an inkjet printer and the role each plays in the printing process.

Inkjet ink cartridges vary in size and shape.

Ink Cartridge

An inkjet printer's *ink cartridge* is more than just the ink supply reservoir. The ink cartridge of an inkjet printer contains one (if monochrome) or more (if CMYK) ink reservoirs and a micro-processor that communicates and coordinates with the printer's controller to supply the correct amount (and color) of ink to the print head, which can often be a part of the ink cartridge itself.

There is no one standard size or shape for inkjet ink cartridges. An inkjet ink cartridge's form factor and construction are unique to the specific inkjet printer, the family of printers, and, always, the manufacturer. Figure 3.7-3 shows inkjet ink cartridges from five different inkjet models, each from a different printer manufacturer.

Print Head

The *print head* for some inkjet printer models is included in the ink cartridge. For others, the print head is a separate component altogether. Regardless of its location, an inkjet printer's print head performs the same function, which is spraying ink onto a variety of media to form characters, numbers, and images.

Unlike most of its predecessors, which are covered later, inkjet print heads don't contact the media. Whereas impact printers are like a rubber stamp and stamp pad or even a paint brush, an inkjet print head is more like a paint spray gun. However, within the general category of inkjet print heads, even though they may produce the same overall result, inkjet print heads can vary in the technology in use. Inkjet printer print heads use one of two different methods—piezo and thermal—for spraying ink onto a medium and it's important to know the differences between them for the Core 1 exam.

Piezo Print Heads   The piezo print method (which gets its name from the piezo crystal producing its charge) involves a very thin film that receives an electric charge. The charge causes the film to bend, which creates pressure on an ink chamber just ahead of a print head nozzle. The amount of charge determines the amount of flex, which in turn determines the amount of ink that is sprayed from the nozzle onto the surface of the medium. A *piezo print head* has 720 print nozzles for each of the colors it prints. High-quality printing can require multiple passes for each print line, which can slow the print speed but can also improve the print resolution.

Thermal Print Heads   Thermal inkjet print heads are the most common type of inkjet printer print heads. A *thermal print head,* as its name suggests, uses heat and water-based inks to produce images on media. In comparison to piezo, which uses an electrical charge to create the pressure that forces the ink from a print head nozzle, thermal applies sufficient heat to the ink held in a chamber behind a nozzle to bring it to a boil. The boiling ink creates a bubble of ink vapor, which is forced through the print head nozzle, causing it to burst and spray the ink onto the medium. The chamber then cools down very quickly so that the process can repeat immediately, if needed.

Print Head Stepper Motor   Regardless of the print head technology used on an inkjet printer, the print head (and ink cartridges) must be moved horizontally across the medium, typically in both directions. This motion is powered by a *stepper motor,* which divides the side-to-side distance of the print area into small individual distances, or steps. Some inkjet printers also use a stepper motor to park the print head when the printer is idle or powered off.

Trays, Rollers, and Feeders

The general design of most inkjet printers includes a *paper tray* either as a snap-in (removable) or as a built-in (nonremovable) component. In either case, the medium is pulled into the print area by a set of *rollers,* which also advance the paper, as directed by the printer controller, after the print head completes printing a line and is ready to move to the next one.

Some inkjet printers have a *feeder* in place of a tray. On an inkjet printer, a feeder snaps open either on the top or back of the printer's chassis. A feeder won't hold as many sheets as a tray, but it is typically able to feed specialty paper types and sizes that a tray may not be able to load. Figure 3.7-4 shows an inkjet printer with both a tray and a feeder included.

FIGURE 3.7-4   An inkjet printer featuring both a paper tray and a document feeder

Carriage Belt

The inkjet printer's print head moves side-to-side under the power of the carriage stepper motor. The print head assembly is attached to the carriage belt, which is directly connected, although not anchored, to the stepper motor. As the stepper motor is instructed to advance or reverse, it moves the carriage belt accordingly, which in turn pulls the print head in the direction it should move.

Duplexing Assembly

As explained earlier in the discussion of laser printers, a duplexing assembly enables a printer to print on both sides of the medium. In general use, the duplexing assembly enables the printer to retract a document after it has been printed on one side back into the printer so that it can be printed on its opposite side.

Inkjet Print Process Summarized

Inkjet printers use a thermal drop-on-demand process that pumps ink from a cartridge reservoir into a small chamber connected to a spray nozzle. The printer then uses either a piezo or a thermal process to spray the ink through a nozzle in the print head and onto the paper. The ink supply is contained in one or more ink cartridges, and the ink is transferred to the paper by the print head. The ink cartridges are unique to the manufacturer and model of the printer, but print heads are one of two types: piezo or thermal.

Inkjet Printer Maintenance and Cleaning

The supplies required when cleaning an inkjet printer are the same as those listed earlier for use when cleaning a laser printer, with one addition: printer oil for lubricating the moving parts of an inkjet. However, if the printer being cleaned has a piezo print head that uses an oil-based ink, you should look for products specifically designed for cleaning this type of inkjet printer.

When cleaning an inkjet printer, focus on the print head (which may be a part of the printer ink cartridge), the ink cartridge, any paper jams or debris from past jams, and the printer's calibration, which is covered next.

The process to clean an inkjet printer varies slightly with the manufacturer and the print process type. Before starting to clean an inkjet printer, review the printer's documentation, looking for any cautions, warnings, or hazards. Unless the documentation prescribes a different cleaning process, these are the steps to follow:

1. *Remove the ink cartridge.* In most inkjet printers, the ink cartridge (or cartridges) is mounted in a caddy that moves along a stabilizer or glide bar. Gently, yet firmly, move the cartridge caddy to the middle of the bar, if the printer doesn't automatically move it there when you open the case. With the caddy in position, power the printer off, remove the power cord from the power source, and remove the ink cartridge.

2. *Clean the print head and cartridges.* With the ink cartridge removed, you should have access to the print head, either on the cartridge or as a separate device attached to the ink cartridge caddy. In either case, apply isopropyl alcohol, a window cleaning solution, or a print head cleaner to a soft paper towel or cotton swab and gently swipe across the print head to remove any dried ink or to clear any clogs on the feed holes. If the printer has removable print heads, you may remove them to clean them in the same way. Wipe the ink flow areas of the ink cartridges to remove any excess ink.

3. *Clean the ink cartridge caddy.* Use a cotton swab to remove any ink or lint from the ink cartridge caddy.

4. *Check the ribbon cables and ink reservoirs.* Ink and paper lint can accumulate on the connecting cables and in recesses of the case. Using a paper towel, swab, or soft-bristle brush, remove any ink/lint debris from the case interior.

5. *Clean the exterior.* Using a cleaning wipe or a towel with alcohol, wipe down the exterior of the printer's case.

6. *Reassemble and test.* Re-insert the ink cartridge and print heads, if necessary, and power up the printer. If available, use the print test function to ensure that the printer is properly reassembled. You should also take the time to recalibrate the printer's alignment.

EXAM TIP   Be sure that you are familiar with the inkjet printer components described in this section as well as the areas and procedures listed in the maintenance process.

Thermal Printers

A *thermal printer,* unlike laser or inkjet printers, doesn't use toner or ink to create characters or images on paper. In fact, it's the paper or a wax or resin transfer that creates the images printed when heat is applied. The two types of thermal printers, both of which use a thermal "print head" to heat the surface of the paper or material, are thermal transfer and direct thermal. A thermal printer has three primary parts: the thermal print head/heating element, a feed roller assembly that moves the medium past the print head, and tensioners that keep the medium and the print head in place.

Thermal Print Head/Heating Element

A thermal print head, or *heating element,* emits electrical signals to generate heat to create images on a medium. The images are created either by melting a material onto or effecting a chemical change of the medium. Thermal printing is a thermal transfer in which text, characters, or images are "printed" on any material or specifically on heat-sensitive chemically treated thermal paper.

A *thermal transfer printer* applies sufficient heat to a ribbon coated with a wax or resin material to melt the coating onto a medium. The melted material is absorbed by the medium, which is matched to the material it receives. The medium absorbs the melted print material, and the image becomes bonded to its surface.

Direct thermal printing, which is also called *thermal printing,* uses heat to create text, characters, and images on special chemically treated thermochromic paper, which is called, obviously enough, *thermal paper.*

Thermal transfer is typically favored over direct thermal for printing on heat-sensitive materials and because it is more durable. Thermal transfer printing is used for a variety of image transfers, including paper, T-shirts, polyester, and other synthetic materials. Figure 3.7-5 illustrates the thermal transfer print function.

Thermal Printer Feed Assembly

One of the primary advantages of a thermal printer is that it's very quiet, which is the reason this type of printer is common in libraries, restaurants, and hospitals. To support its quiet operation, the feed mechanism for the thermal paper must also be quiet. The feed assembly for a thermal printer uses rubberized rollers that grip the chemically treated paper and pull it past the thermal print head and through the print path.

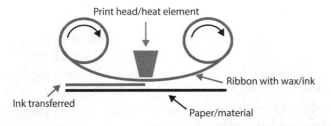

FIGURE 3.7-5   Thermal transfer printers heat the material on a ribbon to transfer it to a medium.

Thermal Paper

Unlike thermal transfer printing, direct thermal doesn't involve anything other than heat and thermal paper. (In other words, no ribbons, toners, inks, or waxy materials are harmed in the production of a direct thermal print.) As the thermal paper passes the print head, heat is applied to the thermal paper and its chemical coating reacts to the heat to form the characters or images being printed.

Because unprinted areas of the thermal paper remain sensitive to heat and light, direct thermal printing isn't durable. Eventually, the images can fade or the paper can darken as a result of the paper being exposed to heat or light for any length of time. Although some two-color thermal paper is available, the majority of direct thermal printing is monochrome (either black or amber).

Thermal Printer Cleaning

The following are the steps used when cleaning a thermal head printer:

1. As should always be done, the first step in cleaning any printer, especially one that gets very hot, is to turn off the printer, remove its power cord from the power source, and let the printer cool down.

2. On most thermal printers, the print head or heating element is reached through a panel that provides access to the print head, the ribbon, a paper or label spool (depending on the type of thermal printer), as well as other parts of the printer.

3. Locate the lever that releases the print head and ribbon. Move the ribbon to the side to expose the print head.

4. Using an activated toner cloth or another type of lint-free cloth dampened with isopropyl alcohol, wipe from side to side across the print head, applying light pressure a few times to remove any built-up residue from the ribbon. Let the print head sit a short while to ensure it dries.

5. Replace the ribbon and print head and then secure the print head release lever back in its locked position.

6. Close and secure the access panel. Run a test print to make sure everything is back where it should be.

Impact Printers

There are two types of printers: impact and non-impact. So far, in this objective we've covered non-impact printers—those that don't make direct forceful contact with the print medium. The basic difference between an impact and a non-impact printer should be obvious—the impact, as in the hit or strike. While most home and small office printers are increasingly non-impact printers, such as laser or inkjet, impact printers can serve a purpose, such as where multiple-part tractor-fed forms are in use.

Impact printers evolved from other impact devices—typewriters, teletypes, and the like—and have been in use since the computer first entered businesses and homes. Over the decades, impact printers were extremely popular for home or small office use. However, the quieter, clear, and often faster non-impact printers of today have replaced them for general use.

 EXAM TIP   Know the components (print head, ribbon, and tractor feed devices) and maintenance processes for impact printers.

Impact printer is a generic name for a family of printer types that create text and characters on paper by striking a metal or plastic print head into an inked ribbon that is pressed against the paper to transfer all or part of a line, character, or symbol on the page. Examples of impact printers (both current and in the past) are impact (also called impact-matrix) printers, ball-strike printers, daisy-wheel printers, line printers, and chain printers.

Impact Print Heads

The print heads in impact printers use either a serial or line pattern to print.

A serial impact print head creates characters in a series of columns, and a line impact print head forms its characters and graphics with dots in rows. The most common of the serial impact printers uses a set of nine print wires, each with a small ball on its striking end, arranged in a single vertical column.

Figure 3.7-6 illustrates an example of a serial impact print pattern. In this example, the shaded areas show the pins used, one column at a time, to print an uppercase letter *E*. In this example, six separate columns of print wire impact patterns produced the image of the letter. This illustrates how the print head strikes with the pins needed for each column and then shifts to the next column on the right. Notice that for the leftmost column, all of the wires are used, and in the next column to the right, only the top, middle, and bottom wires are struck. The only the wires needed for each column are struck to complete the remainder of the character. The dots in the shaded areas of Figure 3.7-6 represent the wires the print head strikes to create the character, nine-wire column by nine-wire column, left to right. While this example used only nine print wires, other impact print heads may use 24 wires.

A line impact printer uses a hammer bank (also referred to as a print-shuttle) in place of the wire matrix of the serial impact printer. Like the serial method, a line impact print head travels from side to side, left to right, but instead of printing a vertical column of dots, it prints a horizontal row of dots to create each character on the print line. Whereas the serial impact print head concentrates on each character being printed, a line impact print head works on each character it prints as a part of one layer of an entire document.

As the print head travels left to right, the hammers needed for each row of each character on the line are struck. The hammer bank of the line impact print head is like turning a serial impact wire set on its side. Each of the hammers in the print head's hammer bank is held in a tensed position by a spring that is released to allow the hammer to strike the ribbon and then

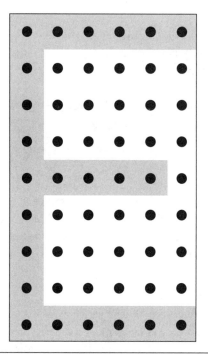

FIGURE 3.7-6   The print wires of an impact printer form a character with a series of columns.

be pulled back into its tense, ready position. Figure 3.7-7 illustrates a character printed by a line impact print head. Each line (indicated by number) is printed as a single strike using only the hammers needed for that line.

 NOTE   A line impact printer is the faster of the two impact print methods.

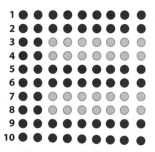

FIGURE 3.7-7   A line impact printer creates characters one row at a time.

A+ Core 1 Exam 220-1101
A+ Core 1 Exam 220-1101

| **FIGURE 3.7-8** | Examples of impact draft mode (top) and near letter quality (NLQ) bottom |

The quality of the print produced by an impact printer varies widely. In draft mode (see Figure 3.7-8), the space between the dots is wide and visible. Near letter quality (NLQ) mode, also shown in Figure 3.7-8, is considered to be nearly as good as the print produced by a typewriter. To produce NLQ print, an impact printer needs a higher wire or hammer count, which means that the wires or hammers are closer together, to reprint each dot after a very slight oscillation in the print head's position.

Impact Components

A impact printer has a few more moving parts than non-impact printers, and all of its major parts work in concert to print documents. Here are the major components, some of which we've already discussed:

- **Platen or tractor feed**   The platen in an impact printer is a rubber-coated roller that pulls a sheet of paper or document up to the printhead and, after each print line is completed, pulls the document up to align the next print line or space with the print head. A tractor feed is a pair of coordinated gear sprockets that use teeth to connect into and pull along a continuous paper stock with a tear-off pinhole track on each side of the stock. Figure 3.7-9 illustrates a tractor feed on an impact printer.

- **Print head**   As discussed earlier, an impact printer uses 9, 18, or 24 pins that are pushed out by a piezoelectric mechanism in a varying pattern to produce one vertical column of a character or graphic.

- **Print ribbon**   When the print head pins are fired out, they strike an inked ribbon and press it onto the paper. Impact ribbons are contained in a cartridge that snaps into the printer. Ribbon cartridges pass the print head in only one direction, and when all of the ribbon has done so, it's time to replace the cartridge. Some legacy printers may still use spooled ribbons, but these are extremely rare.

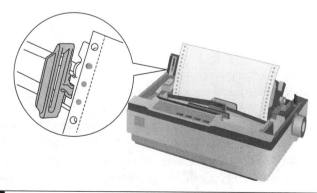

| **FIGURE 3.7-9** | An illustration of a tractor feed unit on an impact printer printing a continuous form |

FIGURE 3.7-10   An example of an impact printer cartridge ribbon

Impact Maintenance

For the A+ Core 1 exam, what you need to know about maintaining an impact printer boils down three items, as follows:

- **Replacing the ribbon**   Most impact printers use a cartridge ribbon, like the one shown in Figure 3.7-10. A ribbon performs two vital functions in an impact printer: it provides the ink transferred to the page when struck by a pin, and it lubricates the print head's pins, which protects them from impact damage.
- **Replacing the paper**   Paper jams can be a problem on impact printers, especially when a multipart form is being tractor-fed. Before each print run, verify the fit and seating of the form or continuous form paper sheet(s).
- **Replacing the print head**   One very common issue with heavily used impact printers is damage to the print head's pins, which can become bent or broken. This issue usually shows up as missing pins in printed characters. The only fix is to replace the print head.

3-D Printers

Additive manufacturing, which is the engineering name for three-dimension (3-D) printing, is the creation of an object by following digital instructions. The 3-D printing process is an additive procedure in which layers are added successively on or to previously applied layers.

A 3-D printer works very similar to an inkjet printer, where material is applied to the object in much the same way an inkjet sprays ink onto a page. However, instead of ink, a 3-D printer "prints" layers of melted thermoplastics or resins and fuses them together with adhesive or UV light. Figure 3.7-11 shows a 3-D printer using a plastic filament to create an object.

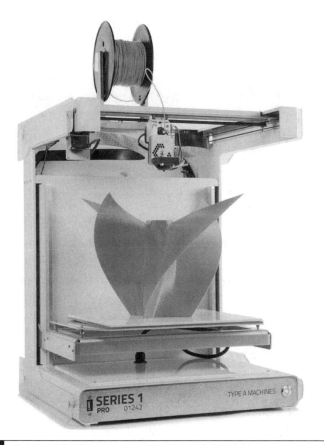

FIGURE 3.7-11 A 3-D printer (image courtesy of LiteWorld, LLC)

3-D Printing Filaments

A 3-D printer doesn't keep a supply of molten material ready like an ink reservoir. Instead, a spool of plastic filament is fed into the printer, which then melts and applies the filament. "Plastic" in 3-D printing can be any *thermoplastic material,* which means that it will melt when heated and solidify when cooled. The types of plastics used in 3-D printers are acrylonitrile butadiene styrene (ABS), polylactic acid (PLA), and, a bit less often, polyethylene terephthalate glycol (PETG). ABS is the material used to make LEGO bricks, PLA is commonly used to make more pliable toys, and PETG is the material of your milk jug. The thermoplastic material comes on spools, is fed into the heating element of a 3-D printer, and then is applied through a nozzle (called an *extruder*) to the object being created.

3-D Printer Bed

An object is built on the print bed of the printer. Print beds may or may not come as a part of the printer itself. In fact, the type of plastic filament can determine the best choice for the print bed. The purpose of the print bed, other than being where the object sits, is to provide an adhesive surface for the first layer (so that the plastic doesn't stick to the extruder) and to prevent the shifting or warping of the object at the start. Most print beds are either glass or aluminum, and some are heated.

 EXAM TIP   For the A+ Core 1 exam, understand how 3-D printers convert filaments and resins into objects on their print beds.

REVIEW

Objective 3.7: Given a scenario, install and replace printer consumables

- Printers use heat, electrical charges, inked ribbons, or plastic filaments to create characters and images on a medium.
- A laser printer uses an electrically charged drum and toner to create and fuse text or images on paper.
- The laser imaging process has seven phases: processing, charging, exposing, developing, transferring, fusing, and cleaning.
- The major components of a laser printer are the imaging drum, fuser assembly, transfer belt, transfer roller, pickup rollers, separation pads, and duplexing assembly.
- Inkjet printers create text and images using drops of ink sprayed onto a page.
- A thermal printer uses thermal transfer and direct thermal.
- An impact printer can use a serial or line impact print head.
- A serial impact print head prints characters as a series of columns.
- A line impact print head forms characters and graphics by printing dots in a series of rows.
- The two most common impact print heads have either 9 or 24 pins.
- The major components of an impact printer are a platen or tractor feed mechanism, the print head, and a print ribbon.
- A 3-D printer uses an additive manufacturing process to create an object by adding successive layers of thermoplastic material or resins to previously applied material.
- Calibrating a printer ensures that the text and images produced are legible and in alignment and, on color printers, that colors are true and don't overlap.

3.7 QUESTIONS

1. Which one of the following is not one of the seven phases of the laser imaging process?
   A. Charging
   B. Fusing
   C. Cleaning
   D. Coloring

2. Which of the following are the coloring agents of a color laser printer? (Choose all that apply.)

    A. Magenta

    B. Cyan

    C. Orange

    D. Black

    E. Yellow

    F. Green

3. The print head technology used by inkjet printers to create characters on a medium is which of the following? (Choose two.)

    A. Piezo

    B. Thermal

    C. Photo-sensitive

    D. Impact

4. Heat is the catalyst in all forms of thermal printers. What is the element that reacts to the heat applied in direct thermal printing?

    A. Dye sublimate

    B. Wax or resin

    C. Thermal paper

    D. Inkjets

5. What is the term for the process of aligning the text, graphics, and colors of a printer?

    A. Line control

    B. Extrusion

    C. Calibrating

    D. Duplexing

3.7 ANSWERS

1. **D** Although color can be an element of the print produced, it is not a process in the laser imaging process.

2. **A B D E** The primary coloring agents are cyan, magenta, yellow, and black (CMYK).

3. **A B** These two technologies vaporize the ink that passes through the nozzle and onto the paper.

4. **B** Direct thermal printers use heat to print an image on specially treated thermal paper.

5. **C** Calibrating a printer ensures a sharper printed output.

Virtualization and Cloud Computing

Domain Objectives

- **4.1** Summarize cloud-computing concepts.
- **4.2** Summarize aspects of client-side virtualization.

 **Objective 4.1** **Summarize cloud-computing concepts**

Cloud computing has become omnipresent, from online storage services and e-mail providers to integrated business apps. In this section, you learn about the different types of cloud services and how to choose the most appropriate cloud model for the work your client or organization needs to do.

Common Cloud Models

It wasn't that very long ago that the "cloud" wasn't much more than a few friendly file-storage services, such as OneDrive, Dropbox, and Google Drive. Today, the cloud offers virtually any service users and enterprises require for infrastructure and applications. The cloud offers a vast array of on-demand computing resources and services from providers such as Amazon, Microsoft, Google, Carbonite, IBM, and myriad others, all on the open Internet.

Cloud Deployment Models

The cloud is conceptually and physically made up of layers of overlapping models. Some models relate to how the cloud is accessed or provided, and others are defined by the type of service or content offered. These models are grouped into two general categories: deployment models and service models. For the A+ Core 1 exam, you need to know what each of these various models defines and understand the services it provides.

Let's start with the deployment models. In simple terms, a cloud deployment model defines who has access to the cloud and its construction. The A+ Core 1 objectives focus on four primary cloud deployment models: public, private, community, and hybrid.

Public Cloud

On the open, public Internet, almost any service anyone who can access and use the resources available is in the *public cloud*. When we talk about the cloud in general terms, we are most likely referring to the public cloud. The resources available in the public cloud are owned by the providers and offered to the public, without cost, restriction, or authorization. Search engines, reference sites, and information and entertainment portals are examples of public clouds.

Private Cloud

A *private cloud,* which is also referred to as an *internal cloud,* is the opposite of a public cloud. Whereas the public cloud is open to all, a private cloud is closed to the public and open to only the members of a select group. The group is typically a company, school, social or political organization, or another type of membership group or organization. Private clouds offer access control, security, and specialization, which are typically minimal in a public cloud.

Community Cloud

A community can be made up of the students and parents of a school district, citizens of a region, the members of an exclusive organization, the businesses in a chamber of commerce, corporations in the same industry, and the like. A *community cloud* is a form of a private cloud, paid for by a community, that allows its members to share information and resources. A community cloud can be likened to a community bulletin board or forum.

Hybrid Cloud

A hybrid anything is made up of parts, usually the best parts, of related elements. A hybrid cloud is a conglomeration of structure, access, and content of public and private clouds (a community cloud is essentially a hybrid cloud to begin with). A *hybrid cloud* is made up of differing amounts of public cloud, private cloud, and onsite resources to create a custom environment.

 EXAM TIP   You need to understand who can access each type of cloud deployment model and who controls them.

Cloud Service Models

When the cloud was first defined by the National Institute of Standards and Technology (NIST) in 2011, it had three service delivery models: Infrastructure as a Service (IaaS), Software as a Service (SaaS), and Platform as a Service (PaaS). Since then, there has been an explosion of "aaS" services defined, each with a narrower scope than the last.

 EXAM TIP   You need to know the common cloud model acronyms—IaaS, SaaS, and PaaS—and associated delivery models for the CompTIA A+ 220-1101 exam.

Infrastructure as a Service

Pronounced as "eye-a-a-ess," *IaaS* is a cloud service that provides service subscribers with a combination of virtualization, protection against data loss and downtime, and the scalability to respond to spikes in demand. *Cloud service providers (CSPs)* enable anyone from individuals to large multinational corporations to launch new virtual servers using a given operating system (OS), on demand, at very low cost. CSPs provide flexible virtualized environments that are capable of driving popular, complex web applications, development environments, and customized operations, including unlimited data storage, database servers, caching, media hosting, and more, all billed by usage. IaaS frees subscribers from managing hardware and operating environments.

Software as a Service

SaaS, which is pronounced as "sass," is the general term for software applications offered on a cloud-based delivery model to the general public by developers and providers. Access to SaaS offerings can be free (with registration), subscribed to via a time-based agreement, subscribed to on a pay-as-you-go basis, or included as part of a membership package. The benefit to the user or subscriber is that the provider has the responsibility for maintaining and updating its SaaS offerings, along with supplying hardware, installation, and access control, thus relieving the user of these responsibilities.

Examples of SaaS model software and applications include word processing, presentations, spreadsheets, e-mail, flowcharting, and audio/video teleconferencing. SaaS offerings are available anywhere there is an Internet connection. However, one of the major tradeoffs of using SaaS applications is that you may need to give up control of your data to the SaaS provider and trust in its security.

Platform as a Service

PaaS, pronounced as "pass," is a cloud service model that provides subscribers with access to a customized bundle of hardware and software resources over the Internet. One of the more common uses for PaaS services is for software development and testing. A PaaS environment can give software developers the tools needed for developing, deploying, administering, and maintaining applications and other software products.

The PaaS CSP constructs an infrastructure, which could be an IaaS, and builds a *platform.* The platform can even be a complete deployment and management system. A PaaS subscription saves the user acquisition and maintenance costs as well as the cost and time of setup, configuration, and maintenance (commonly at the expense of flexibility).

Cloud Characteristics

Cloud computing is in many ways similar to the time-sharing practices of the early days of computing. Time-sharing allowed companies to "rent" time on a centralized computer and to avoid the expense of purchasing computing equipment, which at the time was primarily mainframes. In many ways, the cloud permits a company to "rent" services from a service provider over the Internet, rather than over dial-up lines as before, and not have to bring all of the required hardware and software, and people, in-house. The following sections provide descriptions of some of the features and characteristics of cloud computing.

Shared Resources

One of the benefits of cloud computing is how it enhances the concept of *shared resources.* All networks feature shared resources, such as storage and servers connected to the same LAN. With cloud computing, these and other resources are accessed on the Internet.

When you consider that even a moderately successful CSP may have dozens, if not hundreds or thousands, of subscribers to it services, providing access to its resources must be on a shared basis. Depending on the service model offered, hardware, software, data storage, and other services must be leveraged to provide each of the service subscribers with the resources and access defined in each service level agreement (SLA). To accomplish this, the CSP must implement a virtualized environment.

System, network, and storage virtualizations are essential elements of resource sharing in cloud computing. On the subscriber side, the CSP's virtualized environment is transparent, and each individual or corporate subscriber operates in a "dedicated" space that provides all of the resources required for their needs.

Metered Utilization

A *metered utilization* model is a measured activity method that some CSPs use to track the activities of a subscriber on a cloud service. The metrics show the amount of resource usage, in appropriate units of measure, and provide the CSP with a basis for monitoring, controlling, throttling (limiting), scaling, and, of course, billing the subscriber for that usage.

The service agreement between the CSP and the subscriber defines the rate per unit for the various measures of time (minutes), data transfer amounts (MB or GB), scalability (service levels), data storage space (MB/GB), and other resources and related measurements. For example, should a company need extra servers during the work week only, it can subscribe for the use of IaaS servers and pay for the time, capacity, or data transfer metrics it uses. The company avoids purchasing physical servers that may sit idle nearly 30 percent of the time. Metered utilization services are also known as measured services or "pay-per-use" services.

Resource control and billing are the two primary reasons CSPs use *metering*. Metering captures a subscriber's use of shared resources, such as bandwidth or data storage, as they are consumed. The captured data can then be used for analysis, summarization, scaling or throttling, and billing.

Scaling is the expansion or reduction of the usage thresholds or amounts of a subscribed service based on demand, usage, or isolated events. For example, if a subscriber is constantly at or over their subscribed disk storage limit, they can agree to scaling the disk storage limit to a new higher level. The same scenario could also apply should the subscriber need to reduce their resource requirements. Scalability of resources can also be a standby or as-needed service that is applied on the fly.

Throttling isn't exactly the opposite of scaling, but if scaling is considered to be an expansion, then throttling is a contraction. However, throttling is based on an agreed-to ruleset that defines resource access and usage. A subscriber's actual usage is measured against the throttling rules, which typically define the upper limit of a resource's usage. Throttling is normally used to prevent unlimited use of a resource that is scarce or in high demand.

Billing is based on the actual utilization of resources by a subscriber. The metered usage metrics are used to generate the billing, which is commonly monthly.

Elasticity/Scalability

One of the more sought-after characteristics of the cloud is flexibility, which is expressed as *elasticity* in the A+ Core 1 objectives and *scalability* in many service descriptions. Expanding the capabilities of an in-house system can take more time than is usually available and cost more than it should. A cloud service such as IaaS or PaaS can provide subscribers with the capability of expanding resources as they become required. This elasticity can be instantaneous, with the subscriber unaware of the changes, or the subscriber can be notified for approval before the service increase is applied. Flexibility provides the subscriber with the capability of adding cloud resources and services *on demand,* which empowers the subscriber to scale up or down rapidly to manage spikes or lulls in resource demand. This is known as *rapid elasticity.*

 EXAM TIP   *Rapid elasticity* allows a customer to use more, or fewer, cloud resources, as needed. *On demand* means that a customer can access cloud resources 24/7, as needed.

High Availability

Some companies and organizations must have access to their data and systems at (or very nearly at) all times, 24/7 and 365. Ensuring this capability can be extremely expensive considering the equipment and personnel required. Subscribing to a cloud service that promises this level of support, called *high availability,* involves transferring both the responsibility and trust to a CSP.

Data stored in the cloud, regardless of it being a ready source for interactive commerce or as a backup, is an essential asset that must retain its integrity and be immediately available when needed. The services and security measures of a CSP offering data storage must provide for the high availability, confidentiality, and integrity of its subscribers.

High availability is an umbrella term that is defined by the terms of an SLA between the CSP and the subscriber. Suppose the subscriber needs its data to be instantly available only certain hours and days, such as 7 A.M. to 10 P.M., Monday through Friday, but no less than 99.9 percent of the time during those hours. This, then, is the high availability required by the subscriber. An online shopping website that supports real-time ordering around the clock, seven days a week and 52 weeks a year, could require the same percentage of high availability (99.9 percent), which results in a much higher commitment from the CSP. In comparing these two examples, we can see that the former requires a commitment from the CSP that, during the contracted hours, the SaaS and the subscriber's data cannot be unavailable for any more than one minute per daily session. In the second example, the CSP commits to ensuring that its services cannot be unavailable more than 8.78 minutes per year. Table 4.1-1 provides the upper limits of downtime in the "five-nines" chart for high availability commitments.

TABLE 4.1-1	Downtime Limits by Time Period in the Five-Nines Schedule			
Availability	**Downtime Limit**			
	Year	**Month**	**Week**	**Day**
99.0% (two nines)	87.6 hours	7.3 hours	1.7 hours	14.4 minutes
99.9% (three nines)	8.7 hours	43.8 minutes	10.1 minutes	1.44 minutes
99.99% (four nines)	52.6 minutes	4.4 minutes	1.0 minute	8.6 seconds
99.999% (five nines)	5.3 minutes	26.3 seconds	6.0 seconds	< 1 second

EXAM TIP   You don't need to memorize the information in Table 4.1-1. It's provided only as an illustration for high availability. However, the five-nines approach is commonly used to define availability terms in SLAs.

File Synchronization

File synchronization is fundamentally a form of file backup, where a data file or object is replicated to one or more different storage media. File synchronization differs from just making a copy periodically in that it's designed to keep copies of files and objects coordinated, regardless of their locations. A backup copy of a file is a snapshot taken at a point in time. Until a backup is replaced by a later snapshot of the same file, it remains the same. A synchronized file remains constant to its source, meaning that any change made to the source file is automatically made (on demand) to the synchronized file as well. Backup files are normally stored on a separate medium or device and placed offline in a secured location. A set of synchronized files can be stored on the same device or even on different types of storage media on the same device, attached to its network, or even in the cloud. Typically, though, synchronized files are stored on different devices and usually different media.

A set of synchronized files may have copies on a desktop PC, a mobile PC, and a smartphone, and perhaps other devices as well. On these devices, the files may be on a hard disk, a USB device, and on the Universal Flash Storage (UFS) of a cell phone. If a modification is made to any one of a file's copies, a file synchronization application or service will follow predefined rules and settings to apply the modification to all other versions of the file, regardless of on which device the change was made and on which devices the synchronized files copies are stored. The configuration and settings of the file synchronization software determines its actions: for example, not all copies are updated for any change; some copies are updated only periodically; all synchronized copies are refreshed periodically—plus a variety of other synchronization actions.

File synchronization can be a one-way or two-way process. *One-way synchronization* is also referred to as *mirroring* (in RAID). When a change is made to a base copy of a file, copies of the revised file are sent to designated locations in storage. Only changes to the base file are mirrored. *Two-way synchronization,* which is actually what file synchronization is, applies any modifications to all copies of a file, often by copying the entire file to all the synchronized copies.

Desktop Virtualization

Virtualization, in the context of computing, is a process that simulates hardware elements that exist only as creations of the virtualization software. Although virtual, the simulated hardware is able to function as if it were an actual device. Virtual devices can be computers, network adapters, internetworking devices, and many others, including what you'll likely see on the A+ Core 1 exam: virtual desktops.

Virtual desktops are created in one of two models: hosted desktop infrastructure (HDI) and client virtualization or virtual desktop infrastructure (VDI). The *hosted desktop* model defines virtualized machines and desktops created directly on physical hardware, or what is called "bare metal." Client virtualization, or VDI, can create desktop environments on the premises, on a remote workstation on a local network, or in the cloud.

Desktop virtualization creates (and in many cases, stores) multiple simulated user desktops, all running on a single computer. The *host* device, the computer on which the virtualization software (called a *hypervisor*) is running, could be a physical computer in an organization or a virtual computer in the cloud. Most of the virtualization systems create *persistent* virtual desktops, which means that the system saves the entire virtual desktop's environment so that its user can store it and then later recall it to continue exactly at the point where it was stored. A *nonpersistent* virtual desktop cannot be saved and is completely new each time it's started.

Virtualization systems support three types of desktop virtualizations:

- **Virtual desktop infrastructure (VDI)**   In this type of desktop virtualization, the hypervisor creates virtual machines (VMs), each with its own desktop image, on a data center or cloud server. Users access the virtual desktops remotely from endpoint devices. VDI creates a dedicated VM that creates its own unique operating environment.
- **Remote desktop services (RDS)**   Using RDS, users can access a remote desktop that shares hardware resources as well as system and application software.
- **Desktop as a Service (DaaS)**   DaaS (pronounced as "dass") is very much like VDI, with the major exception that the user's organization doesn't supply the hardware or software on which the virtual desktop is generated, only the endpoint device used to access the DaaS service in the cloud.

REVIEW

Objective 4.1: Summarize cloud-computing concepts

- The major types of cloud services are Infrastructure as a Service (IaaS), Software as a Service (SaaS), and Platform as a Service (PaaS).
- The public cloud provides cloud services to anyone.
- A private cloud limits access to authorized internal users.
- A community cloud is a private cloud with access limited to a specific group of organizations or individuals.
- A hybrid cloud blends features of public and private cloud resources.
- Resources such as VMs, cloud storage, and others can be shared via LANs (internally) or cloud computing (externally).
- Metered utilization tracks computing resource usage via measurements of bandwidth, time, and/or capacity for billing and analysis purposes.
- The ability to add or drop cloud services as needed (on-demand self-service) enables organizations to have rapid elasticity.
- Popular cloud-based services include e-mail, file storage, and file synchronization.
- Virtual desktop infrastructure (VDI) creates a virtual environment that can be accessed locally or on the cloud as a stored, persistent, or renewed standard or nonpersistent desktop image.
- File synchronization is used to keep multiple copies of a file or object in sync, commonly on diverse devices.

4.1 QUESTIONS

1. Company A uses several SaaS products such as Gmail and Google Docs, along with a customized private cloud for its proprietary apps. Which of the following best describes Company A's cloud computing strategy?

   A. Public cloud

   B. Hybrid cloud

   C. Community cloud

   D. VMM

2. Company B operates an around-the-clock real-time sales operation that supports both telephone and online orders. When an order is accepted, the inventory is updated in real time to avoid oversales. What element of the company's SLA with a CSP covers the requirements of this area of its operations?

   A. Bandwidth

   B. Backups and archives

   C. High availability

   D. Metered utilization

3. Your company is going to use cloud services to develop software, and the software will then be available as a cloud service. Which pairing accurately reflects what services will be used, in the correct order?

   A. IaaS, PaaS

   B. PaaS, SaaS

   C. SaaS, IaaS

   D. SaaS, PaaS

4. What is the term for the capability of a cloud service to expand or contract its resources, as required, to serve a subscriber's needs?

   A. DaaS

   B. Synchronization

   C. Rapid elasticity

   D. Metered utilization

5. Your company needs access to unlimited resources to support on-demand swings in resource requirements but wants to pay only for the resources actually used. What service arrangement is your company looking for?

   A. VDI

   B. IaaS

   C. Hybrid cloud

   D. Metered utilization

4.1 ANSWERS

1. **B**   A hybrid cloud combines public cloud (in this case, SaaS) and private cloud solutions.

2. **C**   High availability is a critical element of Company B's operations.

3. **B**   Platform as a Service (PaaS) is the use of a complete cloud-based software development environment. Software as a Service (SaaS) makes the software available for use via the cloud.

4. **C**   Rapid elasticity in a cloud environment is the ability to increase or decrease committed resources, as needed, to meet a subscriber's processing or storage requirements.

5. **D**   Metered utilization provides unlimited access to resources on a pay-for-what-you-use basis.

Objective 4.2   Summarize aspects of client-side virtualization

Virtualization enables a single physical host computer running specialized software to create virtual machines (saved in separate files), also known as *guests,* which replicate other computers, each with its own operating system, settings, apps, and data. Client-side virtualization refers to running a virtual machine (VM) on your local system (in contrast to VMs run elsewhere) regardless of whether the VM file itself might be stored locally or on a central server accessed via the network. The software used to create and manage VMs is known as a *hypervisor.*

Purpose of Virtual Machines

If you aren't familiar with virtualization, the idea can seem a little pointless at first. Why would you need to run an OS inside an OS? Here are a few of the biggest benefits:

- Going virtual enables companies to combine multiple servers onto fewer machines than in traditional computing. This offers tremendous savings on hardware purchases, electricity use, and the space used for computing.

- Because a VM is only a single file or two, a hacked system can rapidly be replaced with a snapshot (a backup) taken of the properly working VM. This is especially useful for getting critical servers back up quickly. Likewise, the minimal file numbers make it easy to duplicate a VM.

- The capability to run many operating systems on a single physical machine makes multiplatform testing and research easier and cheaper than with traditional setups.

Sandboxing

Sandboxing is a virtualization concept in which a newly developed or a suspicious program can be executed as a test or a trial on a virtualized computer. The program running in the sandbox has the resources it needs to completely simulate that it's running in a production environment without any of the risk that might mean.

Another virtual concept that is an extension of a sandbox is the *container.* Sandboxes are created in essentially the same size and with the same resources, which is often more than what's actually needed for its purpose. A container is a sandbox that is fitted to its task.

Another, perhaps lesser known, fact about sandboxes is that a virtual machine is essentially a sandbox, which is something you should know.

EXAM TIP You should know about sandboxes, containers, and VMs for the A+ Core 1 exam.

Test-Driven Development

Test-driven development (or *test development*) is a rapid application development (RAD) technique commonly performed on a VM, which is a perfectly safe environment for the development and testing of apps. In test development, small blocks of programming are tested against an environment that simulates the problem to be solved or an objective to be achieved. The short version of the test development process goes something like this: create a test, write a program, test the program, adapt the programming, and then repeat.

Application Virtualization

Application virtualization is a term that describes one of the major purposes and uses of virtualization in general. Application virtualization describes the interaction of a thin network client running in an application environment on a VM. The virtual environment hosting the virtual application could be a local or remote physical or virtual server. Application virtualization is able to overcome any environment conflicts on a local machine.

Virtual applications are optimized to run in virtual desktop environments on a local machine or in the cloud. A virtual application actually runs on a server but appears to be running on the VM. Another form of application virtualization is *application streaming*. In this method, only portions of an application, its code, configuration, and data are delivered to the VM and then only when they are needed.

Application virtualization managers can streamline the use of virtualized applications. For example, the Microsoft Application Virtualization (App-V) for Windows product manages the delivery of virtual applications to user environments. The virtual applications are stored on central servers and delivered in real time using the as-needed method described earlier. On the virtual desktop, a user accesses the virtual application in the same way as a locally installed application.

NOTE Other available virtual application managers include Citrix Virtual Apps, Parallels Remote Application Server, and the Microsoft Azure Virtual Desktop.

Many companies and organizations cling to older, "legacy" software (most likely with the claim that if it's still working, there's no reason to replace it), despite the fact that the hardware and software environments on which it was originally developed to run may no longer be available. *Cross-platform virtualization,* which is a software-based system emulator, allows these systems to run on a virtual machine configured to provide the required environment.

Virtualization provides the capability for legacy operating systems and applications to continue to be used until newer software can be developed or the processes are brought up to date.

> **EXAM TIP** For the A+ Core 1 exam, know and understand the purpose and use of VMs and their relationships with virtual apps, including sandboxes, application and test development, and VDI.

Resource Requirements

The latest versions of Windows, Linux, and macOS will support a hypervisor or a virtual machine manager (VMM). However, a hypervisor or VMM runs better on a computer with hardware virtualization support. If your computer's CPU and BIOS UEFI include hardware virtualization, it can be enabled or disabled in the system setup utility (see Figure 4.2-1).

Cross-Reference

Hardware virtualization is also covered in Domain 3.0, Objective 3.4.

> **NOTE** AMD and Intel include hardware virtualization to provide better performance when the CPU is supporting multiple VMs and operating systems. AMD's hardware virtualization features are Secure Virtual Machine (SVM) mode and AMD-V. Intel provides VT-x and Intel VT-d. VT-d is separate from VT-x and provides directed I/O (input/output) virtualization for better performance.

In addition to hardware virtualization, two other hardware requirements for efficient virtualization support are RAM and storage space. Each VM requires just as much RAM as the physical machine it's emulating. Even though the RAM assigned to a VM is allocated as needed, the host machine may need sufficient RAM itself to run the hypervisor and, in some cases, the host operating system and perhaps other software. Just how much RAM is needed in total typically requires a bit of research.

A VM can also take up a lot of storage space. A VM's files can consume a considerable amount of storage space because they include everything installed on the VM, which can

NX Mode	Enabled
SVM Mode	Enabled
Intel Virtualization Tech	[Enabled]
Intel VT-D Tech	[Enabled]

FIGURE 4.2-1 UEFI firmware settings for CPU virtualization support on AMD (top) and Intel (bottom) CPUs

amount to anywhere from a few megabytes to as much as dozens of gigabytes. Online calculators can be used to help you calculate the space requirements for configuring a VM in a variety of hypervisors or VMMs.

ADDITIONAL RESOURCES One virtualization calculator you could use is the "Virtualization Calculator" provided by WintelGuy.com at https://wintelguy.com/vmcalc.pl.

Emulator Requirements

In the virtualized world, some hardware is emulated and some is virtualized. Often emulation and virtualization are confused and thought to be the same thing. Although they have many similarities, emulation and virtualization have some differences in how they operate.

When a system imitates the actions of another, it is emulating that system. For example, suppose you have an old game such as *Duke Nukem* that you'd like to play again. Windows 11 won't run the software, but you can access an OS emulator, like OnWorks.com, that emulates a Windows 95 environment through your browser so you can play the game. Your system is still Windows 11, but you're running a browser that is running an emulator on a web application. Emulation is performed by software running on a native environment that mimics another environment. The difference is basically that virtualization runs independent of the base system whereas emulation runs on the base system.

Hypervisors emulate hardware to allow a guest OS to be able to access and use the hardware devices available on a host system. Otherwise, the hypervisor would need to include a device driver for any and all devices a guest OS supports. Emulating a generic version of a device driver allows the guest operating system and any application it runs to use the virtual hardware. The types of hardware being emulated are typically those that are widely supported and those for which the guest OS includes a driver.

In the emulation performed by a hypervisor, the commands given to the virtual desktop hardware device are converted into the appropriate commands used by the physical device.

EXAM TIP Understand that emulating another platform (using a laptop to run Sony PlayStation 5 games, for example) requires hardware several times more powerful than the platform being emulated.

Security Requirements

A virtual machine should be kept as secure as a physical computer. After all, with network and Internet connections present on almost any VM, it can be used (or misused) in the same way as a physical computer. Different users with different levels of access should be set up on a VM that will be used by multiple users. Strong passwords should be implemented.

Antivirus and anti-malware apps should be deployed and kept updated. OS updates should be performed as needed.

> **EXAM TIP**   Virtualized operating systems use the same security features as real ones. You still need to keep track of user names, passwords, permissions, and so on, just like on a normal system.

Network Requirements

The easiest way to network a computer that will be hosting one or more VMs is with the fastest wired Ethernet supported. If you want a wireless connection, you could use a wireless NIC that uses a PCIe slot. Using a USB network adapter is not recommended because of the limited support that USB devices have on most VM software.

Hypervisor

A *hypervisor*, also known as a *virtual machine manager (VMM)*, creates, runs, and manages VMs. There are two types of hypervisors: Type 1 and Type 2.

> **EXAM TIP**   Be sure to know the differences between Type 1 and Type 2 hypervisors.

A Type 1 hypervisor such as Hyper-V, VMware ESXi, or Citrix Hypervisor (formerly known as Citrix XenServer) runs directly on computer hardware in place of a standard operating system. A Type 1 hypervisor is also known as a "bare-metal" hypervisor because there's no other software between it and the hardware. VMs running server operating systems are run on Type 1 hypervisors.

A Type 2 hypervisor such as Oracle VM VirtualBox or VMware Workstation is run on a standard operating system (Linux, Windows, or macOS). Thus, Type 2 hypervisors have an additional layer of software compared to Type 1 hypervisors (see Figure 4.2-2 for an example). Most types of client-side virtualization use Type 2 hypervisors.

> **NOTE**   Although you install Hyper-V after installing Windows Server or enable it after installing a Windows 10 or Windows 11 edition that includes it, it is considered a Type 1 hypervisor. Here's why: after Hyper-V is installed/enabled, it turns the Windows edition that was installed first into a VM running under Hyper-V, and additional VMs can be created. To learn more about the differences between Hyper-V running on Windows versus Hyper-V running on Windows Server, see https://docs.microsoft.com and search for "Hyper-V."

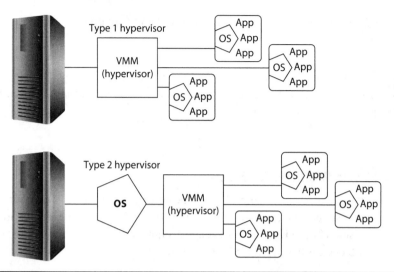

FIGURE 4.2-2   Type 1 hypervisor (top) compared to Type 2 hypervisor (bottom)

Installing a Hypervisor and Creating a Virtual Machine

Installing a third-party hypervisor is like installing any other software—download and execute the hypervisor software and follow its setup wizard. On a Windows system that includes Hyper-V, you can enable it in the Windows Features dialog box (see Figure 4.2-3), which you reach via Control Panel | Programs and Features applet | Turn Windows Features On or Off. After enabling Hyper-V, reboot the system.

After you've installed your hypervisor of choice, you'll have a virtual machine manager that acts as the primary place to create, start, stop, save, and delete guest virtual machines. On pretty much any VMM, you create a new VM by clicking New | Virtual Machine and completing the wizard that opens (see Figure 4.2-4). Most hypervisors have presets to ensure your guest OS has the virtual hardware it needs.

Installing the Guest Operating System

Once you've created the new guest VM, it's time to install a guest operating system. Would you like to use Microsoft Windows in your virtual machine? No problem, but know that Windows (and any other licensed software you install) requires a valid license.

If you don't already have installation media, most VMMs can just treat any ISO file (such as the one you'd use to make your own installation media) as the virtual machine's optical drive. If the VMM recognizes your installation media (see Figure 4.2-5), it may configure the virtual hardware settings (amount of RAM, virtual hard drive size, and so on) automatically; otherwise, you need to set sensible values for these (you can still change them after the VM is created). Next, set the size of the virtual drive (see Figure 4.2-6).

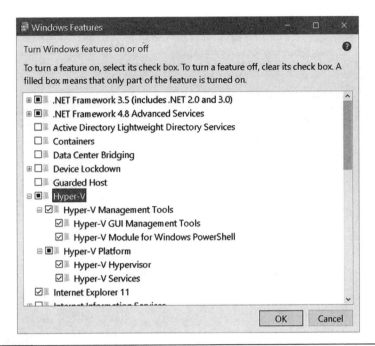

FIGURE 4.2-3   Enabling Hyper-V in Windows

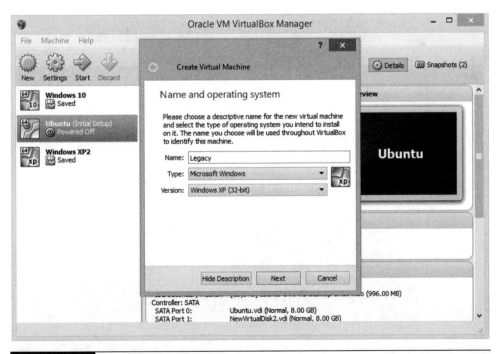

FIGURE 4.2-4   Creating a new VM in Oracle VirtualBox

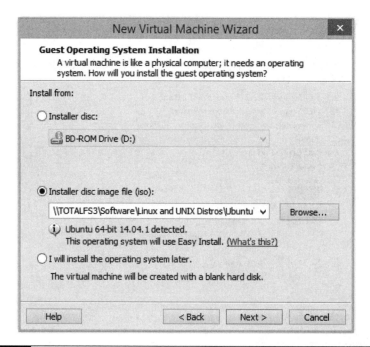

FIGURE 4.2-5   Installer recognizing selected installation media

FIGURE 4.2-6   Setting the virtual drive size

EXAM TIP   After you have set up a VM, installing an operating system into it is just like installing an OS on a normal computer.

You'll also be prompted to name the VM and indicate where to store its data files. If you specified installation media, you'll also have some time to burn while the OS installs. After configuration and installation, you can stop, start, pause, or delete the VM, add or remove virtual hardware, or just interact with the OS and other software inside it.

 NOTE   Use descriptive names for virtual machines, such as "64-Win10-Mark." This will save you a lot of confusion when you have multiple VMs on a single host.

Using a VM is almost exactly like using a real system, except it's contained in a window and some hotkeys differ. VMware Workstation, for example, replaces CTRL-ALT-DELETE with CTRL-ALT-INSERT by default (so you can still use CTRL-ALT-DELETE on your desktop). That, and you can adapt your *virtual desktop* to changing needs without a trip to the store: a good hypervisor can add and remove virtual hard drives, virtual network cards, virtual RAM, and so on. Keep in mind that USB drive support varies between hypervisors and may require special settings or have limited support for USB 3.0 and faster versions.

REVIEW

Objective 4.2: Summarize aspects of client-side virtualization

- Virtualization enables companies to use fewer servers to perform tasks, provides for faster backup, and enables multiplatform testing on a single computer.
- Virtual machines (VMs) can provide for sandboxes and development and testing environments.
- Intel and AMD processors support hardware virtualization with VT-x and AMD-v, which is enabled or disable in BIOS/UEFI setup.
- Virtualization requires sufficient RAM and disk space for each VM as well as for the host OS or hypervisor.
- Hypervisors emulate a wide range of hardware without specific drivers.
- VMs require exactly the same levels of security (passwords, updates, and so on) as the physical computers they replace.
- Application virtualization provides support for legacy applications and cross-platform compatibilities.
- Type 1 hypervisors (a.k.a. bare-metal hypervisors) are installed directly on the hardware and are typically used for VMs in production applications.

- Type 2 hypervisors are installed on an operating system and are typically used for experimenting and educational purposes.
- Hyper-V is a Type 1 hypervisor available on Windows 10 and later that is enabled through the Turn Windows Features On or Off option in the Programs and Features Control Panel applet.

4.2 QUESTIONS

1. What is the term for a virtual machine (VM) environment used to test out new programs in an isolated area away from critical servers and resources?

    A. Type 1 virtualization

    B. Sandbox

    C. VMM

    D. Type 2 virtualization

2. Which of the following statements are true?

    A. A virtual machine is a computer that is walled off from the physical computer on which the virtual machine is running.

    B. Virtual machines provide the capability of running multiple machine instances, each with its own operating system.

    C. The downside of virtual machine technologies is that having resources indirectly addressed means there is some level of overhead.

    D. A and B.

    E. All of the above.

3. Company D has set up virtualization on several late-model Intel and AMD systems running high-performance processors using the recommended settings in the hypervisor for each VM, but the VMs are running very slowly. Which of the following is the most likely cause?

    A. Hardware virtualization support is not enabled in the UEFI firmware.

    B. VMs are using too much RAM.

    C. Hardware virtualization support is not enabled in the OS.

    D. VMs are using too much disk space.

4. Customer E is running Windows 10 Pro and wants to install a Linux-based VM in Hyper-V. Which of the following must the customer do for this to work? (Choose two.)

    A. Turn on Hyper-V in Windows Features.

    B. Run Windows Update.

    C. Scan the host system for viruses.

    D. Restart the system.

5. What operating system can be installed as a VM guest OS?

   A. Windows 10

   B. Linux distro

   C. Windows 11

   D. macOS

   E. All of the above

4.2 ANSWERS

1. **D** Type 2 virtualization runs within an installed operating system and relays requests to the hardware to the host operating system, whereas Type 1 virtualization directly interfaces with the computer's hardware.

2. **E** A VM is segregated from the physical computer, can be one of many instances running on a physical computer with its own OS, and can generate additional operational overhead.

3. **A** High-end Intel and AMD processors have support for hardware virtualization. However, if it is not enabled in the firmware, virtualization would run very slowly.

4. **A D** For this to work, hardware virtualization support must first be enabled in the UEFI/BIOS. Second, Hyper-V needs to be turned on in Windows Features. Finally, enabling Hyper-V requires the system to be restarted.

5. **E** Any of these OSs can be installed in a VM.

Hardware and Network Troubleshooting

Objective 5.1 # Given a scenario, apply the best practice methodology to resolve problems.

The CompTIA *best practice methodology,* also known as the *troubleshooting methodology,* provides you with a process you can use to identify, solve, and document any technology problem.

As you apply this methodology in your day-to-day work (and to scenarios presented in the CompTIA A+ 220-1101 exam), remember to always consider corporate policies, procedures, and impacts before implementing changes.

The CompTIA Troubleshooting Methodology

The methodology has six steps, as shown in the following table. Note that the descriptions and the bullet points are from the official CompTIA objectives with a few comments of our own.

Step #	Description	Details, Tips, and Notes
1	Identify the problem.	• Gather information from the user, identify user changes, and, if applicable, perform backups before making changes. • Inquire regarding environmental or infrastructure changes. Computers, peripherals, and devices are composed of subsystems (hardware, software, and firmware), so look at all possible causes. Conduct user interviews in a professional manner without any attempt to cast blame.
2	Establish a theory of probable cause (question the obvious).	• If necessary, conduct external or internal research based on symptoms. Check vendor and third-party websites and forums, system and peripheral documentation, and internal help desk records. Create a list of possible causes, starting with the simple and moving to the less obvious.

Step #	Description	Details, Tips, and Notes
3	Test the theory to determine cause.	• Once the theory is confirmed, determine the next steps to resolve problem. • If theory is not confirmed, reestablish a new theory or escalate. Change one item at a time and then test the device. If the device still doesn't work, restore it to its previous setting and change another item that is on the list of potential causes. If your scope of knowledge or responsibility is limited, make sure you provide all information to the next-level tech for follow-up.
4	Establish a plan of action to resolve the problem and implement the solution.	• Refer to the vendor's instructions for guidance The plan should list each step necessary. You might need additional resources such as known-good replacement parts. Refer to the vendor's instructions for guidance.
5	Verify full system functionality and, if applicable, implement preventive measures.	Making sure the system works after the solution is applied is essential, but this task is often not performed. Preventive measures help organizations from needing to solve problems repeatedly.
6	Document the findings, actions, and outcomes.	Recording symptoms, solutions, and results helps minimize future outbreaks of similar problems, helps fellow techs who encounter the same issue, and helps track the troubleshooting history of a device.

 EXAM TIP   It is likely you will encounter exam questions directly related to the best practice troubleshooting methodology. Know it well!

REVIEW

Objective 5.1: Given a scenario, apply the best practice methodology to resolve problems   Use the six-part CompTIA best practice methodology to troubleshoot and solve technology problems:

1. Identify the problem.
2. Establish a theory of probable cause (question the obvious).

3. Test the theory to determine cause.

4. Establish a plan of action to resolve the problem and implement the solution.

5. Verify full system functionality and, if applicable, implement preventive measures.

6. Document the findings, actions, and outcomes.

5.1 QUESTIONS

1. After you establish a plan of action, what should you do next?
   A. Test the theory.
   B. Verify full system functionality.
   C. Document findings.
   D. Establish a theory of probable cause.

2. When should you question the obvious?
   A. When identifying the problem
   B. When documenting findings
   C. When testing the theory
   D. When establishing a theory

3. During the process of troubleshooting a printer problem, you created a document that lists the printer drivers needed, how you installed them, and how you tested the printers and the systems involved. Which of the following steps did you perform?
   A. Documenting findings
   B. Establishing a theory of probable cause
   C. Verifying full system functionality
   D. Testing the theory

4. Which step of the troubleshooting methodology is considered to be step 1?
   A. Identify the problem.
   B. Establish a theory of probable cause.
   C. Test the theory to determine cause.
   D. Verify full system functionality and, if applicable, implement preventive measures.

5. What should you always do first before implementing changes?
   A. Conduct external and internal research based on symptoms.
   B. Implement preventive measures.
   C. Consider corporate policies, procedures, and impacts.
   D. Establish a new theory or escalate.

5.1 ANSWERS

1. **B** Establishing a plan of action is step 4, and verifying full system functionality is step 5.

2. **D** Questioning the obvious is a part of establishing a theory of probably cause (step 2).

3. **A** Documenting the findings, which is the final step of the troubleshooting methodology, refers to noting in detail the solutions used and how they were applied.

4. **A** Identifying the problem is step 1.

5. **C** Always consider corporate policies, procedures, and impacts before implementing a change.

Objective 5.2 # Given a scenario, troubleshoot problems related to motherboards, RAM, CPU, and power

Motherboards, RAM, CPUs, and power are the core components of any computer. Troubleshooting and diagnosing a computer problem should start by looking at these subsystems.

Troubleshooting Common Symptoms

Troubleshooting problems with motherboards, RAM, CPUs, and power can be difficult because these components have a number of common symptoms that can have multiple causes. In this objective, you will learn about these symptoms, typical causes, and leading solutions.

The following sections categorize common PC issues identified by one or more symptoms you may encounter on the A+ Core 1 exam (220-1101). These issues and symptoms are listed in the Core 1 exam objectives of the current exam, but a few leftovers from the previous exam (220-1001) are included because you might also see them on the current exam. Information is provided to help you identify the likely issue(s) and solution(s) for each symptom.

Power-On Self-Test Beep Codes

The very first thing a computer does when it is powered on is to run a self-test of its essential components, which are those configured in the BIOS or UEFI. This test has the obvious name of power-on self-test, or as it's commonly called, the POST. Many later systems will display any errors they encounter, but just as many still use POST beep codes, which are just what they sound like (no pun intended). To inform you of a problem encountered during the POST, a predefined serious of internal beeps are sounded. The number of beeps and, in some cases, the

TABLE 5.2-1   Examples of POST Beep Codes from Different BIOS Publishers

| Provider | Beep Signals | | | |
	BIOS ROM	CPU	RAM	Video card
AMI BIOS	9 short	5 short	1 short	1 long + 2 short
AST BIOS	9 short	1 short	1 long + 5 short	1 long + 2 short
Dell	1 short	7 short	4 short	6 short
IBM Bios	2 short	1 long + 1 short		1 long + 2 or 3 short

length of the beep tone indicate audibly what problem the POST encountered. This problem is the first one encountered should there be more discovered later.

One long-time nuisance concerning the POST beep codes is that there is no standard format or pattern to them. Each BIOS publisher uses its own unique code scheme. So, as long as you use the same BIOS on all your computers, there'll be no problems. Table 5.2-1 lists examples of some of the more commonly used BIOS-based POST beep code schemes.

The specific beep code symptoms you should know for the test are included in the following table:

Suspected Issue(s)	Possible Solution(s)
Computer doesn't boot and POST beep codes sound.	POST codes vary with the BIOS providers; refer to the BIOS documentation for the fault identified by the code sounded.
POST beep codes sound, indicating a bad or loose video card.	Power down the system and reconnect the video card. Turn on the system and retest. If the problem persists, replace the video card.
POST beep codes sound, indicating bad or missing RAM.	Power down the system and check RAM. Replace bad RAM or insert new RAM, turn on the system, and retest.

 EXAM TIP   You don't need to memorize the beep code patterns, just know what they are and why you'd hear them. Also be familiar with the beep code symptoms.

Proprietary Crash Screens

The two most infamous screen displays that indicate a system halt or crash due to a serious hardware or software fault are the halt error message display with a blue backdrop, commonly called the *blue screen of death,* or the *BSoD,* on Windows operating systems, and the never-ending spinning pinwheel, commonly known as the *spinning pinwheel of death,* or the *SPoD,* on both Windows and macOS (although it's in color on macOS).

The BSoD error typically indicates two general types of problems: device drivers and/or hardware problems. Another, less common cause is a misconfiguration with overclocking settings. An SPoD indicates on either OS that an application has stopped responding.

Another error condition display is the black screen on boot-up, which doesn't really have a sinister sounding acronym. The issues detailed in the following table relate to this problem.

Suspected Issue(s)	Possible Solution(s)
Black or blank display at or after boot-up	Turn on the display. Check the monitor's power cord.
BSoD: multiple causes	Look up the STOP error code to determine the cause and solution. If the system reboots before you can read the STOP error code, see "Intermittent Shutdowns" for a solution.
macOS SPoD: unresponsive app	Shut down the system and add RAM (if possible). Then restart the system.
	Free up space on the macOS system drive to achieve 10 percent or more free space.
	If a particular app is unresponsive, delete its .plist file.
	Use Force Quit (OPTION-COMMAND-ESC) to stop an unresponsive app.
Bad video driver	If the display works during POST but not after the OS loads, reload the OS in Safe Mode and install an updated video driver.

No Power

This can be one of the absolutely easiest failures to diagnose. If the computer appears to not have power, the first thing to check is that the power cord is inserted into a power source outlet. However, there are other causes, as detailed in the following table.

Suspected Issue(s)	Possible Solution(s)
Power cord is not properly attached.	Reattach the power cord.
Power switch on power supply is turned off.	Turn on the power supply switch.
Power supply with a manual voltage switch has an incorrect voltage setting.	Turn off the power supply switch; change the switch to the correct voltage.

Sluggish Performance

There are many reasons and causes for a Windows system to run slow, lag on some actions or commands, or just run like a slug, including too many programs in the startup list, too many active programs, a damaged Registry, and the swap space being too small. The following table identifies some suspected issues and possible solutions relating to sluggish performance by a PC.

Suspected Issue(s)	Possible Solution(s)
Overheated CPU	See the next section, "Overheating."
Junk files	Temporary files, caches, cookies and Internet histories, as well as a bloated Recycle Bin can quickly add up and occupy a large amount of storage, which could be needed urgently if you have little hard drive capacity (for example, paging file). Use the Windows *Disk Cleanup* app to remove unneeded files.
Malware	Malware and virus software may be running in the background. Scan the system with antivirus/anti-malware software.

Overheating

Heat can be the mortal enemy of a computer. Too much heat can kill a CPU; too little heat can cause slow response. Even the right amount of heat, but on the wrong components, can cause a computer to perform poorly or fail altogether. The following table lists many of the suspected issues and possible solutions relating to overheating.

Suspected Issue(s)	Possible Solution(s)
Power supply fan has failed.	If the fan is not turning, shut off the system and replace the power supply.
Active heatsink on CPU is dirty.	Clean the active heatsink fan and fins with compressed air or a computer-safe vacuum.
Active heatsink fan on CPU has failed or is disconnected.	If the fan is not turning, shut off the system and check the fan connection to the motherboard. If the fan is connected, replace the active heatsink fan.
Air intakes on case are clogged.	Clean the air intakes and fan.
Case or CPU fans are turning too slowly.	Use the PC Health or Hardware Monitor function in the BIOS/UEFI firmware to check fan performance.
System is overclocked.	Reset the system and memory clock speeds to the normal settings in the BIOS/UEFI firmware; if the CPU is overclocked, reset its clock speed to the normal setting.

Burning Smell and Smoke

If you smell something like burning rubber or see smoke coming from your computer, it can't be a good thing, but it may not be as bad as you may think. First of all, it's not an operating temperature problem. If the computer continues to run, it must be within the monitored operating ranges. Therefore, the problem is most likely to be something else. The following table describes some possible issues and their solutions for when you smell or see smoke from a PC.

Suspected Issue(s)	Possible Solution(s)
There's a bad or loose connector.	Check power connectors on internal devices and the motherboard for scorch signs. Replace burned connectors or snug/loose connectors.
Peripheral device inside case is failing.	Operate the device outside of the case. If the odor continues, replace the device.
There's a component failure caused by a capacitor failure.	Check for blown, burnt, or distended capacitors. Replace damaged components that can be replaced.
There's a component failure caused by incorrect voltage levels.	Power down the system and check the connectors to the drives, motherboard, and other components. Make sure the power connectors are not backward.

Intermittent Shutdowns

When a computer starts up, one of the system checks performed is the Power Good (PG) check. The power supply unit (PSU) checks the voltages on its output lines, and if all are carrying the correct voltages, which means the PSU is working correctly, the motherboard is sent a Power Good signal of +5 V and the boot process can continue. The following table provides possible solutions for a few of the suspected issues that may be causing a PC to shut down intermittently.

Suspected Issue(s)	Possible Solution(s)
Power Good line on power supply is out of spec.	Power Good (PG) is the wire at position 8 (usually gray). Normal voltage is +5 VDC. If the PG voltage drops too low, the system will reboot.
CPU is overheated.	See "Overheating," earlier in this objective.
System is overclocked.	See "Overheating," earlier in this objective.
Mobile device battery is faulty.	Test with a known-good battery and possibly replace the faulty battery.
Windows is configured to automatically reboot after BSoD error.	To disable the BSoD automatic restart, run **SystemPropertiesAdvanced.exe** from a command prompt and in Settings for Startup and Recovery, uncheck Automatically Restart.
Surge protector is faulty.	Test with a known-good unit and possibly replace the unit.

Application Crashes

If an installed application does not start, starts and then stops right away, or freezes up or "crashes" while running, but not always in the same place, you definitely have a application issue. The following table identifies a few of the issues that could be causing an application to crash and possible solutions to solve that issue.

Suspected Issue(s)	Possible Solution(s)
Windows app is crashing or not starting.	Enable Windows Store auto-update.
Required resources are not available.	Too many applications are running in the background; close unnecessary jobs.
Updates installed are incompatible with existing device drivers.	Update device drivers.
Faulty devices are causing I/O failures.	Test devices the software is interfacing with to find the faulty device.
Corrupted system files are causing app to fail.	Run the System File Checker tool (DISM.exe) to check for corrupted files and repair them.

Grinding Noise

Other than the hum of the case fan, there should be no loud noises, especially grinding noises, coming from a system case. There is typically only one major thing that could be causing the problem: the power supply or motherboard components are failing, as explained in the following table.

Suspected Issue(s)	Possible Solution(s)
Smoke or a burning smell from the PC and the power supply or motherboard components have failed.	Replace the burnt or smoking component. Should the component be on the motherboard, replace the motherboard. If the smoke is coming from the power supply, it should be replaced immediately.

Capacitor Swelling

Any component on the motherboard that becomes misshaped, as in enlarged or distended, or appears to be burnt may need to be replaced, as explained in the following table.

Suspected Issue(s)	Possible Solution(s)
Swelling of capacitors after installation on motherboard or components	Replace capacitors with solid ones (requires desoldering/ resoldering), replace replaceable components, or replace the motherboard, if needed.

Inaccurate System Date/Time

There is a difference between the system time (kept by the system clock) and the time displayed in the lower-right corner of the Windows GUI. If the system time fails to keep the actual data and time correctly, look at the CMOS battery. As indicated in the following table, the problem may be as simple as the motherboard battery.

Suspected Issue(s)	Possible Solution(s)
Bad battery on motherboard	Power down the system and replace the CMOS battery (usually a CR2032). Turn on the system, enter BIOS/UEFI firmware setup, reset date/time and settings, save changes, and restart the system.

Other Symptoms

The following issues and solutions are leftovers from the previous A+ Core 1 exam (220-1001), but you may still encounter them on the current (220-1101) exam.

Attempts to Boot to Incorrect Device

Suspected Issue(s)	Possible Solution(s)
Nonbootable optical disc or USB flash drive inserted	Remove nonbootable removable media and restart the system.
Incorrect boot sequence settings	Enter BIOS/UEFI firmware setup, reset the boot sequence to include a bootable drive, and restart the system.
Windows or other OS boot drive corrupt	Repair the boot drive using OS tools.

System Lockups

Suspected Issue(s)	Possible Solution(s)
Overheating system	See "Overheating," earlier in this objective.
Corrupt Windows files	Run System File Checker (sfc.exe) and use it to replace corrupt files.
Corrupt temporary files	Delete the contents of \Temp folder (Windows).
Bad RAM	Power down the system, remove RAM, insert one stick/bank, and restart the system. If the system runs and doesn't lock up, swap RAM. If one stick/bank is the problem, replace it.

Intermittent Device Failures

Suspected Issue(s)	Possible Solution(s)
USB device: power supply failing to provide enough power to port	Replace the power supply with a higher-rated model. Connect USB devices to the powered hub.
Internal drives: loose or defective power connectors or power splitters	Replace power splitters. Replace the power supply if power connectors or cables are broken or cracked.
Internal or external devices: power supply voltages out of spec	Use a power supply tester, the PC Health/System Diagnostics window in BIOS/UEFI, or a multimeter to check power supply power levels. Replace the power supply with a higher-rated unit if power levels are out of spec.

Fans Spin, No Power to Other Devices

Suspected Issue(s)	Possible Solution(s)
Secondary power to motherboard (4/8-pin) connector loose or disconnected	Power down the system, plug in the connector, and then power up the system.

Indicator Lights

Suspected Issue(s)	Possible Solution(s)
Indicator lights not working	Power down the system, check the front panel connectors on the motherboard, and reconnect any loose ones as needed. Power up the system.

Log Entries and Error Messages

Suspected Issue(s)	Possible Solution(s)
Error messages (BSoD or others) are displayed in OS system logs.	Open event logs using OS utilities (Event Viewer in Windows, for example) and check for problems and solutions. Check error messages for problems and use the details to research solutions.

EXAM TIP Given a scenario, be prepared to identify and troubleshoot the common systems covered in this objective and listed in the following "Review" section.

REVIEW

Objective 5.2: Given a scenario, troubleshoot problems related to motherboards, RAM, CPU, and power   Common symptoms of problems related to motherboards, RAM, CPUs, and power include the following:

- Power-on self-test (POST) beep codes
- Proprietary crash screens
- No power
- Sluggish performance
- Overheating
- Burning smell and smoke
- Intermittent shutdowns
- Application crashes
- Grinding noise
- Capacitor swelling
- Inaccurate system date/time
- Other symptoms:
  - Attempts to boot to incorrect device
  - System lockups
  - Intermittent device failures
  - Fans spin but no power to other devices
  - Indicator lights
  - Log entries and error messages

Keep in mind that each of these symptoms usually has multiple potential causes.

5.2 QUESTIONS

1. Which of the following causes for overheating can be tested in the system BIOS/UEFI settings?
   A. Clogged air intakes
   B. Power supply fan failure
   C. Case or CPU fan speed slow
   D. GPU overclocking

2. What happens if a power supply is set for 230 VAC and you connect a 115 VAC line to it and turn on the computer?

   A. Overvoltage error appears on screen.

   B. Computer cannot start.

   C. Signal lights turn on but fans do not run.

   D. Smoke and flames appear.

3. You have tested the power supply on a computer that is continuously rebooting, and the Power Good line and other voltage levels test out OK. What else should you check?

   A. Whether Windows is configured to automatically reboot after a STOP error

   B. Whether Windows always reboots automatically after a STOP error

   C. Whether the CTRL-ALT-DEL keys on the keyboard are stuck

   D. Whether the power switch on the power supply is stuck

4. What should you do if a customer's computer resets the BIOS/UEFI time and settings incorrectly every time her computer is powered on?

   A. Reset the boot sequence order.

   B. Check log entries and error logs.

   C. Perform a soft reset.

   D. Replace the CMOS battery.

5. A customer reports that his computer keeps booting to an incorrect device. Which of the following will most likely remedy this situation? (Choose two.)

   A. Change the boot order in the BIOS/UEFI.

   B. Remove any nonbootable disc or USB flash drive.

   C. Run System File Checker (sfc.exe).

   D. Check front panel connectors and reconnect as needed.

5.2 ANSWERS

1. **C**   The BIOS/UEFI screen, commonly called PC Health or Hardware Monitor, displays fan speeds as well as system temperature.

2. **B**   The computer cannot start because the power supply is set for a voltage level twice what is being provided.

3. **A**   Windows can be configured to restart the system immediately in the event of a STOP error; to enable diagnosis of the STOP error, restart the system in Safe Mode and change this setting in System properties.

4. **D**   Power down system and replace the CMOS battery (usually a CR2032). Turn on the system, enter BIOS/UEFI setup, reset BIOS/UEFI time and settings, save your changes, and restart the system.

5. **A B**   Enter BIOS/UEFI setup, reset the boot sequence to include the correct bootable drive, and restart. Remove nonbootable removable media and restart the system.

Given a scenario, troubleshoot and diagnose problems with storage drives and RAID arrays

Hard drives and RAID arrays are where programs and data alike are stored. Solving problems with these subsystems is essential to keeping workstations and servers in order.

Troubleshooting Common Symptoms

The sections in this objective present common symptoms of storage problems, along with the typical causes and leading solutions.

Light-Emitting Diode (LED) Status Indicators

Hard drive light is always on.	Restart the system manually by removing the power source.

Grinding Noises

Fan producing whining noise	System overheating; check cooling system.
Message displayed: • No boot device available • Boot device not found	Unplug AC power. Press Power button for 15 seconds and then restore BIOS/UEFI settings.

Clicking Sounds

HDD failure imminent; noise due to attempts to reread failing sectors.	Back up the drive, replace the drive, and restore data from the backup.

Bootable Device Not Found/Failure to Boot

Drive not bootable	Change the boot order.
Damaged boot sector	Repair the boot sector with OS utilities.
Nonbootable optical or USB removable-media drives inserted	Remove nonbootable media and restart or change the boot order.

Data Loss or Corruption

\<filename\> is not recognized or file format is not recognized.	Run disk error utility, such as SFC or CHKDSK, or restore file from backup.

RAID Failure

RAID controller disabled	Reenable the RAID controller in the BIOS/UEFI firmware setup or add-on card setup.
Bad or loose data cable	Shut down the system, reconnect the data cable, and power up the system. Replace the data cable if the problem persists.
Loose power cable	Shut down the system, reconnect the power cable, and power up the system.
One or more drives in array failed	If using RAID 1, RAID 5, or RAID 10 with one failed drive, replace the drive and rebuild the array from the surviving drives. If using RAID 0 with one failed drive, replace the drive and restore data from backups (array data is lost).

S.M.A.R.T. Failure

Hard drive prediction errors indicate drive failure imminent.	Back up the drive, replace the drive, and restore data to the new drive from the backup.

Extended Read/Write Times and Read/Write Failure

Loose data cable	Shut down the system (if an internal drive), reattach the data cable, and power up the system.
Bad data cable	Shut down the system (if an internal drive), replace the data cable, and power up the system.
Drive failure	Back up the drive, replace the drive, and restore from the backup.
Incorrect speed setting for SATA drive in BIOS/UEFI firmware setup	Check the drive specs and verify the correct SATA drive type/speed setting in BIOS/UEFI firmware setup.
Cable not suitable for SATA 6 Gbps	Shut down the system, replace the SATA cable with a SATA 6-Gbps cable, and restart system.
Bad data cable	Shut down the system (if an internal drive), replace the data cable, and power up the system.

Lack of RAM forcing disk thrashing (virtual memory)	Add RAM to the system.
Long wait time when accessing folders and files Repeated read attempts before successful access	Typical signs of hard drive failure. Test with known-good drive and possibly replace.
Fewer input/output operations (IOPs)	Analyze disk with defrag, disk analysis reporting, or integrity checks.

Missing Drives in OS

Power and data cables are not connected (internal).	Shut down the system, reconnect power and/or data cables, and power up the system.
Incorrect SATA port setting.	Change the SATA port setting to non-RAID (AHCI on most recent systems).
USB or Thunderbolt cable is disconnected.	Reconnect the cable to the port and drive and then retry.
USB port doesn't provide enough power to run the drive.	Plug the drive into the root hub on the system or into a self-powered hub.
File system is not recognized by host operating system.	Windows cannot use drives prepared with file systems normally used by Linux or macOS.
Drive is missing from OS.	Check BIOS/UEFI settings, format the drive, and check hardware connections. Check Disk Management in Windows and try to initialize.

Other Symptoms

OS Not Found

Wrong boot device selected	Change the boot order.
Boot files corrupt	Repair the boot sector with OS utilities.

 EXAM TIP Be sure to know the symptoms, meanings, and solutions covered in this objective and listed in the following "Review" section.

REVIEW

Objective 5.3: Given a scenario, troubleshoot and diagnose problems with storage drives and RAID arrays   Hard drives and RAID arrays can have a variety of problems, symptoms of which include the following:

- LED indicators
- Grinding noises
- Clicking sounds
- Bootable device not found
- Data loss/corruption
- RAID failure
- Self-monitoring, Analysis, and Reporting Technology (S.M.A.R.T.) failure
- Extended read/write times
- Missing drives in OS
- OS not found

Keep in mind that many of these symptoms can have more than one possible cause.

5.3 QUESTIONS

1. A drive in a RAID 0 array stops working. After you replace the defective drive, how can you recover from this error?

    A. Rebuild the array from the working drive.

    B. Restore the most recent backups to the array.

    C. Use Disk Management to rebuild the array.

    D. Replace both drives; the other drive will probably fail right away as well.

2. A 1-TB USB portable drive works fine on a desktop computer running Windows but will not work when plugged into a Windows laptop computer on battery power. What is the most likely cause?

    A. Drive must be reformatted to be recognized by the laptop.

    B. Drive is too large to be used by the laptop.

    C. Laptop USB port is not providing enough power for the drive.

    D. Laptop and desktop computers use different versions of Windows.

3. A computer fails to reboot after a Windows update. The update was provided on a nonbootable USB drive. Which of the following should you try first to get the computer to boot?

   A. Reinstall the update from a bootable USB drive.

   B. Reinstall the update from an optical disc.

   C. Scan the USB drive for viruses.

   D. Disconnect the USB drive and restart the computer.

4. A customer's computer displays a "RAID not found" error on bootup. What can you do to troubleshoot this issue?

   A. Free up space on the system drive to achieve 10 percent more free space.

   B. Reenable the RAID controller in the BIOS/UEFI firmware or add-on card setup.

   C. Repair the boot sector with OS utilities.

   D. Add more RAM to the system.

5. Which of the following indicates drive failure is imminent? (Choose the best answer.)

   A. S.M.A.R.T.

   B. BSoD/pin wheel

   C. Loud clicking noises

   D. Event Viewer alerts

5.3 ANSWERS

1. **B**   RAID 0, despite the name, does not include any redundancy; the data is striped across both drives to improve performance, and thus the loss of a single drive wipes out the array's contents.

2. **C**   Some laptop USB ports do not provide the full power level needed for external hard drives when running on battery power; as a workaround, some drives include a Y-cable to pull power from a second port, or the drive can be plugged into a self-powered USB hub.

3. **D**   Some systems are configured to have a USB drive as the first bootable device to enable diagnostics or operating system installations; by disconnecting the drive, you cause the system to use the next bootable device as set in the BIOS/UEFI firmware.

4. **B**   For "RAID not found" errors, you should reenable the RAID controller in the BIOS setup or add-on card setup. You can also try reconnecting or replacing data and power cables if you encounter loose or bad cables.

5. **A**   S.M.A.R.T. hard drive prediction errors indicate drive failure is imminent.

Objective 5.4 # Given a scenario, troubleshoot video, projector, and display issues

Desktop and laptop computer users interact with their displays as much as with their keyboards or pointing devices. Getting display problems fixed quickly is a high priority.

Troubleshooting Video, Projector, and Display Issues

The sections in this objective cover common symptoms of video, projector, and display issues, along with the typical causes and solutions.

Incorrect Data Source

Required codec missing	Codec files are necessary for encoding and decoding a digital data. Configure Windows Media Player to download the codecs automatically.
Corrupted video or graphic file	Video or graphic files saved on a hard drive, SD card, USB drive, and so on can be corrupted or broken due to malware, a system crash, or malfunction of the playback device. Use a video conversion or repair utility such as VLC media player of Windows Media Player to restore the file.
Data content not compatible with file extension	Use a video file converter to reformat the data.

Physical Cabling Issues

Loose or disconnected video cable	Power down the system and the display, reconnect the video cable, and restart the display and system.

Burned-Out Bulb

Burned-out bulb in projector	Replace the bulb.

Fuzzy or Distorted Image

Corrupted video card (GPU) drivers	Reinstall the latest drivers.

Display Burn-In

Stationary design elements onscreen leave "ghosts" behind on plasma displays.	Don't use plasma displays as monitors. Play a full-screen slideshow for a few hours to remove moderate burn-in.

Dead Pixels

Pixels dead due to manufacturing defects	Replace the display under manufacturer's warranty.
Pixel stuck in "off" mode	Gently massage pixel with a pencil eraser to see if it turns on.

Flashing Screen/Flickering Image

Flashing screen image	Check refresh rate, device driver, or graphics card.
CCFL backlight failing	Replace the backlight or display.

Incorrect Color Display

Overheating video card (GPU)	Check the fan on the video card and replace the fan or card if defective. If the card is overclocked, reset it to normal operations.

Audio Issues

No sound	Check the volume control and speaker connections.
Audio not working after installing update	Run the Windows Playing Audio troubleshooter.
Audio loss intermittently	Check the speaker connection.
Audio services not running	Check the sound settings and device driver in Task Manager.

Dim Image

Backlight failure	Repair or replace the display.
Inverter failure	Replace the inverter or display.
Display brightness too low	Increase brightness.

Intermittent Projector Shutdowns

Intermittent shutdown	Replace the filter.
Projector overheating	Clean the air vents.
Flashing screen and intermittent shutoff	Check the status indicators.
Projector overheated due to clogged air vents	Turn off the projector, vacuum out the air vents, replace or clean the filters, if present, and restart.
Projector fan failure	Repair or replace the projector.
GPU (video card) fan failure	Replace the fan or video card.

Other Symptoms

Artifacts

Overheating video card (GPU)	Check the fan on the video card and replace the fan or card if defective. If the card is overclocked, reset it to normal operations.
Overheating computer	Check the fan on the CPU heatsink and replace the fan if defective. Clean the case fans and air intakes.

Distorted Geometry

Overheating video card (GPU)	Check the fan on the video card and replace the fan or card if defective. If the card is overclocked, reset it to normal operations.

Oversized Images and Icons

System running in VGA (640 × 480) or SVGA (800 × 600) resolutions	Reset the display resolution to the preferred values.
Corrupted video card drivers	Reinstall the video card drivers.
Display scaling set too high	Reset the scaling to 100 percent using the Display menu in Settings

 EXAM TIP   Make sure you are familiar with the symptoms, explanations, and solutions covered in this objective and listed in the following "Review" section.

REVIEW

Objective 5.4: Given a scenario, troubleshoot video, projector, and display issues   Common symptoms of video, projector, and display issues, include the following:

- Incorrect data source
- Physical cabling issues
- Burned-out bulb
- Fuzzy image
- Display burn-in
- Dead pixels
- Flashing screen
- Incorrect color displays
- Audio issues
- Dim image
- Intermittent projector shutdowns
- Other symptoms:
  - Artifacts
  - Distorted geometry
  - Oversized images and icons

Keep in mind that many of these symptoms have multiple potential causes—and solutions.

5.4 QUESTIONS

1. A user has repositioned her desktop computer and now the display no longer has an image on the screen. However, the display and computer power lights are on. Which of the following would you have her check first?

   A. Loose power cord on display

   B. Pressing FN keys to go back to primary display

   C. Loose video cable

   D. Loose network cable

2. A Windows user reports very large text and icons on his screen. In the course of you asking the user what might be the issue, the user reported there was "some sort of an error message" during startup. Which of the following is the most likely cause?

   A. System booted up in Safe Mode.

   B. Video card GPU fan has failed.

   C. CPU fan has failed.

   D. System booted up in STOP mode.

3. You are playing a 3-D game at home and have been experimenting with getting better performance from your video card, and now you see incorrect color patterns onscreen. After checking the fan on your video card and determining it's working properly, what should you do next?

   A. Enable event logging.

   B. Disable overclocking.

   C. Enable Safe Mode.

   D. Enable Airplane mode.

4. How would you resolve a dead pixel display issue? (Choose two.)

   A. Replace the fan on the video card.

   B. Replace the display if under warranty.

   C. Gently message the pixel with a pencil eraser until it turns on.

   D. Clean the case fans and air intakes.

5. A customer is experiencing distorted images on a display. You believe this is a result of driver corruption. Which of the following is likely to fix this?

   A. Install or reinstall the latest video card drivers.

   B. Replace the GPU.

   C. Increase the display resolution.

   D. Replace the inverter.

5.4 ANSWERS

1. **C** Moving the computer could cause the video cable to become loose, causing the loss of picture.

2. **A** Some versions of Windows automatically boot up in Safe Mode if the system didn't boot normally on the previous boot attempt; Safe Mode uses a low screen resolution, resulting in large icons and text.

3. **B** Overclocking video cards or other components can lead to overheating, which is a common cause of incorrect colors onscreen.

4. **B C** Pixels may be dead due to manufacturing defects or being stuck in "off" mode. Replace the display if it is under warranty or gently message the pixel with a pencil eraser to see if it turns on.

5. **A** A common cause for distorted images is corrupted video card (GPU) drivers. You should install or reinstall the latest video card drivers.

Objective 5.5 ## Given a scenario, troubleshoot common issues with mobile devices

Mobile devices such as laptops, smartphones, and tablets are essential tools for today's on-the-go workforce. When they stop working, companies stop working. This objective helps you understand typical mobile device problems and solutions.

Troubleshooting Mobile Devices

The sections in this objective cover common symptoms of mobile device issues, along with typical causes and solutions.

Poor Battery Health/Short Battery Life

Device Type	Cause	Solution
Laptop, smartphone, tablet	Unneeded apps are running.	Close or hibernate unneeded apps.
Laptop, smartphone, tablet	Battery is not charged properly.	Follow the manufacturer's suggestions for discharging and recharging the battery.
Laptop, smartphone, tablet	Battery is defective.	Remove the battery if possible; have the unit serviced or replaced.

Swollen Battery

Device Type	Cause	Solution
Laptop, smartphone, tablet	Overcharged battery	(Prevention) Disconnect the charger after the battery is fully charged. (Solution) Replace the battery and recycle the old battery safely.
Laptop	Charger output voltage too high	Check the charger voltage output; replace the charger if out of spec.
Laptop, smartphone, tablet	Defective battery	Replace the battery and recycle the old battery safely.

Broken Screen

Device Type	Cause	Solution
Laptop	LCD cutoff switch is stuck.	Free up the switch or have the unit serviced.
Laptop	System set to use external display.	Use the display switching key on the keyboard to change to internal display.
Laptop	Inverter has failed.	Replace the inverter (applies to LCDs with CCFL backlights only).
Laptop	Backlight has failed.	Replace the backlight or LCD panel.
Smartphone, tablet	Backlight has failed.	Repair or replace the device.
Laptop	Inverter or backlight has failed.	Use an external display until the unit can be serviced.
Laptop, smartphone, tablet	System is in sleep mode.	Tap the keyboard, mouse button, or touchscreen to wake up the system.
Laptop, smartphone, tablet	Screen is broken.	Check with manufacturer for replacement, take it to repair shop, or accept the broken screen.
Laptop	Inverter is failing.	Replace the inverter (applies to LCDs with CCFL backlights only).
Laptop, smartphone, tablet	Display brightness is set too low.	Increase the display brightness.
Laptop	Inexpensive displays with LED backlights turn them off and on rapidly when dim modes are selected.	Increase the display brightness or replace the display with a higher-quality LED-backlit LCD display.

Improper Charging

Device Type	Cause	Solution
Laptop, smartphone, tablet	Bad AC adapter	Replace the AC adapter and retry.
Laptop, smartphone, tablet	Failed battery	Replace the battery or device.
Laptop, smartphone, tablet	Damaged charging cable	Replace the charging cable or charger.
Laptop, smartphone, tablet	Improper charging	Check for faulty cable, charger, socket, or adapter.

Poor/No Connectivity

No Wireless Connectivity

Device Type	Cause	Solution
Laptop, smartphone, tablet	Wi-Fi radio is turned off.	Turn on the Wi-Fi radio; depending on the device, the radio might be controlled by an external switch or by OS settings.
Laptop, smartphone, tablet	Airplane mode is turned on.	Turn off airplane mode.
Laptop	Wi-Fi antennas not are connected to Wi-Fi radio.	If the laptop was recently serviced, check the Wi-Fi antenna connection to the Wi-Fi radio card.

No Bluetooth Connectivity

Device Type	Cause	Solution
Laptop, smartphone, tablet	Bluetooth is turned off.	Turn on Bluetooth; pair the devices as needed.
Laptop, smartphone, tablet	Airplane mode is turned on.	Turn off airplane mode.

Intermittent Wireless

Device Type	Cause	Solution
Laptop	Wi-Fi antenna wire is loose or disconnected.	Check the Wi-Fi card in the laptop base for loose or disconnected antenna wires and then reconnect them.
Laptop	Wi-Fi card is not properly installed.	Check the Wi-Fi card in the laptop base for proper installation. If the securing screws are loose, tighten them. If the securing screws are missing, replace them.
Laptop, smartphone, tablet	Signal strength received by Wi-Fi radio is low.	Adjust the position of the device or USB Wi-Fi adapter to help improve signal reception.

Liquid Damage

Device Type	Cause	Solution
Smartphone and tablet	Liquid	Access the Liquid Damage Indicator (LDI). Could be unrepairable.
Laptop	Liquid	Remove external power and peripherals; remove battery and internal removable devices; pat dry and allow to air dry.

Overheating

Device Type	Cause	Solution
Smartphone	Case or pocket is causing overheating.	Remove the device from pocket; take off the case if the problem persists.
Laptop, tablet	Vents on underside/rear of device are blocked.	Place the device on a hard surface and clean dirty or clogged vents.
Laptop, tablet	Fans inside device have failed or are running too slowly.	Check fan operation and have the device serviced if the fans have failed; clean the fans if they are running too slowly.
Laptop	Thermal transfer material between CPU and heat sink has failed.	Have the device serviced.

Digitizer Issues

Laptop, smartphone, tablet	Touchscreen digitizer is disconnected.	Have the unit serviced.

Physically Damaged Ports

Device Type	Cause	Solution
Laptop, smartphone, table	Broken or damaged port	Take the device to a professional repair shop.

Malware

Device Type	Cause	Solution
Smartphone and tablet	Malware attacks	Use anti-malware software downloaded to the device or use Enterprise Mobility Management (EMM) services in the device OS.
Laptop	Malware attacks	Install or enable malware protection.

Cursor Drift/Touch Calibration

Device Type	Cause	Solution
Laptop	Misconfigured touchpad	Use the Control Panel mouse or touchpad settings or equivalent.
Laptop	Dirty touchpad sensors	Remove the keyboard to gain access to the touchpad sensors and clean them.
Laptop	Incorrect refresh rate	Use the Control Panel or Settings dialog to reset the refresh rate to the default (usually 60 Hz).
Laptop	Unintentional touches	Adjust the sensitivity of the touchpad.

Other Symptoms

Sticking Keys

Device Type	Cause	Solution
Laptop, Bluetooth keyboard used with tablet or smartphone	Debris or sticky material between or behind keys	Use compressed air to clean between the keys; remove the keyboard to clean spills, and be sure the keyboard is dry before reinstalling it.

No Power

Device Type	Cause	Solution
Laptop	Faulty peripheral device connected to USB, FireWire, and Thunderbolt ports	Disconnect the device and retry.
Laptop, smartphone, tablet	Bad AC power outlet	Try a different AC power outlet.
Laptop, smartphone, tablet	Bad AC adapter	Replace the AC adapter and retry.
Laptop	Bad laptop power jack	Have the laptop serviced.

NUM LOCK Indicator Lights

Device Type	Cause	Solution
Laptop	NUM LOCK or CAPS LOCK key turned on accidentally.	Turn off the NUM LOCK or CAPS LOCK key, as desired; if the problem persists, check BIOS setup, clean the keyboard, or replace the keyboard.

Cannot Display to External Monitor

Device Type	Cause	Solution
Laptop	Display is not plugged into laptop.	Plug the display into the laptop.
Laptop	Laptop is not configured to use external display.	Use the appropriate laptop key or menu selection to use the external display or mirror internal/external displays, as desired.

Touchscreen Nonresponsive

Device Type	Cause	Solution
Laptop, smartphone, tablet	Touchscreen is dirty.	Clean the surface of the touchscreen with a microfiber cloth; do not use liquid directly on the touchscreen.
Laptop, smartphone, tablet	Touch is not registering on icons.	Perform touchscreen calibration per the device operating instructions.
Smartphone, tablet	System is frozen.	Use a soft reset to restart the device.

Apps Not Loading

Device Type	Cause	Solution
Laptop, smartphone, tablet	Too many apps are running in memory.	Close apps that are not in use.
Smartphone, tablet	App doesn't load after you close apps not in use.	Perform a soft reset and then retry the app.
Laptop	App is not compatible with device.	Compare app requirements (OS, RAM, disk space, and so on) with laptop software/hardware specifications; uninstall the app and replace it if the app is not compatible.

Slow Performance

Device Type	Cause	Solution
Laptop, smartphone, tablet	Too many apps running in memory	Close apps that are not in use.
Laptop, smartphone, tablet	Not enough RAM	Install more RAM if possible.
Laptop, smartphone, tablet	Not enough free space on primary drive or internal storage	Free up space on the primary drive or internal storage.
Laptop, smartphone, tablet	Overheating device	Shut down the device, allow it to cool down, and then restart the device.

Unable to Decrypt E-mail

Device Type	Cause	Solution
Laptop, smartphone, tablet	E-mail app doesn't have correct software or decryption key.	Install the correct software or decryption key to open e-mail.

Frozen System

Device Type	Cause	Solution
Laptop, smartphone, tablet	System software or app problem	Perform a soft reset and then retry app.
Laptop, smartphone, tablet	Incompatible or corrupt app	Remove and reinstall the most recent app installed.

No Sound from Speakers

Device Type	Cause	Solution
Laptop, smartphone, tablet	Speaker or headset wire not fully plugged into speaker jack	Turn off the unit, reconnect the speaker, and retry.
Laptop, smartphone, tablet	Bluetooth speaker or headset not working	Make sure the speaker or headset is turned on; pair with the mobile device if necessary.
Laptop	Incorrect audio output chosen	Open the audio mixer and choose the correct output device.

GPS Not Functioning

Device Type	Cause	Solution
Smartphone, tablet	GPS is turned off in device settings.	Turn on GPS.
Smartphone, tablet	GPS is turned off for an individual app.	Change the app settings to use GPS.
Smartphone, tablet	Airplane mode is enabled.	Turn off airplane mode.

EXAM TIP Be sure to know the symptoms, explanations, and solutions covered in this objective and listed in the following "Review" section.

REVIEW

Objective 5.5: Given a scenario, troubleshoot common issues with mobile devices Symptoms of common mobile device issues include the following:

- Poor battery health/short battery life
- Swollen battery
- Broken screen
- Improper charging
- Poor/no connectivity
    - No wireless connectivity
    - No Bluetooth connectivity
    - Intermittent wireless
- Liquid damage
- Overheating
- Digitizer issues
- Physically damaged ports
- Malware
- Cursor drift/touch calibration
- Other symptoms
    - Sticking keys
    - No power
    - NUM LOCK indictor lights
    - Cannot display to external monitor

- Touchscreen nonresponsive
- Apps not loading
- Slow performance
- Unable to decrypt e-mail
- Frozen system
- No sound from speakers
- GPS not functioning

Keep in mind that many of these symptoms have multiple potential causes—and solutions.

5.5 QUESTIONS

1. A user is running a laptop computer in an office that also has an HDTV with a cable connected to the laptop. After dropping the laptop, the user can no longer see anything on the built-in display. What should you try first until you can get the laptop repaired or replaced?
    A. Connect the laptop to the network and try to use remote access.
    B. Have the user press the appropriate key(s) to switch to the external display.
    C. Tell the user to take a day off.
    D. Find an identical laptop and clone the original laptop's Windows installation to it.

2. A laptop's wireless connection is intermittent after it comes back from the repair shop for a screen replacement. Which of the following is the most likely cause of the problem?
    A. Antenna wires are not connected properly.
    B. Keyboard is stuck.
    C. Wi-Fi button on the edge of the laptop was turned off during the repair.
    D. Computer virus was introduced in the repair shop.

3. A customer is experiencing extremely short battery life on a mobile device. What recommendations should you make? (Choose all that apply.)
    A. Close or hibernate apps running in the background.
    B. Perform a hard reset on the mobile device.
    C. Follow the manufacturer's suggestions for discharging and recharging the battery.
    D. Reduce the brightness of the display to help improve battery life.

4. A user finds that she is unable to use the icons on her notebook computer touchscreen to open applications. What action should she take?
    A. Perform touchscreen calibration per device operating instructions.
    B. Change the screen resolution.
    C. Disable an active second screen.
    D. Update the display's device driver.

5. Which of the following are conditions that indicate a possibly broken screen?

   A. LCD cutoff switch stuck

   B. Inverter failure

   C. Backlight failure

   D. Inverter or backlight failure

   E. All of the above

   F. A and C

   G. Only D

5.5 ANSWERS

1. **B** Most laptops can switch between the built-in display and the video port by using a Function key (sometimes requiring the user to also press the FN key).

2. **A** Laptops with built-in Wi-Fi use antennas mounted around the edges of the display panel and connected to the Wi-Fi card inside the body of the laptop; if these cables are not properly connected during reassembly, Wi-Fi connections will be poor or will completely fail.

3. **A C D** Battery life on a mobile device is dependent on the items active on the device that draw power. Another issue could be that the battery is not being charged properly.

4. **A** Performing touchscreen calibration will realign the sensors in the display's touch system.

5. **E** Answers A, B, C, and D are all conditions that could result from a broken display screen.

Objective 5.6 **Given a scenario, troubleshoot and resolve printer issues**

Although organizations have sought the so-called paperless office for decades, printing is still a vital part of computer use in offices of any size as well as in the home. Printer technologies vary, so it's essential to know both the symptoms and the printer type producing the symptoms to solve printing problems.

Troubleshooting Printing Issues

The sections in this objective cover symptoms of common printing issues by printer type, along with typical causes and solutions.

Lines Down the Printed Pages

Impact: Horizontal white bars—dirty or damaged printhead	Clean the printhead. If the problem persists, replace the printhead.
Impact: Characters clipped off—head gap incorrect	Set the head gap to the recommended value for the media type.
Laser: Vertical white lines—toner clogged	Remove and shake the toner cartridge.
Inkjet: Colored bands through output	Enter the correct paper type setting in printer preferences. If the problem persists, clean the printhead.
Laser: Spots at regular intervals caused by a damaged drum or a dirty roller	Check the printer documentation to determine which markings are caused by which problem. Clean the printer rollers with 90 percent or higher denatured alcohol, replace the toner cartridge or drum, or service the printer as needed.
Laser: Random black spots and streaks caused by a worn or damaged cleaning blade	Replace the cleaning blade or toner, depending on where the cleaning blade is located.
Dirty rollers	Clean all rollers with 90 percent or higher denatured alcohol.

Garbled Print

Bad or loose printer cable	Check the printer cable; reconnect it if it's loose or replace it if it's bad.
Corrupt printer driver	Reinstall the printer driver.

Toner Not Fusing to Paper

Laser: Fuser assembly dirty	Clean the fuser assembly with 90 percent or higher denatured alcohol.
Laser: Fuser failure	Replace the fuser, preferably with a maintenance kit that has other replaceable components.

Paper Jams

Incorrect media type or printer setting	Check recommended media types for the printer and any special settings needed.
Paper jams when using duplex function because duplexer not installed correctly or not working	Check duplexer installation and paper separators; repair any broken parts. Print one side at a time as a workaround.
Worn separator pad	Replace the separator pad or use a scouring pad to add texture to the pad by removing the shiny surface.

Faded Prints

Impact: Printer ribbon is worn out or dried out.	If the printer ribbon has an ink reservoir, activate it. Otherwise, replace the ribbon.
Impact: Fresh ribbon produces faint output.	Adjust the head gap. If the head gap is okay, replace the printhead.
Impact: One side of printout is faded.	The platen is out of adjustment; have the printer serviced.
Laser: Toner is running low.	Remove and shake or replace the toner cartridge.
Laser: Toner is out.	Replace the toner cartridge or add toner, as appropriate.
Laser: Toner is not out.	Print the diagnostic page using the self-test. If the page is blank, check the drum to see if the page image is visible there. If it is, the printer's transfer corona or power supply has failed. Replace or service as needed.
Blank page appears between print jobs.	This is a normal spooler setting for networked printers, intended for privacy and security. Adjust the setting in the print spooler if not desired (after checking that corporate security policy doesn't require the blank page).

Incorrect Paper Size

Horizontal misalignment: Misaligned paper feed tray	Adjust the paper feed tray for the correct paper size.
Vertical misalignment: Multiple sheets of paper picked up	Remove the paper, fan it, and make sure the appropriate paper is being used; then reinstall the paper.

Paper Not Feeding

Wrong paper type for printer or paper tray	Use the recommended paper type; use a rear-mounted paper feed if possible.
Paper too damp	Replace the paper with dry paper.
Paper tray not loaded or inserted properly	Remove the paper tray, check the paper level and position, and reinsert the tray correctly.

Multipage Misfeed

Multipage misfeed	Consult the owner's manual to learn which paper is best for the printer.

Multiple Prints Pending in Queue

Printer has a number of print jobs waiting that are not progressing.	Open the Print Spooler service and check the status of print jobs (see Figure 5.6-1); release print jobs that are waiting, delete print jobs that have errors, and then resubmit. Bypass the print spooler and print directly to the printer (see Figure 5.6-2). Restart the Print Spooler service.
Print jobs are not emerging from printer although the printer is online.	Examine print spooler logs for error details. Use the logs to determine possible causes for failures and solutions.

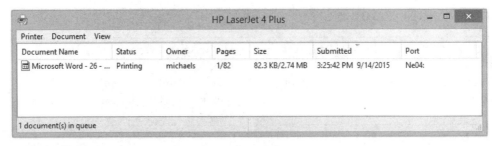

FIGURE 5.6-1 Print spooler's print queue

FIGURE 5.6-2 Print spool settings

Speckling on Printed Pages

Speckling on printed page	Check for faulty ink or toner cartridge or possible faulty photoconductor unit on laser printer.

Double/Echo Images on the Print

Laser: Dark ghosting caused by damaged imaging drum	Replace the toner cartridge if the drum is built in or replace the drum.
Laser: Dark ghosting caused by toner starvation	Prevention methods: • Lower the resolution (print at 300 dpi instead of 600 dpi). • Change the image/pattern completely. • Avoid 50 percent grayscale and "dot-on/dot-off patterns." • Change the layout so that grayscale patterns do not follow black areas. • Make dark patterns lighter and light patterns darker. • Print in landscape orientation. • Adjust the print density and RET settings. • Insert a blank page in the print job before the page with ghosting. • Check the temperature and humidity in the printer location and adjust them if they are out of the recommended range.
Laser: Light ghosting caused by worn or damaged cleaning blade	Replace the toner cartridge if the cleaning blade is built in, or replace the blade.
Image double prints or overlaps another image	Hard-reset the printer and check the calibration.

Incorrect Color Settings

Printer calibration or realignment needed	Rerun automatic alignment or calibration.
Corrupt driver	Reinstall the latest printer driver.
Defective printer	Have the printer serviced or replace the printer.
Inkjet: Printheads clogged	Run the printhead test and cleaning utility provided by the vendor.

Grinding Noise

Printer makes grinding noise when printing.	Use one or more of the following actions: • Check paper feed. • Clean rollers. • Replace cartridges. • Update printer device driver. • Clean the print head.

Finishing Issues

Staple jams	Power off printer; remove all paper from machine; pull jammed paper in print direction; remove any debris.
Hole punch	Empty hole punch bin; replace hole punch device driver.

Incorrect Page Orientation

Page is printing with incorrect orientation.	Check the Layout | Orientation settings and the preferences or settings of the printer setup. Check the Print settings in the Advanced Settings of the Microsoft Office applications (File | More |Options |Advanced).
Page orientation fails in multipage two-sided document with mixed page orientation.	Change the Flip settings in the Microsoft Office application print settings to match the page orientation.

Other Symptoms

No Connectivity

Bad or loose printer or network cable	Check the printer or network cable and reconnect it if it loose or replace it if it is bad.
Printer set for incorrect data port	Check the printer input setting and set it to the correct source.
Bad network configuration	Check the wired or wireless network settings.
Printer taken offline	Put the printer back online at the printer or with the spooler app.

Low Memory Errors

Laser: Too many fonts or graphics on page causes printer to run very slowly or print part of page after displaying an error message or error lights (user might need to eject page manually).	Upgrade printer memory if possible. Workarounds: Reduce printer resolution, simplify the page (fewer fonts, fewer or smaller graphics), and turn off RET or other print enhancements.

Access Denied

Shared printer cannot be used.	Verify the user account has access to the printer (check Security tab in Printer Properties). Some accounts might have access only during specified times.

Printer Will Not Print

Incorrect paper in tray compared to printer setting in OS	Change the paper setting on the printer to match the OS paper setting.
Print queue backed up	See the "Multiple Prints Pending in Queue" symptom in this objective.
Printer set for incorrect data port	Check the printer input setting and set it to the correct source.

Unable to Install Printer

User lacks permission	Provide administrator or superuser credentials to install the printer.
Printer not detected	Local: Check the printer cable and power to the printer. Network: Check the network settings on the printer.

No Image on Printer Display

Display frozen	Turn off the printer, unplug it for a few minutes, and then turn it back on. If the display is still frozen, have the unit serviced.

 EXAM TIP   Make sure you are familiar with the symptoms, causes, and solutions covered in this objective and listed in the following "Review" section. Note that to solve many of these problems, you first need to correctly identify the printer type in use.

REVIEW

Objective 5.6: Given a scenario, troubleshoot and resolve printer issues   Common symptoms of problems with printers of all types include the following:

- Lines down the printed pages
- Garbled print
- Toner not fusing to paper
- Paper jams
- Faded print
- Incorrect paper size
- Paper not feeding
- Multipage misfeed
- Multiple prints pending in queue
- Speckling on printed pages
- Double/echo images on the print
- Incorrect color settings
- Grinding noise
- Finishing issues
  - Staple jams
  - Hole punch
- Incorrect page orientation
- Other symptoms
  - No connectivity
  - Low memory errors
  - Access denied
  - Printer will not print
  - Unable to install printer
  - No image on printer display

5.6 QUESTIONS

1. A user is reporting that her print jobs are displaying dark ghost patterns. From this description, which of the following types of printers is in use?

   A. Virtual

   B. Laser

   C. Impact

   D. Inkjet

2. A user reports that when he prints envelopes, the envelopes are creased and misaligned. Which of the following steps is most likely to help?

   A. Change the printer to single-sided printing.

   B. Adjust the tractor feed.

   C. Adjust the paper guides.

   D. Use RET in the printer preferences.

3. A user reports paper jams at the rear of the printer when he tries to print double-sided pages. Which of the following components is most likely the cause?

   A. Rear paper feed

   B. Ink cartridges

   C. Duplexer

   D. RET

4. A laser printer is printing blank pages. Which of the following solutions should you apply to fix this problem? (Choose two.)

   A. Replace the printhead.

   B. Bypass the print spooler and print directly to the printer.

   C. Replace toner cartridge.

   D. Attempt to print a diagnostic page using self-test.

5. A user's printer has a number of print jobs backed up and waiting in the print queue. Which of the following measures should you take to get the print jobs printing again?

   A. Verify the user account has access to the printer.

   B. Restart the Print Spooler service.

   C. Calibrate the printer.

   D. Reinstall the latest printer driver.

5.6 ANSWERS

1. **B** Dark ghost patterns only occur on malfunctioning laser printers.

2. **C** Paper guides must be set correctly for the paper or media width installed; if they are set too wide, the paper/media will not feed straight.

3. **C** The duplexer at the rear of the printer is used to flip the paper for printing on the reverse side.

4. **C D** If a laser printer prints blank pages, you should replace the toner cartridge or add toner, as appropriate. If it is not out of toner, print a diagnostic page using the self-test. If the page is blank, check the drum to see if the page image is visible there. If it is, the printer's transfer corona or power supply has failed and should be replaced or serviced, as needed.

5. **B** Of the listed answers for addressing a backed-up print queue, restarting the Print Spooler service is the best option.

Objective 5.7 **Given a scenario, troubleshoot problems with wired and wireless networks**

Today's offices, home offices, and home entertainment systems rely on networking, so the odds of running into network problems are high.

Troubleshooting Network Issues

Make the odds of solving network problems in your favor by learning the common symptoms and solutions covered in the following sections.

Intermittent Wireless Connectivity

Bad or loose network cable	Reconnect the cable if it's loose or replace it if it's bad.
Bad NIC	Power down the system, remove the NIC, and reseat it in the slot (if it's a card). Replace the NIC if it's bad. Install the appropriate driver.
Marginal Wi-Fi signal	Change the position of the Wi-Fi antenna (move the laptop) to get closer to a wireless router or AP. Change to a less-crowded channel on the router or AP.
Too much network congestion on selected channel (particularly with 2.4 GHz)	Choose the least crowded of channels 1, 6, and 11. Use a Wi-Fi analyzer app on an Android or iOS device to find the network channels in use.
Long distance to wireless router or AP	Move the device closer to the router or AP.
Poor position of wireless antennas on device	Change the position of antennas (laptop display if built-in Wi-Fi). If USB Wi-Fi or Bluetooth is used, connect the adapter to a USB extension cable and move it as needed to improve signal.

Slow Network Speeds

Wired: Manual speed/duplex settings slow down network.	Use automatic negotiation of speed/duplex settings.
Wired: Non-standard or marginal wiring for the desired performance.	Use Cat 5 only for Fast Ethernet (100 Mbps). Use Cat 5e or 6 for Gigabit Ethernet (1000 Mbps). Use Cat 6a or greater for 10-Gbps Ethernet.
Wired: Hub used instead of a switch.	Hubs broadcast to all connected devices and subdivide bandwidth. Replace any remaining hubs with switches.
Wireless: Long distance to wireless router or AP.	Move the device closer to the router or AP. Use repeaters or mesh networking to improve performance.

Limited Connectivity/No Connectivity

APIPA IP address only allows local LAN connections; DHCP server connection not available.	Check the status of the DHCP server (often a function of the router or AP on the network). Restart the router or AP. Open a command prompt in Windows and use **ipconfig/release** and **ipconfig/renew** to obtain a new IP address, one from the DHCP server. Restart the device if necessary to get the DHCP IP address.
Wired: Network cable might be loose or defective.	Check the NIC or switch signal lights to see if they indicate physical connectivity. If no lights are displayed, swap the patch cable. Use a known-good network port.
Wired: NIC might not be enabled or the proper driver not installed.	Check Device Manager or the hardware listing for the NIC. If the NIC is not found, install the driver. If the NIC is disabled, enable it.
Wired: NIC might not be sending or receiving signals.	Test the NIC with a loopback plug. Disconnect the network cable and insert the loopback plug. If the NIC is bad, replace it.
Wired: Cable might not be connected or might be defective.	Check that the network cable is plugged into a wall socket; if it is, check the other end of the cable for a working connection. If it is connected at both ends, use a cable scanner to test the cable. Replace the cable if it's bad.

Wired: NIC MAC address doesn't have permission to use network.	Add the NIC's MAC address to permitted addresses (whitelist) in the router configuration. If the router uses a blacklist of blocked MAC addresses, remove the address from the blacklist, if applicable. If the device is connected to a managed switch, check MAC filtering settings on the switch.
Wireless: Airplane mode is enabled.	Turn off airplane mode.
Wireless: Wi-Fi is turned off.	Turn on the Wi-Fi radio using the physical switch on the device or the software switch in the OS.

Jitter

Increased or intermittent latency	Add a jitter buffer, upgrade the Ethernet cable, or upgrade the gateway devices.

Poor VoIP Quality

Poor voice quality	Reduce the jitter or upgrade the internal network.

Port Flapping

Port flapping	Look for a loop in the network or a rogue device added to the network.

High Latency

High latency on network	Apply one or more of the following to reduce network latency: <ul><li>Replace or add a router to reduce network contention.</li><li>Use a wired connection instead of wireless or high-volume transfers.</li><li>Apply QoS protocols to high-bandwidth demand requirements.</li></ul>
Wireless latency	Lay out the network to avoid interference and place APs in locations that provide maximum coverage.

External Interference

Wireless: Wi-Fi overlap	Change the Wi-Fi channel or move the router.
Electromagnetic interference (EMI)	Apply filtering, shielding, or grounding.

Other Symptoms

Unavailable Resources: Internet

User or group is not granted Internet access.	Check the domain controller user/group configuration and change it if necessary.
APIPA IP addresses don't allow Internet connections.	See the "Limited Connectivity/No Connectivity" symptom earlier in this objective.
Router has failed.	Shut down and restart the router. Update the firmware. Release and review the IP address at each device. Replace the router if it fails again.
Broadband modem has failed.	Shut down and restart the modem, followed by the router. Update the modem firmware. Replace the modem if it fails again.

Unavailable Resources: Local Resources

Unable to access local resource via network shortcut	Access the local resource through normal means, not as a network device.
Shares, printers: Incorrect user name/password	Workgroup/shared resource: Use the correct user name/password if the account is already set up on the device. If not, set up accounts for users on shared resource.
	For a domain resource, check with the network manager for a list of accessible shares.
Workgroup printer: Share not available	Check if the printer is online.
	Restart the print spooler or clear the print spooler and try again.
Shares, printers: Incorrect network, homegroup, or domain settings	Check the workgroup or domain name setting in System Properties and change it as needed.
E-mail: Incorrect user name/password for e-mail	Check with the e-mail provider to verify you are using the correct user name/password. Change the settings as needed.
E-mail: Incorrect configuration for e-mail provider	Check with the e-mail provider to verify you are using the correct e-mail settings (server type [SMTP, POP, IMAP], port addresses, encryption, and so on). Change the settings as needed.

APIPA/Link Local Address

The device has an IP address in the range 169.254.0.1–169.254.255.254.	The DHCP server (which provides IP addresses automatically) is not working. Check the device providing the DHCP service (usually a router) and restart the DHCP server. Release and renew the IP address on each device with an APIPA address or restart them.

IP Conflict

Two or more devices have same IP address.	Release and renew the IP addresses if they are provided by DHCP. If the IP addresses are set manually, change each conflicting device to its own IP address in the appropriate range.

SSID Not Found/Multiple SSIDs

Hidden SSID	Enter the correct name of the SSID and provide the encryption key.
Airplane mode enabled	Turn off airplane mode. If Wi-Fi is still turned off, turn it on again manually.
More than one available SSID	Select the SSID with the strongest signal. Sign off of the weaker network signal and sign in to the stronger signal, if permitted.

 EXAM TIP   Be sure to know the symptoms, causes, and solutions for the network issues covered in this objective and listed in the "Review" section.

REVIEW

Objective 5.7: Given a scenario, troubleshoot problems with wired and wireless networks   The following wired and wireless network problems can have multiple causes and, sometimes, more than one solution to try:

- Intermittent wireless connectivity
- Slow network speeds:
  - Limited connectivity/no connectivity
  - Jitter

- Poor VoIP quality
- Port flapping
- High latency
- External interference
- Other symptoms:
  - Unavailable resources: Internet and local resources: shares, printers, e-mail
  - APIPA/link local address
  - IP conflict
  - SSID not found/multiple SSIDs

5.7 QUESTIONS

1. Which of the following solutions possibly would not resolve a slow wireless network connection speed?
   A. Moving client devices to a new location to minimize obstacles between the router and the clients
   B. Changing the AP channel setting on the router to a non-overlapping channel
   C. Updating the firmware and device drivers on the client and wireless AP or router
   D. Removing other non-network wireless devices in the area that may use the same frequency bands
   E. Changing the DHCP settings

2. What is the IPv4 address range used for APIPA assignments?
   A. 169.254.0.1–169.254.255.254
   B. 10.0.0.0–10.255.255.255
   C. 127.0.0.1–127.255.255.255
   D. 224.0.0.0–239.255.255.255

3. A workstation is able to connect to the router but is unable to obtain an IP address. Which of the following is likely the cause of this problem? (Choose all that apply.)
   A. Router requires a reset.
   B. Windows Fast Startup.
   C. Recent update was applied to the router.
   D. Internet service is not available from the ISP.
   E. All of the above could be the issue.

4. What is the primary cause for poor quality service on a VoIP network?
   A. Bandwidth
   B. Throughput
   C. Jitter
   D. Transfer speed

5. Which of the following is the better solution for slow throughput on a wired network?

   A. Using automatic negotiation for speed duplex settings

   B. Using manual settings for speed duplex

   C. Upgrading the cabling standard installed

   D. Replacing all switches with hubs

5.7 ANSWERS

1. **E** All of the other available options could individually or together resolve speed issues on a wireless connection.

2. **A** IP addresses starting with "169." are assigned automatically when an IP address cannot be received from a DHCP server.

3. **E** All of the options listed could be the cause of this issue.

4. **C** Jitter is the most common cause of issues on a VoIP connection.

5. **A** Automatic negotiation for speed duplex settings allows the system to regulate the transfer speed of the network.

About the Online Content

This book comes complete with:

- TotalTester Online practice exam software with practice exam questions for exam 220-1101, as well as a pre-assessment test to get you started
- More than an hour of sample video training episodes from Mike Meyers' CompTIA A+ Certification video series
- More than 20 sample simulations from Total Seminars' TotalSims for CompTIA A+
- Links to a collection of Mike Meyers' favorite tools and utilities for PC troubleshooting

System Requirements

The current and previous major versions of the following desktop browsers are recommended and supported: Chrome, Microsoft Edge, Firefox, and Safari. These browsers update frequently, and sometimes an update may cause compatibility issues with the TotalTester Online or other content hosted on the Training Hub. If you run into a problem using one of these browsers, please try using another until the problem is resolved.

Your Total Seminars Training Hub Account

To get access to the online content you will need to create an account on the Total Seminars Training Hub. Registration is free, and you will be able to track all your online content using your account. You may also opt in if you wish to receive marketing information from McGraw Hill or Total Seminars, but this is not required for you to gain access to the online content.

Privacy Notice

McGraw Hill values your privacy. Please be sure to read the Privacy Notice available during registration to see how the information you have provided will be used. You may view our Corporate Customer Privacy Policy by visiting the McGraw Hill Privacy Center. Visit the **mheducation.com** site and click **Privacy** at the bottom of the page.

Single User License Terms and Conditions

Online access to the digital content included with this book is governed by the McGraw Hill License Agreement outlined next. By using this digital content you agree to the terms of that license.

Access   To register and activate your Total Seminars Training Hub account, simply follow these easy steps.

1. Go to this URL: **hub.totalsem.com/mheclaim**

2. To register and create a new Training Hub account, enter your e-mail address, name, and password on the **Register** tab. No further personal information (such as credit card number) is required to create an account.

   If you already have a Total Seminars Training Hub account, enter your e-mail address and password on the **Log in** tab.

3. Enter your Product Key: `dqvf-v30w-ngxh`

4. Click to accept the user license terms.

5. For new users, click the **Register and Claim** button to create your account. For existing users, click the **Log in and Claim** button.

   You will be taken to the Training Hub and have access to the content for this book.

Duration of License   Access to your online content through the Total Seminars Training Hub will expire one year from the date the publisher declares the book out of print.

Your purchase of this McGraw Hill product, including its access code, through a retail store is subject to the refund policy of that store.

The Content is a copyrighted work of McGraw Hill, and McGraw Hill reserves all rights in and to the Content. The Work is © 2023 by McGraw Hill.

Restrictions on Transfer   The user is receiving only a limited right to use the Content for the user's own internal and personal use, dependent on purchase and continued ownership of this book. The user may not reproduce, forward, modify, create derivative works based upon, transmit, distribute, disseminate, sell, publish, or sublicense the Content or in any way commingle the Content with other third-party content without McGraw Hill's consent.

Limited Warranty   The McGraw Hill Content is provided on an "as is" basis. Neither McGraw Hill nor its licensors make any guarantees or warranties of any kind, either express or implied, including, but not limited to, implied warranties of merchantability or fitness for a particular purpose or use as to any McGraw Hill Content or the information therein or any warranties as to the accuracy, completeness, correctness, or results to be obtained from, accessing or using the McGraw Hill Content, or any material referenced in such Content or any information entered into licensee's product by users or other persons and/or any material available on or that can be accessed through the licensee's product (including via any hyperlink or otherwise) or as to non-infringement of third-party rights. Any warranties of any kind, whether express or implied, are disclaimed. Any material or data obtained through use of the McGraw Hill Content is at your own discretion and risk and user understands that it will be solely responsible for any resulting damage to its computer system or loss of data.

Neither McGraw Hill nor its licensors shall be liable to any subscriber or to any user or anyone else for any inaccuracy, delay, interruption in service, error or omission, regardless of cause, or for any damage resulting therefrom.

In no event will McGraw Hill or its licensors be liable for any indirect, special or consequential damages, including but not limited to, lost time, lost money, lost profits or good will, whether in contract, tort, strict liability or otherwise, and whether or not such damages are foreseen or unforeseen with respect to any use of the McGraw Hill Content.

TotalTester Online

TotalTester Online provides you with a simulation of the CompTIA A+ Core 1 exam, 220-1101. The exam can be taken in Practice Mode or Exam Mode. Practice Mode provides an assistance window with hints, explanations of the correct and incorrect answers, and the option to check your answer as you take the test. Exam Mode provides a simulation of the actual exam. The number of questions, the types of questions, and the time allowed are intended to be an accurate representation of the exam environment. The option to customize your quiz allows you to create custom exams from selected domains, and you can further customize the number of questions and time allowed.

To take a test, follow the instructions provided in the previous section to register and activate your Total Seminars Training Hub account. When you register, you will be taken to the Total Seminars Training Hub. From the Training Hub Home page, select your certification from the list of "Your Topics" on the Home page, and then click the TotalTester link to launch the TotalTester. Once you've launched your TotalTester, you can select the option to customize your quiz and begin testing yourself in Practice Mode or Exam Mode. All exams provide an overall grade and a grade broken down by domain.

Pre-Assessment

In addition to the sample exam questions, the TotalTester also includes a CompTIA A+ pre-assessment test to help you assess your understanding of the topics before reading the book. To launch the pre-assessment test, click **Pre-Assessment Test** for the Core 1 exam. The A+ Pre-Assessment test is 50 questions and runs in Exam Mode. When you complete the test, you can review the questions with answers and detailed explanation by clicking **See Detailed Results**.

Mike's CompTIA A+ Video Training Sample

Over an hour of training videos, starring Mike Meyers, are available for free. Select **CompTIA A+ Core 1 Passport (220-1101) Resources** from the list of "Your Topics" on the Home page. Click the TotalVideos tab. Along with access to the videos, you'll find an option to purchase Mike's complete video training series from the Total Seminars website www .totalsem.com.

There are over an hour of free videos available for study. You can purchase Mike's complete video training series from the Total Seminars website www.totalsem.com.

TotalSims Sample for CompTIA A+

 From your Total Seminars Training Hub account, select **CompTIA A+ Core 1 Passport (220-1101) Resources** from the list of "Your Topics" on the Home page. Click the TotalSims tab. There are over 20 free simulations available for reviewing topics covered in the book. You can purchase access to the full TotalSims for A+ with over 200 simulations from the Total Seminars website, www.totalsem.com.

Mike's Cool Tools

Mike loves freeware/open-source PC troubleshooting and networking tools! Access the utilities mentioned in the text by selecting **CompTIA A+ Core 1 Passport (220-1101) Resources** from the list of "Your Topics" on the Home page. Click the Book Resources tab, and then select **Mike's Cool Tools**.

Technical Support

For questions regarding the TotalTester or operation of the Training Hub, visit **www.totalsem .com** or e-mail **support@totalsem.com**.

For questions regarding book content, visit **www.mheducation.com/customerservice**.

Index